I0763258

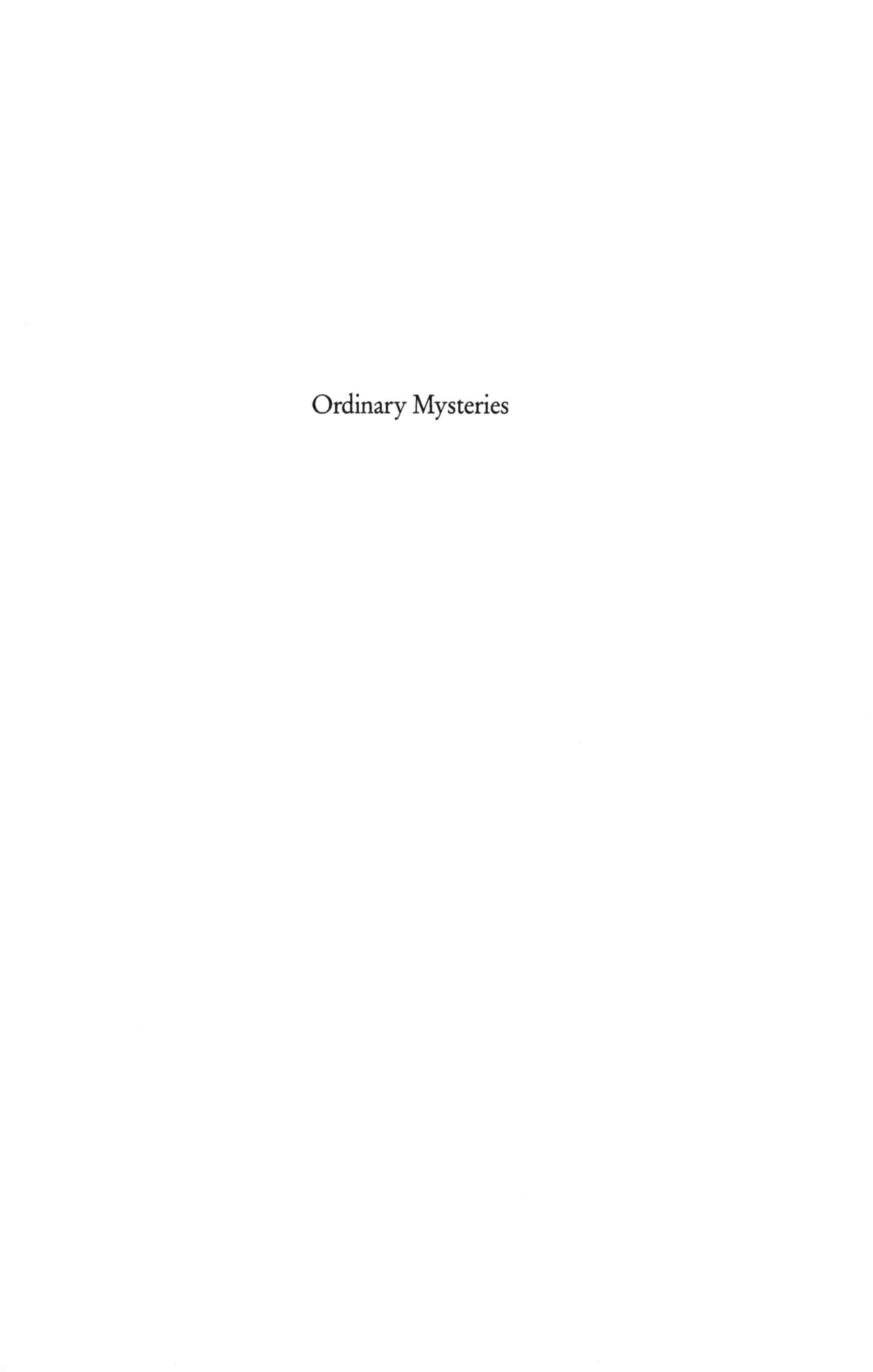

Ordinary Mysteries

Ordinary Mysteries

The Common Journal of Nathaniel and Sophia Hawthorne 1842–1843

Edited by
Nicholas R. Lawrence and Marta L. Werner

American Philosophical Society
Philadelphia • 2005

Memoirs of the American Philosophical Society
Held at Philadelphia
For Promoting Useful Knowledge
Volume 256

ISBN-10: 0-87169-256-2
ISBN-13: 978-0-87169-256-6
US ISSN: 0065-9738

Library of Congress Cataloging-in-Publication data

Hawthorne, Nathaniel, 1804–1864.
Ordinary mysteries: the common journal of Nathaniel and Sophia Hawthorne, 1842–1843 / edited by Nicholas R. Lawrence and Marta L. Werner.
p. cm. — (Memoirs of the American Philosophical Society held at Philadelphia for promoting useful knowledge, ISSN 0065-9738 ; v. 256)
Includes bibliographical references and index.
ISBN-13: 978-0-87169-256-6 (cloth)
ISBN-10: 0-87169-256-2 (cloth)
1. Hawthorne, Nathaniel, 1804–1864—Diaries. 2. Hawthorne, Sophia Peabody, 1809–1871—Diaries. 3. Novelists, American—19th century—Diaries. 4. Authors' spouses—United States—Diaries. 5. Concord (Mass.)—Social life and customs. I. Hawthorne, Sophia Peabody, 1809–1871. II. Lawrence, Nicholas R., 1964– III. Werner, Marta L., 1964– IV. Title. V. Memoirs of the American Philosophical Society ; v. 256.

Q11.P612 vol. 256
[PS1881]
813′.3—dc22
[B] 2005048347

Project management: Book Production Resources

Printed in Canada.

Contents

Allegories of Collaboration:

The Common Journal of Nathaniel and Sophia Hawthorne

FROM THE SUMMER OF 1842 through the fall of 1843, Nathaniel and Sophia Hawthorne kept a common journal of their daily lives in a notebook currently housed in the Pierpont Morgan Library and catalogued as MA 580. Intended solely for their own eyes, the journal records the ordinary events and activities that occupied them as newlyweds: walks through the countryside around Concord, appraisals of their new home, encounters with neighbors and visitors, descriptions of the weather and the changing seasons, and most persistently, expressions and probings of the happiness they found in each other—all, save the last, material that Hawthorne would later draw on for the preface to his second collection of tales, *Mosses from an Old Manse* (1846). Elaborating on a theme begun earlier in their correspondence, the couple cast themselves as citizens of Paradise—a new Adam and Eve, redeemed from the fallen state of solitude and single life.

In keeping with its collaborative occasion, MA 580 tells at least two stories. The first is the story of a year during which the Hawthornes reinvented themselves through the medium of each other. It is a leisurely narrative, spirited on Sophia's part, playful on Nathaniel's, absorbed in the texture and minutiae of days lived without fixed schedules or pressing deadlines. Scholars and critics have generally read this chapter in the Hawthornes' lives as a sunny one. Yet it was not without its tensions: beneath the give-and-take dynamic of the newlywed couple there is an occasional hint of power plays and the clash of wills; Sophia's tendency toward transcendentalist enthusiasm for nature (nurtured in the Peabody family through contact with such figures as Emerson and Margaret Fuller) sits uneasily alongside Nathaniel's penchant for allegorizing nature's lessons; and the contradictions inherent to journalizing life in Paradise become more apparent as the labor of professional writing takes up more of Nathaniel's time and pregnancy takes up Sophia's. The fiction that Hawthorne wrote during this period, too, offers a different perspective: in tales such as "The Birth-Mark" and "Rappaccini's Daughter," paradisial settings reveal blighted undersides, the promise of heavenly bliss is poisoned by obsession and meddlesome intervention. Having put aside experimental schemes of communal living and a protracted and secret engagement, the couple now faced the challenge of adapting a union conceived in the terms of Romantic idealism to an emerging Victorian dispensation of pious domesticity. As with Hawthorne's fiction, among the more suggestive aspects of the common journal is what it reveals, in its quotidian record, about the strains involved in the consolidation of gender roles and middle-class identity during this turbulent period in American social history.[1]

The second story contained in MA 580 is that of its afterlife—the story of its editorial transformation from a private document to a public one. Just as a photograph is developed twice—first in rendering an image from its negative, then in rendering the meaning of the image over time—so the significance of the common journal underwent a fundamental change when, through Sophia's agency, it was incorporated into Hawthorne's oeuvre after his death. In selecting portions of the journal to publish while keeping other parts to herself, Sophia became entangled in an allegorical struggle displacing the earlier Edenic fantasy of her honeymoon year—a posthumous collaboration embodying all the tensions accompanying the mediation of public and private worlds, letter and spirit, writing and editing. The drama of her struggle is recorded negatively in the changes and omissions she effected in her husband's text, and positively in the marks she made on the manuscript itself. Sophia's edits are made visible in this edition for the first time; they suggest a powerful drive to preserve the mystery of intimacy even at the cost of destroying its record.

Sophia's agon over publication of this document of a marriage, at once ordinary and extraordinary, recalls Keats's remark concerning the figurative life lived by the writer: "A man's life of any worth is a continual allegory—and very few eyes can see the Mystery of his life—a life like the scriptures, figurative. . . . Shakespeare led a life of Allegory: his works are the comments on it—."[2] Given Sophia's habit of comparing Hawthorne to Shakespeare, as well as of extracting spiritual significance from even the slightest of her husband's actions, she might easily have applied this insight to her own work as collaborator and editor. Yet to turn the specificities of ordinary life into universal allegory puts a heavy burden on both text and reader, as Hawthorne, troubled allegorist, well knew. Even the most banal particulars are pressed into the service of an enobling interpretation. At the same time, the obscurity of the allegorical relation between life and works — its availability to "very few eyes" — means that it courts a second risk, that of utter incomprehension. Julian Hawthorne wrote after his father's death that he was "unable to comprehend how a man such as I knew my father to have been could have written such books." In more than one sense, Keats's stress on the hidden import of the representative life—or a life made over as representative—provides a useful entry point for considering the ambiguities in MA 580 and its history.

Looking Backward: 1870–1868–1864

"When a person breaks in, unannounced, upon the morning hours of an artist, and finds him not in full dress, the intruder, and not the surprised artist, is doubtless at fault. —S.H. Dresden, April 1870."[3] So ends the "Preface" to *Passages from the English*

Note-Books of Nathaniel Hawthorne, and with it Sophia Hawthorne's public silence as editor of her late husband's journals. Although a subsequent version of the preface would excuse the editor as a "friend" rather than an "intruder,"[4] it's worth pausing to consider this extraordinary statement by the author's spouse of twenty-two years, the "inmost wife" and collaborator who, Nathaniel once informed a correspondent, "speaks so near me that I cannot tell her voice from my own" (*CE* 18: 256). Seeking to deflect criticism of the notebooks themselves, Sophia represents her editorial self as an impersonal "person," divorced from her usual role as protector and first reader of her husband's work, who flouts Victorian decorum by uncovering to the public what should remain private.[5] Her language echoes most immediately a *New-York Times* review of *Passages from the American Note-Books*, published in 1868: "Here in the Note-Books, we come upon Hawthorne's genius in undress—taken, perhaps, somewhat at a disadvantage—caught unawares—or, at all events, not always set off with the adornments and trappings of his art." (The *Times* review had, in addition, complained of the lack of "a word of preface or explanation of any kind" accompanying the text.)[6] At the same time, the radical alienation detectable in Sophia's choice of metaphor has its precedent in her own words, for example the stunned eulogy she wrote to her friend Annie Fields upon Nathaniel's death in May 1864: "In the most retired privacy it was the same as in the presence of men. The sacred veil of his eyelids he scarcely lifted to himself. Such an unviolated sanctuary as was his nature, I his inmost wife never conceived nor knew. . . ."[7] Months later, responding to publisher James T. Fields's pleas to allow him to publish excerpts from the notebooks in *The Atlantic Monthly*, she wrote: "The veil he drew around himself no one should lift. . . . He gave all he wished to give. Who shall wrench more from him?" (letter to Annie Fields, n.d.). In turning to the quasi-religious image of the veiled oracle whose enigma demands respect, Sophia is of course echoing Hawthorne's own favored metaphor for the mystery of subjectivity: "So far as I am a man of really individual attributes, I veil my face," as the narrator explains in "The Old Manse" (*CE* X: 33). To try to lift the veil of the "inmost Me" that the author himself repeatedly promises not to divulge is to risk turning "Hawthorne," if not ourselves, into a character from one of his tales.

Nowhere is the strangeness of Sophia's preface more apparent than in relation to the journal they kept in common during the first year of their marriage.[8] The Old Manse journal remains the most intimate document, outside correspondence, of the Hawthornes' early years together; on page after page it records the intertwined mutuality of feeling and perception that fed their sense of unique partnership, later to become the basis of the public image of their marriage as unusually happy and well attuned. Despite the intensity of Sophia's part in the collaboration, however, her entries went unpublished for over a century and a half; as T. Walter Herbert remarks, "The notebooks have become a record of her husband's singular genius, and their original shape and meaning have been obliterated" (xiii). It was not until 1996 that Patricia Dunlavy Valenti published Sophia's portion of the journals she and Nathaniel kept in common;[9] in spite of her pioneering work, the journal as it has come down to us duplicates the severe separation of gendered spheres that marked domestic ideology in the nineteenth century. Additionally, the interplay of spousal address and exchange present in MA 580 has itself been veiled by a series of ink-blottings and scissored excisions performed on the manuscript, presumably by Sophia herself. The intimacy of her editorial engagement with the text, doubling the intimacy of its contents, could hardly be further removed from her self-characterization as careless intruder at the close of the 1870 preface.

The passage of MA 580 from private to public document cost Sophia no small effort. Just as Hawthorne's preface "The Old Manse," when published, invited the reader to inspect the author's house and grounds without mentioning his wife (except in its use of the unspecified "we"), so Sophia continued the labor of self-effacement when copying excerpts for *The Atlantic*: "I have now finished the Old Manse records," she wrote to Fields in 1866, "—all that I could copy. It has been difficult to leave myself out, but I think I have been pretty skillful" (18 February 1866). The double meaning of Sophia's difficulty is clear: it was doubtless troublesome to remove all specific references to herself in her husband's text without compromising its flow, but in a deeper sense, difficult also to remove her own text—a frequently rhapsodic testament to the bond she was experiencing anew as editor of his words. At the same time, the activity of copying was for her a euphoric labor of communion with the Nathaniel of 1842, a Nathaniel who had long since vanished by the time of his death, and hence a way of retrieving the self-styled paradise of the couple's early, relatively carefree life together. Editing the notebooks was thus rife with paradox: in attempting to reestablish contact with the spirit of her dead husband, Sophia had to remove evidence of that contact in the letter of the document she was editing; in presenting the Old Manse journal as continuous in tone and texture with Hawthorne's solo notebooks, she had to suppress the collaborative occasion that distinguished it from them.[10]

This doubleness of intention—making the private public while retaining its privacy—echoes, in turn, the multiple levels of address engaging Sophia as she applied herself to the task of editing. In addition to the specter of an intimate yet dead past and the all-too-contemporary public audience of *Atlantic* readers, her work on the manuscripts was directed at a posterity that presumably included her own children, for whom certain passages in MA 580 had to be blotted out, excised, rendered illegible or invisible. The result is a published text that both reveals and conceals layers of editing like a series of nested Chinese boxes; a private document that wears occasional veils of black ink or empty space so as to produce, even now, a sense of hiddenness or mystery within an apparently mundane record of bourgeois daily life in mid-nineteenth century America.

Allegory

Sophia's double task as editor is reflected not only in the dual character of MA 580 but in a persistent duality structuring much of Hawthorne's writing. Generations of commentators, beginning most famously with Melville and Henry James, have remarked on the peculiar mode of coexistence between the metaphysical and the ordinary in the Hawthornian corpus.[11] On the one hand, as J. Hillis Miller notes,

James is perplexed by the "banal literalism" of Hawthorne's private notebooks, their tendency to record quotidian facts and trivial events rather than delve into speculation or self-scrutiny. On the other hand, Hawthorne's imaginative writing in the tales and novels notoriously betrays "a fatal tendency to fall into the abstraction of allegory," especially an allegory that overreaches itself by setting up an almost humorously incongruous relation between tenor and vehicle—as if, in James's words, "the kernel had not assimilated its envelope" (368). Making the commonplace appear portentous, or portents commonplace, is, implies James, the occupational hazard of a writer of Hawthorne's sensibility, particularly in a society as literal-minded and alienatingly unresonant as antebellum America. Indeed, in James's reading, allegory serves as a compensatory or escapist device—precarious at best—for producing meaning in the face of an unremitting national preoccupation with the ordinary, the literal, the materialistic, the opaque.

What James's perusal of the notebooks overlooks, however, is the way that portents and commonplaces exist side by side throughout Hawthorne's early notebooks, most notably in the form of vividly figurative story ideas and, to use Sophia's phrase, passages of straightforward "word-painting":

> All the dead that had ever been drowned in a certain lake to arise.
>
> The history of a small lake from the first, till it was drained.
>
> An autumnal feature,—boys had swept together the fallen leaves from the elms along the street in one huge pile, and had made a hollow, nest-shaped, in this pile, in which three or four of them lay curled, like young birds. (*CE* VIII: 179)
>
> A fairy tale about chasing Echo to her hiding-place. Echo is the voice of a reflection in a mirror.
>
> Fringed gentians, found the last, probably, that will be seen this year, growing on the margin of the brook. . . .
>
> To symbolize moral or spiritual disease by disease of the body;—thus, when a person committed any sin, it might cause a sore to appear on the body;—this to be wrought out. (*CE* VIII: 222)
>
> A house to be built over a natural spring of inflammable gas, and to be constantly illuminated therewith. What moral could be drawn from this? It is carburreted hydrogen gas, and is coaled from soft shale or slate, which is sometimes bituminous, and contains more or less carbonate of lime. It appears in the vicinity of Lockport and Niagara Falls, and elsewhere in New York. . . . (*CE* VIII: 166)
>
> Some most secret thing, valued and honored between lovers, to be hung up in public places, and made the subject of remark by the city,—remarks, sneers, and laughter. . . .
>
> A ground-sparrow's nest in the slope of a bank, brought to view by mowing the grass, but still sheltered and comfortably hidden by a blackberry-vine trailing over it. At first, four brown-speckled eggs,—then two little bare young ones, which, on the slightest noise, lift their heads, and open wide mouths for food,—immediately dropping their heads, after a broad gape. The action looks as if they

> were making a most earnest, agonizing petition. In another egg, as in a coffin, I could discern the quiet, death-like form of the little bird. The whole thing had something awful and mysterious about it. (*CE* VIII: 185)

Read consecutively, such entries show a more persistent bifocal perspective on the ordinary and the allegorical than James was willing to credit, and suggest that their relationship for Hawthorne went beyond that of drab empiricism and compensatory gothic. Indeed, the embryos of allegory are frequently detectable in passages of otherwise ordinary description.

What James would have been unable to see, given the omissions in Sophia's edition of *Passages from the American Note-Books*, is that the relation between allegory and mundane realism in Hawthorne undergoes a change in the notebooks that he and Sophia produced collaboratively. There, for the first time, the allegorical and the mundane occupy the same space, revealing themselves to be continuous with one another in the manner of a Mobius strip. Instead of entries that read, as James puts it, "like a series of very pleasant . . . letters, addressed to himself by a man who, having suspicions that they might be opened in the post, should have determined to insert nothing compromising" (James 350), the common journals inaugurate a form of self-allegorization that is evidently a function of their address to someone other than the author. Adam, a formerly solitary namer of things, had found his Eve.

Yet the suspicion emerges over the course of MA 580 that Hawthorne's addressee both is *and* isn't Sophia—that even here, in a seemingly private document, his mode of address remains inescapably, uncannily dualistic. Hawthorne's remarks concerning his ideal reader in "The Custom House"—"When he casts his leaves forth upon the wind, the author addresses, not the many who will fling aside his volume, or never take it up, but the few who will understand him, better than most of his schoolmates and life-mates"—suggest that the schism between public and private spheres of reception unavoidably structures even the most intimate authorial address. Directed at the same time inward, to the center of his domestic universe, and outward, to a shadowy public beyond the confines of the Old Manse, Hawthorne's self-allegorizing in this journal betrays an ambiguity that Sophia would come to appreciate only when editing the notebooks a quarter of a century later. In MA 580, it might be said, the Hawthornes together create a playful yet unequal allegory of ordinary married life that plays itself out in unforeseen ways.

Paradise

> "Love is and ever has been one of the great scenes of textuality."
>
> —Jerome McGann, *The Textual Condition*

Concord, July 1842: After their wedding on July 9th, having leased the Old Manse from Samuel Ripley, a relative of Emerson's, Nathaniel and Sophia take up residence in their new home and soon begin writing in the same notebook.[12] The journal they keep together functions variously as a means of "daguerrotyp[ing] & painting the hours" (MA 569: 7 September 1852), the nineteenth-century equivalent of snapshot albums or home movies; as an extension of their domestic space, furnished with observations of their surroundings and housing joint reflections on their newly married state; and more fancifully, as a purported book of Paradise, in which they figured themselves as sole inhabitants, enjoying an Edenic solitude together.

"Externally, our Paradise has very much the aspect of a pleasant old domicile, on earth," writes Nathaniel in the first of his entries:

> I must not forget to mention that the butcher comes twice or thrice a week; and we have so far improved upon the custom of Adam and Eve, that we generally furnish forth our feasts with a portion of some delicate calf or lamb, whose unspotted innocence entitles them to the happiness of becoming our sustenance. Would that my wife would permit me to record the ethereal dainties, that kind Heaven provided for us, on the first day of our arrival! Never, surely, was such food heard of on earth—at least, not by me. (5 Aug. 1842)

Nathaniel's sly reference to sexual manna from heaven represents an early indication of the way in which the journal both offers and withholds details even in the act of composition. The disabling paradox of writing Paradise is that it needs no record; the very act of recording signifies a fallen state. Much of Nathaniel's subsequent play with the Adam-and-Eve theme consists in rueful acknowledgment of this paradox: Sophia must "banish" him from her company and issue a "strict command" in order to get him to perform the labor of journalizing their existence together, yet there are some things (the "ethereal dainties" provided on the first day of their honeymoon) that she apparently won't permit him to record. The editing of the journal is coincident with its writing.

Unmentionable specificities thus find only oblique expression in the notebook; wordless experience is veiled first in words. Sophia's initial, truncated contribution to MA 580, beginning the extant journal in medias res, offers a small narrative of transgression and punishment that prefigures expulsion from the Garden of Eden:

> wife. I could not comprehend why. When I came to him, he told me I had transgressed the law of right in trampling down the unmown grass, & he tried to induce me to come back, that he might not have to violate his conscience by doing the same thing. And I was very naughty & would not obey, & therefore he punished me by staying behind. This I did not like very well, & I climbed the hill alone. We penetrated the pleasant gloom & sat down upon the carpet of dried pine leaves. Then I clasped him in my arms in the lovely shade, & we laid down a few moments on the bosom of dear mother Earth. Oh how sweet it was! And I told him I would not be so naughty again, & there was a very slight diamond shower without any thunder or lightening, & we were happiest. (n.d.)

For all the suggestiveness of Sophia's language in this passage, ranging as it does from transgression to violation to penetration to the climactic shower, it is the first, fragmentary word "wife" and its followup that signify most here. As the journal stands, this broken-off opening expresses much more about the oxymoronic project of keeping Eden's books than anything the writers could positively include. Sophia closes her entry with an echo of the Milton that Nathaniel read to her during their evenings at the Old Manse:[13]

> There was no wind & the stillness was profound. There seemed no movement in the world but that of our pulses. The Earth was still before us. It was very lovely but the rapture of my spirit was caused more by knowing that my own husband was at my side than by all the rich variety of plain, river, forest & mountain around & at my feet. (MA 580: n.d.)

Paradise Lost thus installs itself within the intimate circle of wedded paradise ("The World was all before them, where to choose/Thir place of rest, and Providence thir guide . . ."). But though the world was all before them, the evidence of MA 580 suggests that the priority of the new Adam and Eve lay in excluding the social world wherever possible. In this the journal reveals itself essentially as a version of pastoral, where despite the increasing encroachment of outside trouble (bad weather, unpaid debts, annoying visitors) and internal disturbance (spousal absence, the necessity of labor, the presence of death), a fictive equilibrium is precariously maintained, primarily through the solace of nature. If Nathaniel's Brook Farm period is styled in his previous journal as a socialist experiment to restore a pagan Golden Age, harking back to Virgil's *Georgics*,[14] here the passage to a Biblically inflected rural retreat draws in all the complications attending the bourgeois vision of a paradise built for two.

Long before the conclusive moment of expulsion—"Our landlord has driven us out of our Paradise at Concord" (*CE* 16: 126)—the material signs of trouble in the paradise of MA 580 occur both as "flitting shadow[s] of earthly care" and as gaps—gaps in the chronological record of days, gaps in what is intentionally or unintentionally withheld from inclusion. Months pass without an entry; anxieties, including those concerning Sophia's health during pregnancy, are registered only to be set aside. As a labor of leisure, the journal had to compete for time with other, more pressing forms of labor, including Nathaniel's professional writing, household upkeep, work on the garden, and the separate journalizing that occupied them both apart from MA 580. The fiction of complete and Edenic mutual transparency that appears to underwrite the project of the common journal is belied by these latter efforts, which record thoughts and experiences that aren't, initially at least, shareable.[15] A passage from one of Hawthorne's tales of this period, "The Birth-Mark," recounts how the heroine Georgiana peruses her husband's scientific logbook:[16]

> The book, in truth, was both the history and emblem of his ardent, ambitious, imaginative, yet practiced and laborious, life. He handled physical details, as if there were nothing beyond them: yet spiritualized them all, and redeemed himself from materialism, by his strong and eager aspiration towards the infinite. In his grasp, the veriest clod assumed a soul . . . The volume, rich with achievements that had won renown for its author, was yet as melancholy a record as ever mortal hand had penned. It was the sad confession, and continual exemplification, of the short-comings of the composite man—the spirit burthened with clay and working in matter. . . .
>
> "It is dangerous to read in a sorcerer's books," said [Aylmer], with a smile, though his countenance was uneasy and displeased. . . .
>
> "It has made me worship you more than ever," said she. (*CE* X: 49)

If indeed it contained nothing beyond the physical details, both the spirit and the letter of married life would remain opaque, withholding their significance—like open letters written to oneself.[17] It is against the threat of this form of materialism that Sophia's redemptive enthusiasm periodically asserts itself. The final entry of MA 580 closes with a typical paean to her husband that eerily prefigures the lament she wrote years later (in the letter to Annie Fields) while sitting beside his corpse:

> He is as unfathomable as any other counsel of GOD; for it is only when men insist upon holding up their own minute reflectors to Truth that they shut it out & nail platforms over the depths of the soul, & such people are tedious & soon tire. We cannot get farther than the platform & who can stand always on that? But to be drawn forever into the lower deeps, seeing only space beyond space, this is the true enchantment, the endless communion, & this is his—this is my mystery. (19 Nov. 1843)

Sophia's self-correction here is both wish-fulfillment and recognition: a wish for immediate, eternal, and boundary-dissolving communion in a paradise of souls, and a recognition of the infinite regress of "space beyond space," surface beyond surface, in the mystery of the intimate other's distanced presence. As in Hawthorne's fiction, the allegorical impulse to endow meaning on an inert, unresponsive universe may result in something closer to a hall of mirrors than a key to Eden.

MA 580 breaks off abruptly on November 19, 1843, eight months before the Hawthornes' second wedding anniversary. It is likely that the journal ends at this juncture simply because the notebook has been filled, but it ends on a high point; Sophia's language in the final entry goes well over the border of idolatry. "If we lived in a world of angels instead of prosaic men—what a glory would they be to publish," wrote Sophia to Fields of Nathaniel's love-letters, years later. "Why am I not already transfigured into a Shining One by such a love, so expressed?" (31 May 1867). With the onset of an ensuing period of trouble—a miscarriage, unpaid debts, ejection from the Old Manse Eden followed by years of child-rearing and travel abroad—it was only after Nathaniel's death that Sophia was able to return her attention fully to the mystery of her husband's legacy.

Remembering and Dis-membering the Text of Paradise: 1864–1868

> During these closing years of her life she had occupied much of her time in transcribing her husband's journals for publication. This work was a great pleasure to her, for . . . much of it recalled scenes and events in which they had participated; so that it seemed as if they were still conversing together. Indeed, from a short time after his departure until the hour came for her to join him, she always had a feeling that he was near her,—that their separation was of the senses only, not spiritual. —Julian Hawthorne, *Hawthorne and His Wife*

> I was excessively agitated in copying this first little book [MA 580] . . . I do not seem to have had undimmed eyes.
>
> —Sophia Hawthorne to James T. Fields, November 1865

Collaboration, which takes one form while both husband and wife are alive, necessarily takes another in the wake of death. Between 1864 and 1868, Sophia reverses the trajectory of Nathaniel's death and her loss by re-reading and copying his notebooks as well as the notebooks they kept together.[18] Her buoyant assumption during this phase is one of spiritual contact beyond death, a frictionless communication she achieves paradoxically through painstaking transcription of his words. In this she reaffirms one of the great dreams of the nineteenth century, an idealist vision of communication as the immaterial communion of souls.[19]

I am imagining a table at the Wayside—the table on which Sophia Hawthorne places the notebooks she is about to prepare for publication. Perhaps the table she uses to copy is the same table she leaned on to write in the common journal. Perhaps she copies at Hawthorne's desk, abandoned to her after his death. In order to edit the journals she must re-read them; she must return to texts not opened, presumably, for twenty years, since 19 November 1843. When she re-opens the journal after a twenty years' absence, does she read from the beginning? Is she engaged in an act of re-reading or of reading for the first time? At what hours does she turn over the leaves of the notebooks? Does she read and copy during the day, when the light is strong, or at dusk, Hawthorne's favored hour for reverie? Does the hand of the dead writer control the hand of the living amanuensis?

The history of Sophia's work on the notebooks can be understood as a passage in which several states of mind succeed one another: the "trembling" re-entry into the world after a period of sorrow, the unfolding of a sense of joy occasioned by the rediscovery of Hawthorne's journals, a physical reaction to the transference of the notebooks from the private to the public sphere, and, near the end of the process, the threat of illness, cessation of copying, and the abandonment of the America depicted in the notebooks. Although all of Hawthorne's notebooks were in Sophia's possession, she did not initially work through them systematically in the order of their composition. Rather, after several months of hesitation over the propriety of publishing Hawthorne's private papers, she significantly began the work of copying/mourning with the first of the notebooks they wrote in common, MA 580.[20] By December of 1864, the act of copying that began in a privacy of grief issued in an experience of delight. The pleasure of copying was for a time its own end, unrelated to the larger venture of publishing the notebooks. In the first of a series of ecstatic letters to Fields, she wrote, "I wish to copy, copy, copy—Perhaps nothing will do to print—but I must copy all the same" (5 December 1864). Copying keeps the circuit of desire open—"To copy . . . is a great joy. My hours sing" (14 October 1865)—and fuels the fantasy of what Milton called "wondrous sympathy." If the difficulty of communication is a measure of fallenness, the effortlessness of communication achieved through the act of transcription may be taken as a mark of grace: as long as Sophia copies, she knows no break in contact with her husband. Unlike writing, which necessarily involves the production of difference, copying leads to the production of "perfect" transparency. The painful division between self and other is briefly erased as copying enables her return to the paradise of life with Hawthorne in 1842: "And now I live all day with my husband, pouring [*sic*]over his records" (13 October 1865).[21]

The psychology of Sophia's copying is the psychology of idolatry: in the act of copying, she situates her identity absolutely in the absent beloved:[22] "I have," she wrote Annie Fields in a strange moment of prescience in the year before Hawthorne's death, "a fearful power of being another" (Herbert 250). This psychology, as Samuel Coale observes, "did not appear out of nowhere,"[23] but is intimately linked to nineteenth-century spiritualism and to the cultural phenomena of mesmerism and automatic writing—both of which involve logical, if extreme, extensions of the collaborative ethos. At times, Sophia seems to have copied in a trance in which her external senses are suspended and even the passage of time makes no impression on her: "I have written since breakfast and now it is eight, evening" (4 October 1865); "I cannot tell in the least about whether you would wish such MSS or not. I become a penwoman and do not judge" (12 October 1865). Like the mesmerized subject in the final stage of communion, she is granted a clairvoyance unavailable to her in her waking life. "I think," Sophia writes to Fields, "he reveals himself exquisitely in these papers" (14 October 1865) and, a few days later, "As I copy I seem to . . . see, through his eyes, what I might not see with my own" (20 October 1865). Copying is tantamount to second sight.

It is the rhetorical trope of prosopopoeia, the figure Paul de Man has defined as "the fiction of an apostrophe to an absent, deceased, or voiceless entity, which posits the possibility of the latter's reply and confers upon it the power of speech"[24] that initially drives Sophia's copying. But, as media historian John Peters notes, "As communicators the dead are a particularly enigmatic bunch. They tend not to respond to our entreaties. Their words are fixed and invariant" (149). Copying may not be the same as "conversing together" after all. Repetition is deadly; repetition makes death appear. When Sophia copies the last of the notebooks, she knows (again? for the first time?) Hawthorne is dead. When "the fiction of the voice-from-beyond-the-grave" fails, the initial joy copying furnished Sophia gives way to physical injury, illness, and debilitating doubt. The work of copying, once a way of enabling Hawthorne's presence to express itself through her, now serves to remind Sophia—often sharply—of her own painful survival in the aftermath—"My hand is just now beyond penning for this day" (8 October 1865); "My right thumb felt lame, and it hurts me to write" (11 January 1866); "I should think you would be curious to see how the dead-alive look" (12 June 1868)—and of the absolute threshold separating the silent, inert, and perfectly unresponsive body of the dead writer from the laboring, mourning body of the copyist.

In 1865, Sophia wrote to Fields, "What a history to be sure we are creating! Nothing was ever so stupendous, so grand, so appalling – so glorious – " (18 April 1865). It is a measure of Sophia's absorption in copying that it is unclear whether she refers here to the publication of the notebooks or to the conclusion of the Civil War. And yet Sophia's transformation from elation to illness, from euphoria to doubt may be correlated with the changing status of MA 580 from a private document to a public one. As the contents of the notebook become more and more public, her malaise becomes more marked. When the printing of excerpts from MA 580 in the *Atlantic* and, later, *Passages from the American Note-Books* led to its distribution in a marketplace beyond Sophia Hawthorne's control, her letters to Fields register her growing unease about the project—her fear that paradise, only so recently regained, will be lost again.[25] On July 4, 1866 (Hawthorne's birthday), she insists on seeing all the proofs, "especially," she writes, "as I may find it imperative to omit some things copied." At the same time, Sophia's anxieties may stem from her own transformation from "inmost wife" to objective reader that editing compelled. "You will see I have made wild havoc with the proof," she writes Fields, "but I have grown wiser and look at the MSS from a less inward point of view and so can adapt it better to the public. . . . I think I lost my head when I was copying the Old Manse Journal, and perhaps others – I seemed to forget that the delicious music must not be piped to all ears – As it is, perhaps I leave too much on the page" (24 July 1866). Although she continues to insist on her privileged relationship to Hawthorne and to distinguish herself from readers in general—"but I am not the public" (12 October 1865)—she also implicitly acknowledges her growing remoteness from him.

On the surface, such acts of censorship seem aimed at reasserting the boundaries of private and public discourse. And so they may be. But what Sophia leaves in is often as private as what she edits out, and her forebodings apropos publication and circulation are not wholly explicable in these terms. Can anything in a private document be printed with impunity? It seems more likely that Sophia's fears are linked to her realization that the years of labor devoted to her absent collaborator/correspondent will necessarily go unacknowledged by him and to her recognition that the *Atlantic* and *Passages* publish only "dead letters." The epistolary relation is grounded in time and exposed to time: the printed passages circulate and circulate but always in a whirlwind beyond the reach of their original addressee. "The communicative stance to the dead," notes Peters, "can only be one of dissemination" (149). The intimate dialogical relation Sophia wished to preserve "explodes" as *Passages* enters a new economy of contingencies where, in Paul Ricoeur's words, "instead of being addressed to just you, the second person," it is addressed to everyone, to "unknown" and "invisible" readers.[26] At times, the fanning out of the address of Sophia's letters/passages results in their delivery not into the hands of the "insiders . . . having . . . immediate access to the mystery" alluded to in the final entry of MA 580 but into the hands of "outsiders . . . randomly scattered across space and time."[27] In place of the response she longed for from Hawthorne, came these divinations from unauthorized interpreters: "Hawthorne's note book, doing so little justice to the genius of the writer, is again opened for people to gape over and wonder how such a man could write such commonplace things" (*Christian Register* 1868); "He was unquestionably of the second order" (*Saturday Review* [England], 26 [5 December 1868], 752); "One might fancy he inherited . . . a passionless curiosity which is very little agitated by sympathy" ("Nathaniel Hawthorne's Note-Book," *Spectator* [England], 62 [January 1869], 14); "Alas! At the critical moment it always turns out that his back is towards us" ([James Russell Lowell], "Hawthorne's American Note-Books," *North American Review*, 108 [January 1869], 323-5).[28]

The failure to receive a message from Hawthorne—his back was towards her as well—and not only the negative reviews of *Passages from the American Note-Books*, pitches Sophia into doubt: "It makes me shudder to think I may have done what Mr. Hawthorne would not have approved" (16 May 1866); "I am subject to some awful doubts" (4 July 1866); "I am not at all sure whether it can be printed" (5 August 1866); "Above all things I would be loyal to what Mr. Hawthorne would approve. I had rather starve than do what he might think an impropriety" (30 January 1868). In the end, Sophia's copying had proved unprofitable in both spiritual and material terms. Ultimately, the breakdown of dialogue between the living and the dead reduced her to silence. Her alienation from Hawthorne is signaled most eerily in the bibliographical codes of *Passages*: although she had spent the better part of four years preparing Hawthorne's notebooks for publication her name does not appear on the title page of the volumes; rather, it appears on the following page in a statement identifying her only as the individual responsible for entering *Passages* into the public record: "Entered according to the Act of Congress, in the year 1868, by SOPHIA HAWTHORNE, in the Clerk's Office of the District of Massachusetts."[29] Moreover, in the face of the critics' continual demands for an explanation of her editorial ideology, as well as their calls for a biography of Hawthorne, she maintains her silence. Only in the brief, unsatisfactory "Preface" to *The English Note-Books* does Sophia offer a public defense of her role as editor of the notebooks—and, implicitly, of the notebooks themselves: "The Editor has been severely blamed and wondered at, in some instances, for allowing many things now published to see the light; but it has been a matter of both conscience and courtesy to withhold nothing that could be given up. . . . The Editor has transcribed the manuscripts just as they were left, without making any new arrangement or altering any sequence—merely omitting some passages, and being especially careful to preserve whatever could throw light upon his character" (vi). To "withhold nothing that could be given up," to make "no alterations" but "merely omit some passages" is to render the notebooks reifiably unreadable—open and closed at the same time.

> Fancy my emotion when I removed the wrappings and saw the sacred beloved name —and then opening the box found the beautiful books with the Hawthorne vine and the very elegant cloth outside, and then the lovely paper within! I cannot thank you. I should like to weep for joy. . . . There is a grave and perfect elegance in these volumes. It seems as if he would like to see them. —Sophia Hawthorne to James T. Fields, n.d.

Sophia Hawthorne's account of unwrapping her first copy of *Passages from the American Note-Books* may equally double as a description of the unsealing of a letter, or a grave. Here, not the carnal remains, but the commodified textual body, perfected, is transformed into an object of redemption. The processes of both canonization and reification are complete for Sophia in the delivery of this volume, at once living epistle and lettered tombstone.

Much has been made of Sophia's bowdlerization of Hawthorne's texts in *Passages*, but even Randall Stewart, the first indignant critic to note the discrepancy between

Hawthorne's manuscript and the published text, later acknowledged that Sophia's alterations fell within the established protocols for Victorian editing and would most likely have been approved by Hawthorne himself.[30] In general, Sophia Hawthorne's editing of the American notebooks takes two basic forms: silent omissions and unmarked editorial alterations, and omissions indicated by ellipses. The former category involves edits that are invisible to the public; the latter seems to make the machinery of editing visible.

In both cases, Sophia's edits involve the displacement—"leaving out"—of her presence in the text. Yet the play of invisibility and visibility in *Passages* mirrors, perhaps, Sophia's uncertain shifting between the desire to efface herself in order to serve the spirit of her husband and the conflicting desire to inscribe herself in a text she had co-authored. In the silent alteration of phrases such as "the medium of her spirit" to "the medium of *another* spirit"; "my little wife expressed its character" to "expressed by *some one*"; and "my little wife" to "*others*" (italics added) she enacts her own estrangement from Hawthorne—as well as from her former self—and discovers, in the words of Emerson, "the condition of infinite remoteness" between people.[31] In marking omissions by means of ellipses, however, Sophia not only inscribes the trace of her self in *Passages,* thus signaling her private privilege as an insider in Hawthorne's text, but points to that self as a deeply secreted force within the text, the force of an alterity that cannot be completely assimilated within Hawthorne's discourse. In a suggestive letter to Fields, written in July 1866, she hints at the ineffable depths of the text, the power of what is withheld: "But what word-painting of Nature this is!. . . . All the heavenly spring time of my married life comes back in these cadences—so rich and delicate—and what I cannot copy at all is still sweeter than the rest. The stars in their courses do not cover such treasures in Space—as do the dots I substitute for words sometimes" (Stewart 308). For Sophia, the ellipses that serve as her vanishing points in *Passages* shimmer like a Barthesian punctum, a "something the reader can't locate and yet can't stop seeing," an absence she wishes us to receive "right here in our eyes."[32] For Sophia, ellipses point to aporias in the text that are themselves figures for her understanding of the soul, an understanding that, as Terry Eagleton among others has argued, is characteristic of nineteenth-century ideologies of selfhood, whereby the self, an occulted mystery, is readable only through the signs of its absence.[33]

Sophia's experience of the ellipses, however, would not have been shared by contemporary readers of the printed volumes who, familiar with editing conventions of the day, most probably imagined that the ellipses concealed no great secret but only personal names, slightly unflattering portraits, or even passages of little interest. Indeed, the eye floats effortlessly and mechanically from line to line over the uniform surface of *Passages*. What strikes us most forcefully is the continuity of the text, its smoothness, not its gaps. In many cases, the omissions in this section of *Passages* can be restored by revisiting the manuscript of MA 580. Yet the descent into the interior of the manuscript is ultimately disappointing: "characterized by an extraordinary blankness," in the words of James, the passages omitted are as banal and quotidian as those retained:

I possess such a human and heavenly lily, and wear it in my bosom. Heaven grant that I myself may not be symbolized by its yellow companion. (6 Aug. 1842)

My wife should have the credit of introducing this improvement into the arrangement of pond-lilies. She has, in perfection, the love and taste for flowers, without which a woman is a monster—and which it would be well for men to possess, if they can. (6 Aug. 1842)

May the powers of the upper regions always keep guard over my heart's treasure, whether I am at her side, or afar off! (7 Aug. 1842)

. . . for no man can know what home is, until, as he approaches it, he feels that a wife will meet him at the threshold. (7 Aug. 1842)

. . . —and afterwards, in due season, to bed. Then came my dear little wife to her husband's bosom, and slept sweetly, I trust; for she is a beloved woman—which is more than can be said of every wife in the world. Pray Heaven that Mrs. Hillard had a good night's rest in our guest-chamber; but I hardly think that she slept so sweetly as my lily. (15 Aug. 1842)

. . . which would have saddened me, only that my sunny wife shone into my heart, and made it warm and bright . . . (15 Aug. 1842)

But let my wife describe the day; —she should be able to do it well; for she made it, or, at least, must have had something to do with its manufacture, since she prophesized it so truly. (30 Aug. 1842)

A wagon came at about eleven o'clock to carry my Dove to the stage-house. I helped her in, and stood watching her on the door-step, till she was out of sight. (7 April 1843)

I would like to see my wife! (8 April 1843)

. . . but the thought of thee—the great thought of thee—was among all other thoughts, like the pervading sunshine falling through the branches and boughs of a tree, and tingling every separate leaf. Not that I was very cheerful either . . . (9 April 1843)

Surely thou shouldst not have deserted me without manufacturing a sufficient quantity of sunshine to last to my return! Art thou not ashamed? (10 April 1843)

Methinks my little wife is twin-sister to the Spring; so they should greet one another tenderly; for they both are fresh and dewy, both full of hope and cheerfulness, both have bird-voices always singing out of their hearts, both are sometimes overcast with flitting mists, which only make the flowers bloom brighter; and both have a power to renew and re-create the weary spirit. I have married the Spring!—I am husband to the month of May! (26 April 1843)

My dearest wife has almost toiled herself to death with endeavors to purify her empire within the house. (26 April 1843)

❧

What every artifact displays is the residue of an unequal contest: the effort of a human being to transcend the human, an effort constantly thwarted by physical

> realities. Even a document with a text of the sort not generally regarded as art—a simple message to a friend, for example—illustrates the immutable condition of written statements: in writing down a message, one brings down an abstraction to the concrete, where it is an alien, damaged here and there through the intractability of the physical.
>
> —G. Thomas Tanselle, *A Rationale of Textual Criticism*[34]

The levels of editing Sophia performed on the manuscript of MA 580 are another matter altogether. Although Hawthorne's entries in the notebook significantly outnumber Sophia's, the extant notebook, as Patricia Valenti observes, "presents itself primarily as Sophia's text" (116). Ironically, it is her defacement of the manuscript that fixes her claims upon it. For the damages perpetrated against MA 580 affirm the radical privacy of the Hawthornes' original account of paradise and the impossibility of its full translation into the public sphere. At least nine leaves are lost to cuts and blots, while the violence of Sophia's alterations weakened even the binding of the notebook, compelling the book conservators at the Morgan to make extensive repairs simply to keep it intact.

I am imagining a table at the Wayside again—the table on which Sophia Hawthorne places the notebooks she is about to prepare for publication—the table on which she copies, blots, and cuts out the entries of a notebook she composed twenty years earlier with her husband, now dead. "The self who reads past entries," writes Judy Simons, "is significantly different from the self who initially wrote those entries."[35] *When Sophia re-opens the notebook after twenty years, does she recognize the hand—her hand—in the notebook, or does she only identify it, distinguish it from the other hand in order to keep working? Nowhere in her surviving papers does she mention the labor of blotting and cutting. Perhaps she works at night, cutting away leaves under the cover of darkness. Perhaps she works in the day when the light is strongest and shows her what to save (his writing) and what to wipe out (hers). At what moment does she cut out the opening leaves of the journal so that the last word of a lost sentence—"wife"—becomes the first word of a new text about estrangement? No secret copy of MA 580 is saved just for herself. After she cuts and blots out the entries written by her own hand—is it still her own hand?—her reading of the journal will be marked by pathos, that always impossible longing to form an originary relationship to an absent text.*

MA 580 is yet another example of a strange phenomenon in the field of textual studies—i.e., that documents edited for a private audience compel more radical programs of censorship than those edited for a public one.[36] While the omissions in *Passages* are largely recoverable and thus provisional—indeed, they point us back to the original document and the (false) promise of transparency inherent in all original documents—the deletions made on the manuscript through the violation of its surface are almost always irrevocable. At times, ultraviolet light or the application of ink thinners reveals certain of the words hidden beneath the smears and ink blots, leaving a stuttering code whose pitch toward the ineffable is wholly in keeping with Sophia's intact entries:

My
with the
GOD
she has any one yet,
GOD'S infinite
plan of His Providence!
this
?other?
GOD
, & then
life before ! What ! (9 July 1843)

And at times, the texts bordering a blotted out or excised entry offer clues as to what has been lost. A passage from Hawthorne's 31 March 1843 entry, for example, alludes to Sophia's recent miscarriage and also tells us that she recorded the incident in an entry since excised. More often, however, the scissored and blotted pages remain dark before an editor's understandable desire to bring them to light.

In the end, it may be this desire to dispel the darkness, rather than the darkness itself, that is misguided. In remaining partly unrecoverable, MA 580 illuminates the condition of all documents as fallen—paradises lost and then lost again. Paradoxically, our alienation from the text—whether the effect of damage or distance in time and culture—may lead us away from the mournful idealism in G. Thomas Tanselle's account of textual transmission to Jerome McGann's more salutary thought that "the textual condition's only immutable law is the law of change," and that "in this way, time, space, and physicality are not the emblems of a fall from grace, but the bounding conditions of gracefulness abounding."[37]

The mystery of subjectivity embodied in MA 580 as it now stands is ultimately the result of neither editorial concealment nor Romantic codes of disclosure. In his remarkable memoir *The Motion of Light in Water*, writer and critic Samuel Delany points out that, at least since the advent of self-conscious modernity, private narratives of desire and silence always accompany public ones of legitimation, and that it is a categorical mistake to assume that the former constitute the "truth" of the latter, that subjectivity, in all its rich contradictoriness, can be simply conflated with privacy. Rather, as Delany argues,

> if it *is* the split . . . that constitutes the subject, it is only after the Romantic inflation of the private into the subjective that such a split can even be located. That locus, that margin, that split itself first allows, then demands the appropriation of language—now spoken, now written—in both directions, over the gap.[38]

Recognizing the performative role of the public-private divide becomes, in effect, a prerequisite for any editorial strategy that probes, rather than assumes, the facts of subjectivity in their material embodiment on the page. The latest stage in the process of socializing the Hawthornes' fragmented collaborative text might thus be appropriately an attempt to render the complexity of its surfaces and successive stages without positing any necessary secret behind its veils. Just as the nascent development of telemedia in the 1840s forecast a revolution in the relationships between the near and the distant,[39] so the extension of web technology in the 1990s has served to further complicate if not dissolve distinctions between private and public. For these reasons, among others, MA 580 has become freshly available to us as a test-case in the ongoing revisionary allegory that constitutes the politics of editing.

Notes

Notes: We refer throughout to "Sophia" and "Nathaniel" as historical persons, and to "Hawthorne" in the latter's guise as an author function. As our argument suggests, however, the line of division is a porous one.

Citations to Nathaniel Hawthorne's writings are from *The Centenary Edition of the Works of Nathaniel Hawthorne,* ed. William Charvat et. al. (Columbus: Ohio State UP, 1972).

1. For the most extensive treatment of middle-class family ideology in Hawthorne's work, see T. Walter Herbert, *Dearest Beloved: The Hawthornes and the Making of the Middle Class Family* (Berkeley: University of California Press, 1993). See also Joel Pfister, *The Production of Personal Life* (Stanford: Stanford University Press, 1991) and Lauren Berlant, *The Anatomy of National Fantasy: Hawthorne, Utopia, and Everyday Life* (Chicago: University of Chicago Press, 1991).

2. John Keats, *Selected Letters of John Keats,* ed. Grant F. Scott (Cambridge, Mass.: Harvard University Press, 2002), 261. In his discussion of this passage, Gordon Teskey comments: "[Keats] may have meant that the the events of a worthy life are . . . both exemplary in themselves and indications of a higher, remote ideal. Or, as is more likely, he may have meant that the mind of a worthy man has an absolute value to which his achievements are only the traces and signs, unreadable to all but the like-minded few." *Allegory and Violence,* 1.

3. "Preface" to *Passages from the English Note-books of Nathaniel Hawthorne,* vol. 1., ed. Sophia Hawthorne (Boston: James R. Osgood & Company, 1871), viii. For more on the Hawthornes' personal views regarding propriety and states of undress, see Herbert, *Dearest Beloved,* 231, 237, 267.

4. In a revised version of the preface composed for Strahan's English edition, Sophia deletes the reference to herself as "intruder" and insists instead that "apologies are unnecessary" and even "might be thought unbecoming on either side." See Carol Hanbery MacKay, "Hawthorne, Sophia, and Hilda as Copyists: Duplication and Transformation in *The Marble Faun,*" *Browning Institute Studies: An Annual of Victorian Literary & Cultural History* 12 (1984): 119, n. 31.

5. See Donald H. Reiman, *The Study of Modern Manuscripts: Public, Confidential, and Private* (Baltimore: The Johns Hopkins University Press, 1993) for an extended discussion of the editorial meanings of "public" and "private."

6. *Nathaniel Hawthorne: The Contemporary Reviews,* eds. John L. Idol, Jr. and Buford Jones (Cambridge: Cambridge University Press, 1994), 314.

7. Sophia Hawthorne to Annie Fields, May 1864, qtd. in Herbert, *Dearest Beloved,* 278. Annie Adams Fields was one of Sophia's most intimate correspondents outside of her immediate family circle. Between 1861 and 1868, Sophia wrote at least 107 letters to Annie and more than 120 letters to her husband, the publisher James T. Fields. Sophia's portion of the correspondence is currently housed at the Boston Public Library. For a comprehensive breakdown of the correspondence, see Edwin Haviland Miller, "A Calendar of the Letters of Sophia Peabody Hawthorne," in *Studies in the American Renaissance,* ed. Joel Myerson (Charlottesville: The University Press of Virginia, 1986), 199–281. All quotations from Sophia Hawthorne's letters to the Fieldses are from BPL Microfilm Ms.C.1.11 or from Herbert, *Dearest Beloved.* For a generous selections of letters from Sophia Hawthorne to James Fields, see also Randall Stewart's "Editing Hawthorne's Notebooks: Selections from Mrs. Hawthorne's Letters to Mr. and Mrs. Fields," *More Books* XX (Sept. 1945): 299–315.

8. Collaboration, whether between married couples or other writers, remains an under-theorized topic in literary and cultural studies. Just what "collaboration" means in the Hawthornes' case can only be explored fully within the context of other nineteenth-century pairings that include George Eliot and George Heney Lewes, the Wordsworths, the Brownings, the Stevensons, and, most importantly, the Shelleys. For groundbreaking work in the area of collaboration, see

Jack Stillinger, *Multiple Authorship and the Myth of Solitary Genius* (New York: Oxford University Press, 1991). See also Bette London, *Writing Double: Women's Literary Partnerships* (Ithaca: Cornell University Press, 1999) and Wayne Koestenbaum, *Double Talk: The Erotics of Male Literary Collaboration* (New York: Routledge, 1989).

9. For an overview of the publication history of the American notebooks, including MA 580, see Claude M. Simpson's "Textual Commentary" in *The Centenary Edition of the Works of Nathaniel Hawthorne*, 705–08. See also Patricia Dunlavy Valenti's "Sophia Peabody Hawthorne's *American Notebooks*," in *Studies in the American Renaissance*, ed. Joel Myerson (Charlottesville: University Press of Virginia, 1996), 115–185.

10. Eight of Nathaniel Hawthorne's American notebooks, including the two he composed jointly with Sophia, are extant. The earliest surviving notebook dates from 1835; the last American notebook concludes in 1853. Two of Hawthorne's solo notebooks overlap with the notebooks he and Sophia kept together: MA 577 contains entries from September 26, 1841 to 1852; and MA 579 contains entries from May 5, 1850 to June 1853. The *Atlantic* publication of the journal entries corresponding to the period of the common notebooks makes no mention of Nathaniel and Sophia Hawthorne's recent marriage.

11. See Melville's famous review, "Hawthorne and His Mosses," in Idol and Buford, *Reviews*, 104–115, and James's monograph *Hawthorne* in *Essays on Literature: American Writers, English Writers*, ed. Leon Edel (New York: The Library of America, 1984), 315–457. J. Hillis Miller provides an illuminating commentary on James's reading of Hawthorne in *Hawthorne and History: Defacing It* (Cambridge: Blackwell, 1991), 51–56.

12. See James R. Mellow, *Nathaniel Hawthorne in His Times* (Baltimore: Johns Hopkins University Press, 1998).

13. Sophia alludes to Hawthorne's reading of Milton to her in a letter to her sister Elizabeth Palmer Peabody written on February 16, 1851: "And you know his wonderful reading! Certainly I never heard such reading—I felt it first when he read aloud all Shakspere to me during the first winter of our marriage. . . . For the first time I realized Shakspere. So then I first knew Milton [.] Eden bloomed afresh. Adam first raised his kingly brow & the Son of the morning fell from the heavenly hosts" (qtd. in "Sophia Hawthorne as Literary Critic and Educator: A Letter," ed. N. Luanne Jenkins Hurst, *The Nathaniel Hawthorne Review* 18.2 [Fall 1992]: 5). See also Marion L. Kesselring, *Hawthorne's Reading, 1828–1850: A Transcription and Identification of Titles Recorded in the Charge-Books of the Salem Athenaeum* (Folcroft, PA: Folcroft Press, 1969).

14. For Hawthorne's record of his impressions of Brook Farm, see *CE* VIII, 196–314.

15. In the sixteen months covered by MA 580, the Hawthornes made fifty-nine entries—forty of these are by Nathaniel, nineteen by Sophia. Initially, Nathaniel Hawthorne wrote almost daily entries in the journal, while Sophia's entries appeared more infrequently and irregularly; later, Sophia's entries seem to dominate. At different times, moreover, both Sophia and Nathaniel absented themselves from the collaborative project. Nathaniel made no entries between 24 November 1842 and 31 March 1843, 27 April and 2 June 1843, and 31 July and 6 September 1843; Sophia suddenly fell silent between 8 September and 11 December 1842, then again between 12 December 1842 and mid-April 1843, and a final time from 2 September and 19 November 1843. Often their absences from MA 580 can be explained partly by their commitment to other projects. Nathaniel Hawthorne kept at least one private journal at the same time as the "common journal" (MA 577, September 26, 1841–[n.d.] 1852) and composed several tales for publication, including "The Birth-mark" and "Rappacini's Daughter." Sophia's lapses are more difficult to account for: no private journal by her exists for this period, though it is possible that she was already engaged in the painting that would be one focus of the private journal she began in December 1843 (Berg Collection), only a few weeks after abandoning the common journal. This journal, composed between 1 December 1843 and 5 January 1844, consists of eleven unbound and unnumbered sheets folded once and within one another to make a single, folio-style gathering. Here, Sophia both affirms the dream of spiritual union central to MA 580—"Were we two persons?" (January 2, 1844) and undermines that dream through her repeated expressions of loneliness and vulnerability—"I felt desolate & nervous & as if I wanted to sit down & weep a river" (December 30, 1843). Like MA 580, moreover, the journal is a damaged record, marked by internal lacunae and missing leaves. For a transcription of the text of Sophia's solo journal from this period, see McDonald, "A Sophia Hawthorne Journal," 1–30.

16. For readings of Sophia's influence on Nathaniel Hawthorne's writings from the Old Manse period, see, for example, Nina Baym's *The Scarlet*

Letter: A Reading (Boston: Twayne Publishers, 1986), Louise de Salvo's *Nathaniel Hawthorne* (Brighton, Sussex: Harvester Press, 1987), Leland S. Person Jr.'s *Aesthetic Headaches: Women and a Masculine Poetics in Poe, Melville, and Hawthorne* (Athens: University of Georgia Press, 1988), Gillian Brown's *Domestic Individualism: Imagining Self in Nineteenth-Century America* (Berkeley: University of California Press, 1990), and John L. Idol, Jr. and Melinda M. Pinder's *Hawthorne and Women: Engendering and Expanding the Hawthorne Tradition* (Amherst: University of Massachusetts Press, 1999).

17. While the journal entries often mime the direct address of letters—on April 9, 1843, for example, Hawthorne begins an entry, "Dear little Wife" and signs it "Thy truest Husband," while on August 29, 1843, Sophia writes to the absent Hawthorne, "My darling husband, I have been thinking whether I could send thee another letter or write to thee here—And I concluded to do the last; for thou mightest not get another letter in Salem before leaving"—they remain separate, at least in the minds of the Hawthornes, from the epistolary category. This separation is in marked contrast with Sophia Hawthorne's early and extended blurring of journalistic and epistolary genres in her "Cuba Journal" of 1833–35—a series of 56 letters bound into a three-volume home-made book by Sophia's mother and sisters. For information on the "Cuba Journal," see Claire Badaracco, "The Night-blooming Cereus: A Letter from the 'Cuba Journal' 1833–35 of Sophia Hawthorne Peabody, With a Check List of Her Autograph Materials in American Institutions," *Bulletin of Research in the Humanities* 81 (1978): 56–73. On the importance of letters in the Hawthornes' courtship, see also Leland S. Person, Jr., "Hawthorne's Love Letters: Writing and Relationship," *American Literature* 59.2 (May 1987): 211–227 and Julie M. Norko, "Hawthorne's Love Letters: The Threshold World of Sophia Peabody," *American Transcendental Quarterly* 7.2 (June 1993): 127–139.

18. As Claire M. Badaracco notes, during the nineteenth century "editing the papers of a great public man—whether author, minister, or statesman—frequently was the occupation of widows"; see Badaracco's "Pitfalls and Rewards of the Solo Editor: Sophia Peabody Hawthorne," *Resources for American Literary Study* 11.1 (Spring 1981): 92. Mary Shelley's posthumous editing of P. B. Shelley's writings offers an especially interesting case against which to read Sophia's editing of Nathaniel Hawthorne's writings; see, for example, Syndy M. Conger, Frederick S. Frank, and Gregory O'Dea, eds., *Iconoclastic Departures: Mary Shelley after Frankenstein: Essays in Honor of the Bicentenary of Mary Shelley's Birth* (Madison, NJ: Farleigh Dickinson Press, 1997) and Betty T. Bennett and Stuart Curran, eds., *Mary Shelley in Her Times* (Baltimore: Johns Hopkins University Press, 2000).

19. For a first-rate analysis of nineteenth-century ideologies of communication, see John Durham Peters, *Speaking into the Air: A History of the Idea of Communication* (Chicago: University of Chicago Press, 1999).

20. Sophia Hawthorne's letters to James T. and Annie Fields offer clear evidence of her early copying of MA 580. As Claire Badaracco notes in "Pitfalls and Rewards of the Solo Editor," after spending the spring of 1865 reading and rereading Hawthorne's notebooks, "That fall she began editing the papers out of sentiment: one day she copied three pages from an early journal of their married life, at another time twelve pages from the Brook Farm Journal, then several pages from his American Notebook, and random passages from 'Footprints on the Sea Shore" (93). At the same time, Sophia's letters to James T. Fields allude to the initial haphazardness of the copying process. In November 1865, she wrote, "And now let me say that there is not to be this great trouble for you in all the manuscripts. I am sure I grow more careful soon"; and in February 1866, she complained: "For I began to copy selections, and then we concluded it would be better to go straight on from the beginning, and so everything was thrown into Chaos. I have now entirely forgotten how much or what I copied after the Brook Farm papers. . . . I wish I could estimate how many papers there will eventually be. But . . . I cannot form the least idea" (8 February 1866).

21. Sophia Hawthorne's motives for copying the notebooks changed over time. While initially she copied in order to reanimate her relationship with Hawthorne, later, her copying was agitated by financial setbacks. In a letter of December 9, she wrote James Fields, "And if you decide to print anything, I could never have the need of pay for the MSS more than now—alas me! Because I hate to say it. How you must hate everybody who speaks of a written word!"

22. In many ways, Sophia Hawthorne's psychology of copying is continuous with her psychology of composition in MA 580, less a record of daily life than an instance of what Linda Kauffman calls "amorous epistolary discourse";

see Kauffman's *Discourses of Desire: Gender, Genre, and Epistolary Fictions* (Ithaca: Cornell University Press, 1986).

23. Samuel Coale, "The Romance of Mesmerism: Hawthorne's Medium of Romance," *Studies in the American Renaissance*, ed. Joel Myerson (Charlottesville: University Press of Virginia, 1994): 271. Sophia's experience of copying in a trance-like state in the 1860s recalls, uncannily, her experience of reading in the 1840s. In a typically hyperbolic entry in MA 569, the second of the "common" journals, Sophia writes to Nathaniel of the effects his letters have on her: "The next thing I remember was . . . [the servant] rushing up to me after dinner as I lay extended on the floor with the letter I wanted in her hand. The revulsion of joy was so immense that my head almost burst asunder & all the rest of the day it ached so desperately that I had to hold it together while my heart was dancing for joy" (September 13, 1852). While Nathaniel had expressed horror at Sophia's experiments in mesmerism—"There would be an intrusion into thy holy of holies—and the intruder would not be thy husband!" (*CE* XV: 588)—he seems to have acted as a kind of mesmerist to Sophia both during their lives and after his death. Mesmerism, of course, plays a significant role in Hawthorne's third novel, *The Blithedale Romance* (1852).

24. See Paul de Man's "Autobiography as De-Facement" in his *The Rhetoric of Romanticism* (New York: Columbia University Press, 1984), 75–77.

25. Sophia was especially anxious about publishing excerpts from the notebooks in periodical form. On at least two occasions in letters to James T. Fields, she compares journal publication with book publication, noting that the threat of exposure is greater in the first than in the second: "[Julian] may not be willing to be put before the world even at four years old—even in a book—which seems less public than a periodical" (5 August 1866); "Will not some other portion do as well?. . . .[T]here is a certain intimateness of revelation in even these extracts from the letters, which I cannot bear to have go into a public journal. It seems to me as if they would be more sheltered in the volumes" (3 November 1867).

26. Paul Ricoeur, *Hermeneutics and the Human Sciences: Essays on Language, Action, and Interpretation*, trans. John B. Thompson (Cambridge: Cambridge University Press, 1981), 202–03; qtd. in Peters, *Speaking into the Air*, 150.

27. Frank Kermode, *The Genesis of Secrecy: On the Interpretation of Narrative* (Cambridge: Harvard University Press, 1979), xi.

28. For the full text of these and other reviews of *Passages*, see John L. Idol, Jr. and Buford Jones, eds., *Nathaniel Hawthorne: The Contemporary Reviews*: 307, 319, 317. The 1868 review from the *Christian Register* is quoted by Sophia Hawthorne herself, in a May 1866 letter to James T. Fields (qtd. in Stewart, "Editing Hawthorne's Notebooks," 307).

29. *Passages from the American Note-Books of Nathaniel Hawthorne*. 2 vols. Boston: Ticknor and Fields, 1868.

30. See Randall Stewart's "Mrs. Hawthorne's Revision of the American Notebooks" and "Mrs. Hawthorne's Revisions of the English Notebooks" in *The English Notebooks,* ed. Randall Stewart (New York: Modern Language Association, 1941), xxi. For a detailed examination of Sophia Hawthorne's "bowdlerization" of the American notebooks, see Claude M. Simpson, "Alterations in the Manuscript," in the *Centenary Edition* VIII: 739–789.

31. See Ralph Waldo Emerson, "Nature" (1844), in *Selected Writings of Emerson,* ed. Donald McQuade (New York: Modern Library, 1981), 403. Sophia's discovery is also related to Paul Ricoeur's notion that the text is not merely a "particular case of intersubjective communication," but, rather, "the paradigm of distanciation in communication"; see Ricoeur, *Hermeneutics and the Human Sciences,* 202–03.

32. Roland Barthes, *Camera Lucida: Reflections on Photography,* trans. Richard Howard (New York: Hill and Wang, 1981), 49, 43.

33. See Terry Eagleton, *Ideology of the Aesthetic* (Oxford: Blackwell, 1990).

34. G. Thomas Tanselle, *A Rationale of Textual Criticism* (Philadelphia: University of Pennsylvania Press, 1989), 64–65.

35. Judy Simons, *Diaries and Journals of Literary Women from Fanny Burney to Virginia Woolf* (London: Macmillan, 1990), 13.

36. The mutilation of Emily Dickinson's fascicles by her brother, Austin Dickinson, or her editor, Mabel Loomis Todd, offers a ready example of this phenomenon. See Martha Nell Smith, *Rowing in Eden: Rereading Emily Dickinson* (Austin: University of Texas Press, 1992) and Marta Werner, "Entre censure et contre-écriture: Emily Dickinson, Traversée et traces de rapture." *Genèse, censure, autocensure*, ed. Catherine Viollet and Claire Bustarret. Paris: CNRS Editions, 2005: 131–148.

37. Jerome J. McGann, *The Textual Condition*, 9.

38. Samuel R. Delany, *The Motion of Light in Water: Sex and Science Fiction Writing in the East Village, 1960–1965*. New York: Richard Kasak Books, 1993, 69.

39. On the role of telemedia in the 1840s, see Nicholas Royle, *Telepathy and Literature: Essays on the Reading Mind* (London: Basil Blackwell, 1990) and Peters, *Speaking into the Air.*

Textual Introduction

The Common Journal of
Nathaniel and Sophia Hawthorne

Background

THE TEXTUAL HISTORY OF MA 580 is, to say the least, complex. Nathaniel Hawthorne's contributions to the journal were printed in part in *The Atlantic Monthly* (August-October 1866) and *Passages from the American Note-Books* (Boston: Ticknor and Fields, 1868), and were reissued virtually unchanged through numerous printings and editions until Randall Stewart produced his restored and corrected edition of the American notebooks in 1932. Stewart's work became the basis for the updated Centenary Edition, which published Hawthorne's MA 580 entries in full in Volume 8 of *The Centenary Edition of the Works of Nathaniel Hawthorne* (Ohio State University Press, 1972). Sophia Hawthorne's contributions to MA 580 were finally printed in 1996, when Patricia Dunlavy Valenti edited them for publication in *Studies in the American Renaissance.*[1] While Valenti's work of recovery fills a crucial gap in the American notebooks, it also highlights the absence of a comprehensive edition of MA 580.

Our first aim has been to produce a facsimile edition of MA 580 that restores the material integrity of the notebook largely obscured by all previous editions. By providing high-quality photographic facsimiles along with diplomatic transcriptions of the journal's leaves, this edition offers readers intimate access to the Hawthornes' collaborative scene of writing and reveals the complexity of their textual exchanges during the first year of their marriage. By making visible the literal traces of the journal's composition, *Ordinary Mysteries* encourages greater critical attentiveness to the variegated materiality of writing, the rhythms of inscription and inspiration, in a document whose seeming casualness and intimacy belies the torturous history of publication and censorship to which it gave rise.

The edition also foregrounds a principal question of interest raised by the notebook as a whole: how does it challenge us to reassess the definitions of "private," "public," and "intimate," as they are commonly applied in the classification of manuscripts?[2] The difficulty of determining the documentary and generic status of the journal is reflected in its editorial and publication history. Thus the second principal aim of this edition has been to represent the alterations made to the journal throughout its initial metamorphosis from private record to public property. These alterations were carried out by Sophia Hawthorne, most likely when she was first preparing selections from her husband's entries for publication in the mid-1860s.[3] The most visible—and also most violent—of Sophia's alterations were executed directly on the notebook's leaves. Here, cancellations—both simple overinkings and more extensive scissorings—function as inscriptions of Sophia's conscious struggle to construct a narrative of the Hawthornes' lives and writing that would be acceptable to her children (and heirs) as well as to a larger Victorian audience, and of her unconscious negotiation between the desire to speak and the need to repress what was forbidden in this account of intimate life. Moreover, the physical traces of Sophia's editing reveal that even as she transformed MA 580 from a record of relatively carefree private life to a narrative of bourgeois decorum, she was herself transformed from an intimate collaborator into a repressive censor—a kind of double agent whose most serious transgressions ultimately effected her own erasure from the collaborative project. Finally, while Sophia's physical marking of the notebook resulted in the distortion and partial destruction of this private document, her publication of extracts from MA 580 alongside extracts from other notebooks and letters in *Passages from the American Note-Books of Nathaniel Hawthorne* resulted in the destruction of the original reading context for the common journal. No longer part of an ongoing dialogue with an intimate interlocutor, the printed extracts reappear as Nathaniel Hawthorne's individual pensées—a textual situation perpetuated at least in part even in the Centenary Edition, which also omits Sophia's contributions to the notebook. By illuminating the early publication history of the common journal, this edition should stimulate new investigations into the complexities involved in the editing of "private" or "intimate" texts, while also offering a richer awareness of the ways in which all texts are historically contingent in the circumstances of their production, reception, and reconstruction in the present.

The Manuscript

In its original state, the common journal measured 7 by 9 5/16 inches and was bound between green marbled hard covers. Although the physical evidence is now ambiguous, MA 580 appears to have been bound in eight gatherings of varying numbers of sheets: gatherings 1 and 2 consist of four folded sheets; gatherings 3, 5, 6, and 7 consist of five folded sheets; gathering 4, the center gathering, is somewhat problematic, though it probably originally consisted of five folded sheets; and gathering 8, the final gathering, consists of one folded sheet only. Of the apparently sixty-eight leaves originally belonging to the notebook, between nine and eleven leaves have been entirely, and five others partially, excised and destroyed (see Appendix 2). Leaves are missing at the following locations: one or two leaves are missing between the front fly-leaf and the first extant leaf of the notebook currently numbered 2; one or two leaves are missing between the leaves currently numbered 8 and 9; one leaf is missing between the leaves currently numbered 14 and 14a; three or four leaves are missing between the leaves currently numbered 24 and 25; two or three leaves are missing between 30 and 30a; and one leaf is missing between the leaves currently numbered 48 and 49.[4] Five other leaves were cut out of the notebook but preserved and later tipped in: 29, 30, 49, 50, and 59. In addition to the excisions made to the notebook, numerous passages in MA 580 were obliterated via an aggressive process of over-inking with either black or blue ink or altered through the careful superimposition of text (see Appendix 3). The author of the excisions, obliterations, and superimpositions is generally assumed to be Sophia Hawthorne.[5]

Sophia edited the notebook between 1864 and 1868 while living at The Wayside in Concord. In a letter to James T. Fields she writes in reference to the journals, "I have a double-tin box in which I keep everything of this kind for fear of fire."[6] There is no record of the notebook's whereabouts, however, between 1868, the year *Passages* appeared in print and also the year the Hawthornes left The Wayside for Europe, and 1871, the year of Sophia Hawthorne's death in London. She may have taken the notebook with her to Dresden and later to London, or she may have left it behind in Concord.[7] After her death, however, this notebook, along with Nathaniel Hawthorne's other American notebooks, passed into the hands of Julian Hawthorne, who drew haphazardly, and often misleadingly, on its contents in his 1884 biography *Nathaniel Hawthorne and His Wife*.[8] Some two decades after the publication of the biography, in 1903, Julian apparently sold the American notebooks to Stephen Wakeman. Six years later, in 1909, the notebooks entered the collection of J. Pierpont Morgan as part of the Wakeman Collection, which Morgan purchased from George S. Hellman through the New York Cooperative Society. Upon Morgan's death in 1913, his collections passed on to his son, J. P. Morgan, Jr., who made the Pierpont Morgan Library a public institution in 1924. The notebook MA 580 became part of the Morgan Library's collection at this time.

The Morgan Library's records do not indicate the condition of MA 580 at the time of acquisition. We do know, however, that some time after the common journal entered the collection, the library's conservation staff foliated the notebook, numbering the leaves 1-59 before disbinding and then rebinding them anew. The original leaves and boards were retained, while the sewing and leather (spine and corners) were replaced in order to stay deterioration. It is possible that many of the passages originally blotted out in blue water-soluble ink were at this time deliberately lightened through the dry-cleaning process to reveal the text beneath. Additionally, two leaves—51 and 52—previously glued together, probably by Sophia, were separated.[9] The preservation work executed on the notebook resulted in one error: the two leaves previously excised and tipped in before the notebook's arrival at the Morgan Library were there incorrectly numbered 29 and 30 and misbound following the leaf currently numbered 28, creating a fault in the chronological sequence of the notebook's entries. In this edition of the notebook we follow Patrica Valenti's pioneering transcription of Sophia Hawthorne's portions of MA 580 by restoring the manuscript leaves to where they apparently belong chronologically—i.e., following the leaf currently numbered 37.

Note on the Facsimiles: The facsimile pages for this edition were photographed initially as eight-by-ten-inch halftone prints and then digitally retouched to simulate the color of the paper in the manuscript. The color of the ink in the original is closer to a faded brown than black, especially in Sophia's entries. The corrections made on the manuscript pages vary from blottings using the same ink as the entries to (presumably later) coverups using a dark blue ink; these latter have been lightened in places during restoration of the notebook. It is important for the purposes of our argument in this edition that a facsimile be regarded not as the faithful reproduction of an original artifact, but as a motivated intervention within the context of a complex editorial and publishing history.

The Transcription

This edition offers a limited diplomatic transcription of the notebook, corresponding to it leaf by leaf, line by line, rendering precisely the orthography and punctuation of the writers, and emphasizing the journal's fundamentally antiphonal structure. To this end, journal entries composed by Nathaniel Hawthorne appear in Garamond Roman, 14 pt., black, while journal entries composed by Sophia Peabody Hawthorne appear in Garamond Roman, 14 pt., brown. Alterations and emendations on the manuscript judged to have been made by the writers during the course of composition are, wherever possible, represented graphically; for example, interlineated text, often indicated by the Hawthornes with carets, is indicated in the transcript with up and down arrows; cancellations of text that remains legible are indicated with the ~~strike through~~ feature; and cancellations of text that is now illegible are indicated with the strike through feature as follows ~~XXXXX~~. The only compositional practice not represented graphically in the transcription or detailed in the textual notes is the writers' use of overwriting. While Sophia Hawthorne rarely altered her text via overwriting, Nathaniel Hawthorne frequently did so. For a comprehensive record of instances of overwriting in Nathaniel Hawthorne's entries, see the Textual Notes for volume 8 of the *Centenary Edition of the Works of Nathaniel Hawthorne.* The few instances of editorial superimposition of text are detailed in the Textual Notes.

The compositional dynamics of the authors as reflected on the manuscript leaves differ significantly—perhaps indicating their different conceptions of the journal as a public or private document as well as their different experiences of print. While Nathaniel Hawthorne's entries feature largely standard uses of punctuation and paragraphing, Sophia Hawthorne's entries often feature unconventional usage. Most notably, Sophia frequently uses dashes in place of periods. Here, rather than standardize Sophia's end-punctuation, we have evaluated these marks on a case-by-case basis, rendering them sometimes as dashes, sometimes as periods depending on the lengths and angles of the marks. Moreover, when Sophia suspended the closure of sentences altogether, we have not added end punctuation of any kind. Finally, unlike Nathaniel Hawthorne, who almost always clearly indicated the beginning of each new paragraph via indentation, Sophia Hawthorne did not consistently indent at the beginning of paragraphs. At times, a blank space at the end of a line seems to suggest a textual transition; at other times, there are no visual clues as to the beginning and ending of paragraphs. Here, unless the text is clearly indented, it appears flush left. By treating Sophia's text in this manner, we hope to have preserved at least some of the original expressiveness of her hand in our print transcription.

On three occasions Sophia Hawthorne interpolates drawings into the body of her text. These drawings, though not represented graphically in the transcript, are listed in Appendix 4.

In addition to representing the dynamics of composition, this edition seeks to illuminate the dynamics of editing. Alterations, emendations, cancellations, overwriting, and all other markings on the manuscript judged to have been made by Sophia Hawthorne in the course of preparing selections from the journal for print are highlighted in blue, and further information concerning the nature of the editorial interventions is reported in the Textual Notes. In addition to simple corrections, cancellations, and obliterations, a series of pencil cross marks and asterisks appear throughout the journal. Their precise significance is not known, though they seem to be part of a private system of notation employed by Sophia Hawthorne in her editing of the text.[10] Although these marks take at least two different forms, in the transcription they are represented uniformly as "x"s.

Notes made by hands other than Nathaniel and Sophia Hawthorne—heirs, previous owners, library conservators, and cataloguers—as well as page headings, appear in black Linotype Cochin and are identified, whenever possible, in the Textual Notes. Dates added above the transcriptions appear in brackets. When the manuscript was foliated at the Morgan, page numbers were added to the rectos of each of the notebook's extant leaves; for greater clarity, we have added verso page numbers. Similarly, we have added line numbers on each leaf to facilitate the location of corresponding textual notes.

Finally, editorially supplied text, including dates, in the Hawthornes' journal entries is placed in square brackets [ ] in the transcript even when there is reasonable assurance of the text's or date's accuracy.

Textual Notes

The Textual Notes, organized by date of entry, author, leaf and line numbers, reflect the focus of this edition—i.e., the notebook's transition from private to public document. Two categories of textual notes accompany each journal entry made by Nathaniel Hawthorne: notes detailing Sophia Hawthorne's editorial alterations (excisions, overinkings, superimpositions) to the material document; and notes summarizing the substantive textual variants between the manuscript and the earliest printed versions of the manuscript edited by Sophia Hawthorne and printed in *The Atlantic Monthly* (August-October 1866) and *Passages from the American Note-Books*, 2 vols., Boston: Ticknor and Fields (1868). We have not attempted to report the many and often fascinating alterations in punctuation between the manuscript and the earliest printed versions, though representative examples of these important variants are found in Appendix 5. Since Sophia Hawthorne's entries were not edited or published during her lifetime or under her supervision, the textual notes accompanying her entries focus primarily on those editorial changes, largely excisions and overinkings, she made on the manuscript.

This edition has six appendices: Appendix 1: A Calendar of Sophia and Nathaniel Hawthornes' Journal Entries, 1842-43; Appendix 2: Entries with Wholly or Partly Excised Leaves; Appendix 3: Entries with Obliterated Passages; Appendix 4: Entries with Sophia Hawthorne's Editorial Marks, Emendations, and Drawings; Appendix 5: Examples of Published Entries in *The Atlantic* and *Passages;* and Appendix 6: Excerpts from the Sophia Hawthorne/James T. and Annie Fields Correspondence, 1864-1868.

Acknowledgments

We gratefully acknowledge the assistance of Christine Nelson, Curator of Rare Books and Manuscripts at the Pierpont Morgan Library. Without the generous cooperation of Ms. Nelson and her staff this edition of the Hawthornes' common notebook could not have been completed. They permitted close study of the notebook, provided high-quality black and white facsimiles of the notebook's leaves, and answered numerous questions concerning the notebook's provenance and history. Christine Nelson's conviction, moreover, that MA 580 should be re-edited encouraged us throughout the period of our research. Grateful acknowledgment is also due to manuscript specialists at the Boston Public Library and at the New York Public Library who made available critical peripheral materials, including microfilms of the Sophia Peabody Hawthorne/ James T. Fields correspondence, 1864-1868.

We are much indebted to the work of other scholars both on Hawthorne and on textual matters, particularly Patricia Valenti, Joel Myerson, T. Walter Herbert, James R. Mellow, Jerome J. McGann, Donald Reiman, Randall Stewart, and the editors of *The Centenary Edition of the Works of Nathaniel Hawthorne.* Julie Hall and Monika Elbert read early drafts of the introductory essay and offered valuable criticism. Robin G. Schulze provided advice and encouragement during a late stage in the project. The Nathaniel Hawthorne Society, The Society for Textual Scholarship, and The Society for the History of Authorship, Reading, and Publishing gave us opportunities to share our research with colleagues working in different disciplines. Florine Melnyk assisted us with great patience in proofreading the transcription.

The Faculty Research Fund of D'Youville College and the Humanities Research Fund of the University of Warwick awarded us grants to cover final publication costs. Our greatest debt is to the American Philosophical Society, which provided a grant-in-aid toward the research expenses of this edition of the Hawthornes' common journal.

Notes

1. See Patricia Valenti, "Sophia Peabody Hawthorne's American Notebooks," *Studies in the American Renaissance*, edited by Joel Myerson (Charlottesville: University Press of Virginia, 1996), 115–185.

2. See, for example, Donald Reiman's *The Study of Modern Manuscripts: Public, Confidential, and Private* (Baltimore: Johns Hopkins University Press, 1993); for an analysis of the historical and theoretical implications of the idea of the "public" in modern culture, see Michael Warner's *Publics and Counterpublics* (New York: Zone Books, 2002).

3. For representative critical responses to Sophia Hawthorne's editing of her husband's notebooks see Randall Stewart's "Editing Hawthorne's Notebooks: Selections from Mrs. Hawthorne's Letters to Mr. and Mrs. Fields, 1864–1868," *More Books: The Bulletin of the Boston Public Library* (September 1945): 299–315; Sterling Elsiminger's "Mrs. Hawthorne's Editing of the French and Italian Notebooks," *Nathaniel Hawthorne Journal* 8 (1978): 89–93; Claire M. Badaracco's "Pitfalls and Rewards of the Solo Editor: Sophia Peabody Hawthorne," *Resources for American Literary Study* 11.1 (Spring 1981): 91–100; and Carol H. MacKay's "Hawthorne, Sophia, and Hilda as Copyists: Duplication and Transformation in The Marble Faun," *Browning Institute Studies* 12 (1984): 93–120.

4. Christine Nelson notes that the collation of MA 580 is especially challenging and that any conclusions about the notebook's original state are necessarily provisional. An anomaly of the volume is that some gatherings consist of four folded sheets and some of five folded sheets. If, originally, all the gatherings with the exception of the final one consisted of five folded sheets, as the editors of the Centenary seem to believe, there would be an additional two leaves each missing from the first and second gatherings, though precisely where in those gatherings is unclear (Christine Nelson, private correspondence, December 2001, July 2003).

5. A 1903 note by Julian Hawthorne, now affixed to the inside front cover of MA 580, states, "All pages of Mrs. Hawthorne's part of this journal which are not included in those herewith appended, were destroyed, as well as cut out, by her, when she transcribed the volume for publication 35 years ago." Although Julian's narrative of his mother's destruction of manuscript evidence has been accepted and repeated by almost all later scholars, it is not wholly above suspicion. The notebooks were in Julian's possession even longer than they were in Sophia's, and his radically misleading use of their contents in his biography of his parents (see note 9, below) raises questions about his handling of the journals. For further speculation on this issue, see John MacDonald's introduction to "A Sophia Hawthorne Journal, 1843–1844," *The Nathaniel Hawthorne Journal* (1974): 1–30.

6. Sophia Hawthorne to James T. Fields, October 27, 1867 (BPL microfilm).

7. Sophia Hawthorne carried at least some of her husband's papers with her when she went abroad: until the time of her death, she was working on preparing a draft of his abortive romance *Septimus Felton* for publication; her daughter Una, assisted by Robert Browning, completed the work.

8. See Julian Hawthorne's *Nathaniel Hawthorne and His Wife: A Biography*, 2 vols. (Boston: Houghton Mifflin, 1884). In volume I, pp. 288–293, Julian prints extracts from the following entries made in MA 580: August 13, 1842; March 31, 1843; April 9, 1843; April 10, 1843; April 26, 1843; April 15, 1842; August 30, 1842; September 1, 1842; April 7, 1843; April 8, 1843; April 7, 1843; September 2, 1842. The extracts, listed above in the order in which they appear in the biography, are printed without regard for chronology or context. Interestingly, Julian seems to have sought to print those passages specially marked by Sophia for omission: in eight of the twelve passages selected, Sophia's editorial cross-marks appear nearby.

9. We are grateful to Christine Nelson for her careful reconstruction of the notebook's transmission history and treatment at the Pierpont Morgan Library.

10. In a letter to James T. Fields on the protocol for correcting proofs, Sophia Hawthorne writes, "I shall put a cross to whatever I refer" (BPL microfilm).

Facsimile and Transcription of MA 580

Note - 1842-3 Journal.

All pages of Mrs. Hawthorne's part of this journal which are not included in those herewith appended, were destroyed, as well as cut out, by her, when she transcribed the volume for publication 35 years ago.

Julian Hawthorne

New York, April 9, 1913.

A
V-2 Old Manse
10
A

Note – 1842-3 Journal.

All pages of Mrs. Hawthorne's part of this journal which are not included in those herewith appended, were destroyed, as well as cut out, by her, when she transcribed the volume for publication 35 years ago.

Julian Hawthorne

New York, April 9, 1903.

v.1 Journal kept by Nathaniel Hawthorne & his wife 1842–1843 1

Concord — 1842. — 1843. to November 19

This diary was kept conjointly by Hawthorne and his wife and Mrs. H seems to have effaced all of his part —
~~It was~~ this part commenced less than a month after their marriage when they went to live at the Old Manse and ~~the diary as~~ this volume of the journal was continued up to the time they left there —
It is full of terms of endearment used by Hawthorne in reference to his wife all of which Mrs. H — cut out (and much

The Common Journal of Nathaniel and Sophia Hawthorne

v.1 Journal kept by Nathaniel Hawthorne & his wife 1842–1843

Concord 1842 – 1843 to November 19

This diary was kept conjointly by Hawthorne
and his wife and Mrs. H. seems to have
spared all his part –
~~It was~~ ↑His part↓ commenced less than a month after
their marriage when they went to live at the
Old Manse and ~~the diary was~~ this volume of
the journal was continued up to the time
they left there –
It is full of terms of endearment used by
Hawthorne in reference to his wife all
[of] which Mrs. H - cut out (and much

(verso of pastedown)

other matter) when she "edited" and prin[ted]
the journals –
This is the only volume of the diaries
written in this familiar family manner ~~all the others are as~~ which is natural as
practically their whole period at the
Old Manse was a honey-moon –

This outline can be filled in to advantage

[Note by Mr. Wakeman]

wife. I could not comprehend why. When
I came to him, he t'd me I had transgressed
the law of right in trampling down the
unmown grass, & he tried to induce me
to come back, that he might not have to
violate his conscience by doing the same
thing. And I was very naughty & would not
obey, & therefore he punished me by staying
behind. This I did not like very well, &
I climbed the hill alone. We penetrated
the pleasant gloom & sat down upon the
carpet of dried pine leaves. Then I clasped
him in my arms in the lovely shade, &
we laid down a few moments on the
bosom of dear mother Earth. Oh how sweet
it was! And I told him I would not be
so naughty again, & there was a very slight
diamond shower without any thunder or
lightning, & we were happiest. We walked
through the woods, & came forth into an
open space, whence a fair, broad
landscape could be seen, our old Manse
holding a respectable place in the plain,
the river opening its blue eyes here &
there, & waving mountainous ridges
closing in the horizon. There we
plucked whortleberries & then sat down.
There was no wind & the stillness was
profound. There seemed no movement in
the world but that of our pulses. The
earth was still before us. It was very lovely
but the rapture of my spirit was caused more
by knowing that my own husband was at my
side than by all the rich variety of plain,
river, forest & mountain around & at my feet.

wife. I could not comprehend why. When I came to him, he told me I had transgressed the law of right in trampling down the unmown grass, & he tried to induce me to come back, that he might not have to violate his conscience by doing the same thing. And I was very naughty & would not obey, & therefore he punished me by staying behind. This I did not like very well, & I climbed the hill alone. We penetrated the pleasant gloom & sat down upon the carpet of dried pine leaves. Then I clasped him in my arms in the lovely shade, & we laid down a few moments on the bosom of dear mother Earth. Oh how sweet it was! And I told him I would not be so naughty again, & there was a very slight diamond shower without any thunder or lightning, & we were happiest. We walked through the forest, & came forth into an open space, whence a fair, broad landscape could be seen, our old Manse holding a respectable place in the plain, the river opening its blue eyes here & there, & waving mountainous ridges closing in the horizon. There we plucked whortleberries & then sat down There was no wind & the stillness was profound. There seemed no movement in the world but that of our pulses. The [Ear]th was still before us. It was very lovely but the rapture of my spirit was caused more by knowing that my own husband was at my side than by all the rich variety of plain, river, forest & mountain around & at my feet.

August 5th. Friday. 1842. A rainy day—a rainy day—and I do verily believe there is no sunshine in this world, except what beams from my wife's eyes. At present, she has laid her strict command on me to take pen in hand; and, to ensure my obedience, has banished me to the little ten-foot-square apartment, misnamed my study; but she must not be surprised, if the dismalness of the day, and the dullness of my solitude, should be the prominent characteristics of what I write. And what is there to write about at all? Happiness has no succession of events; because it is a part of eternity; and we have been living in eternity, ever since we came to this old Manse. Like Enoch, we seem to have been translated to the other state of being, without having passed through death. Our spirits must have flitted away, unconsciously, in the deep and quiet rapture of some long embrace; and we can only perceive that we have cast off our mortal part, by the more real and earnest life of our spirits. Externally, our Paradise has very much the aspect of a pleasant old domicile, on earth. This antique house (for it looks antique, though it was created by Providence expressly for our use, and at the precise time when we wanted it) stands behind a noble avenue of Balm of Gilead trees; and when we chance to observe a passing traveller, through the sunshine and the shadow of this long avenue, his figure appears too dim and remote to disturb our sense of blissful seclusion. Few, indeed, are the mortals who venture within our sacred precincts. George Prescott, who has not yet grown earthly enough, I suppose, to be debarred from occasional visits to Paradise—comes daily to bring three pints of milk, from some ambrosial cow;—occasionally, also, he makes an offering of mortal flowers, at the throne of a certain angelic personage. Mr. Emerson comes sometimes, and has been so far favored as to be feasted (with a gnome, yclept Ellery Channing) on our nectar and ambrosia. Mr. Thoreau has twice listened to the music of the spheres, which, for our private convenience, we have packed into a musical box. Elizabeth Hoar (who is much more at home among spirits than among

August 5th. Friday. ↑1842↓ A rainy day – a rainy day – and I do verily believe there is no sunshine in this world, except what beams from my wife's eyes. At present, she has laid her strict command on me to take pen in hand; and, to ensure my obedience has banished me to the little ten-foot-square apartment, misnamed my study; but she must not be surprised, if the dismalness of the day, and the dulness of my solitude, should be the prominent characteristics of what I write. And what is there to write about at all? Happiness has no succession of events; because it is a part of eternity; and we have been living in eternity, ever since we came to this old Manse. Like Enoch, we seem to have been translated to the other state of being, without having passed through death. Our spirits must have flitted away, unconsciously, in the deep and quiet rapture of some long embrace; and we can only perceive that we have cast off our mortal part, by the more real and earnest life of our spirits. Externally, our Paradise has very much the aspect of a pleasant old domicile, on earth. The antique house (for it looks antique, though it was created by Providence expressly for our use, and at the precise time when we wanted it) stands behind a noble avenue of Balm of Gilead trees; and when we chance to observe a passing traveller, through the sunshine and the shadow of this long avenue, his figure appears too dim and remote to disturb our sense of blissful seclusion. Few, indeed, are the mortals who venture within our sacred precincts. George Prescott – who has not yet grown earthly enough, I suppose, to be debarred from occasional visits to Paradise – comes daily to bring three pints of milk, from some ambrosial cow; – occasionally, also, he makes an offering of mortal flowers, at the shrine of a certain angelic personage. Mr. Emerson comes sometimes, and has been so far favored as to be feasted (with a gnome, yclept Ellery Channing) on our nectar and ambrosia. Mr. Thorow has twice listened to the music of the spheres, which, for our private convenience, we have packed into a musical box. Elizabeth Hoar (who is much more at home among spirits than among

3

fleshly bodies) came hither a few times, merely to welcome us to the ethereal world; but lately she has vanished into some other region of infinite space. One rash mortal, on the second Sunday after our arrival, obtruded himself upon us in a gig. There have since been three or four callers, who preposterously think that the courtesies of the lower world are to be responded to by people whose home is in Paradise. I must not forget to mention that the butcher comes twice or thrice a week; and we have so far improved upon the custom of Adam and Eve, that we generally furnish forth our feasts with a portion of some delicate calf or lamb, whose unspotted innocence entitles them to the happiness of becoming our sustenance. Would that my wife would permit me to record the ethereal dainties, that kind Heaven provided for us, on the first day of our arrival! Never, surely, was such food heard of on earth — at least, not by me. Well; the above-mentioned persons are nearly all that have entered into the hallowed shade of the avenue; — except, indeed, a certain sinner who came to bargain for the grass in our orchard, and another who came with a new cistern; for it is one of the drawbacks upon our Paradise, that it contains no water fit either to drink or to bathe in; so that the showers of Heaven have become, in good truth, a godsend. I wonder why Providence does not cause a clear, cold fountain to bubble up at our doorstep; — methinks it would not be unreasonable to pray for such a favor. At present, we are under the ridiculous necessity of sending to the outer world for water. Only imagine Adam trudging out of Paradise with a bucket in each hand, to get water to drink, or for Eve to bathe in! Intolerable! I shall absolutely think myself wronged, unless I find the aforesaid fountain bubbling at our doorstep the next time I look out. In other respects, Providence has treated us pretty tolerably well; but here I shall expect something further to be done. Also, in the way of future favors, a kitten would be

fleshly bodies) came hither a few times, merely to welcome us to the ethereal world; but latterly she has vanished into some other region of infinite space. One rash mortal, on the second Sunday after our arrival, obtruded himself upon us in a gig. There have since been three or four callers, who preposterously think that the courtesies of the lower world are to be responded to by people whose home is in Paradise. ~~XXXXXXXXXXXXXXXXXXX~~

~~I'm~~ I must not forget to mention that the butcher comes twice or thrice a week; and we have so far improved upon the custom of Adam and Eve, that we generally furnish forth our feasts with a portion of some delicate calf or lamb, whose unspotted innocence entitles them to the happiness of becoming our sustenance. Would that my wife would permit me to record the ethereal dainties, that kind Heaven provided for us, on the first day of our arrival! Never, surely, was such food heard of on earth – at least, not by me. Well; the above mentioned persons are nearly all that have intruded into the hallowed shade of ↑our↓ avenue; – except, indeed, a certain sinner who came to bargain for the grass in our orchard, and another who came with a new cistern; for it is one of the drawbacks upon our Paradise, that it contains no water fit either to drink or to bathe in; so that the showers of Heaven have become, in good truth, a godsend. I wonder why Providence does not cause a clear, cold fountain to bubble up at our doorstep; – methinks it would not be unreasonable to pray for such a favor. At present, we are under the ridiculous necessity of sending to the outer world for water. Only imagine Adam trudging out of Paradise with a bucket in each hand, to get water to drink, or for Eve to bathe in! Intolerable! I shall absolutely think myself wronged, unless I find the aforesaid fountain bubbling at our doorstep, the next time I look out.

In other respects, Providence has treated us pretty tolerably well; but here I shall expect something further to be done. Also, in the way of future favors, a kitten would be very acceptable. Animals (except, perhaps, a pig) seem never out of place, even in the most paradisiacal spheres. And, by the bye, a young colt comes up our avenue, now and then, to crop the seldom-trodden herbage; and so does a company of cows, whose sweet breath well repays us for the food which they obtain. There are likewise a few hens, whose quiet cluck is heard pleasantly about the house. A black dog sometimes stands at the farther extremity of the avenue, and looks wistfully towards the house; but when I whistle to him, he puts his tail between his legs, and trots away. Foolish dog!— if he had more faith, he should have bones enough.

August 6th. Saturday. Still a dull day, threatening rain, yet without energy of character enough to rain outright. However, yesterday there were showers enough to fill our washing-tubs, which we eagerly set forth to receive the beneficent down-pouring. As to the new cistern, it seems to be bewitched; for while the spout pours into it like a cataract, it still remains almost empty. I wonder where Mr. Hosmer got it,— perhaps from Tantalus, under the eaves of whose palace it must formerly have stood; for, like his drinking-cup in Hades, it has the property of filling itself for ever, and never being full.

After breakfast, I took my fishing-rod, and went down through our orchard to the river-side; but as three or four boys were already in possession of the best spots along the shore, I did not fish. This river of ours is the most sluggish stream that I ever was acquainted with. I had spent three weeks by its side, and swam across it every day, before I could determine which way its current ran; and then I was compelled to decide the question by the testimony of others— not by my own observation. Owing to this torpor of the stream, it has nowhere a bright pebbly shore, nor is there so much as a narrow strip of glistening sand, in any part of its course; but it slumbers along between broad meadows, or kisses the tangled grass of mowing fields and pastures, or bathes the overhanging boughs of elder bushes, and other water-loving plants. Flags and rushes grow along its shallow margin; the yellow water lily spreads its broad flat leaves upon

very acceptable. Animals (except, perhaps, a pig) seem never out of place, even in the most paradisaical spheres. And, by the bye, a young colt comes up our avenue, now and then, to crop the seldom trodden herbage; and so do a company of cows, whose sweet breath well repays us for the food which they obtain. There are likewise a few hens, whose quiet cluck is heard pleasantly about the house. A black dog sometimes stands at the farther extremity of the avenue, and looks wistfully towards the house; but when I whistle to him, he puts his tail between his legs, and trots away. Foolish dog! – if he had more faith, he should have bones enough.

August 6th. Saturday. Still a dull day, threatening rain, yet without energy of character enough to rain outright. However, yesterday there were showers enough to fill our washing-tubs, which we eagerly set forth to receive the beneficent downpouring. As to the new cistern, it seems to be bewitched; for while the spout pours into it like a cataract, it still remains almost empty. I wonder where Mr. Hosmer got it; – perhaps from Tantalus, under the eaves of whose palace it must formerly have stood; for, like his drinking-cup in Hades, it has the property of filling itself forever, and never being full.

After breakfast, I took my fishing-rod, and went down through our orchard to the river-side; but as three or four boys were already in possession of the best spots along the shore, I did not fish. This river of ours is the most sluggish stream that I ever was acquainted with. I had spent three weeks by its side, and swam across it every day, before I could determine which way its current ran; and then I was compelled to decide the question by the testimony of others – not by my own observation. Owing to this torpor of the stream, it has nowhere a bright pebbly shore, nor is there so much as a narrow strip of glistening sand, in any part of its course; but it slumbers along between broad meadows, or kisses the tangled grass of mowing fields and pastures, or bathes the overhanging boughs of elder bushes, and other water-loving plants. Flags and rushes grow along its shallow margin; the yellow water lily spreads its broad flat leaves upon its surface; and the fragrant white pond-lily occurs in many favored spots, generally selecting a situation just so far from the river's brink, that it cannot be grasped, except at the hazard of plunging in. But thanks be to the beautiful flower for growing at any rate. It is a marvel whence it derives its loveliness and perfume, sprouting as it does from the black mud over which the river sleeps, and from which, likewise, the yellow lily draws its unclean life and noisome perfume. So it is with many people in this world;—the same soil and circumstances may produce the good and beautiful, and the wicked and ugly;—some have the faculty of assimilating to themselves only what is evil, and so they become as noisome as the yellow water-lily. A few assimilate none but good influences; and their emblem is the spotless and fragrant pond-lily, whose very breath is a blessing to all the region roundabout. I possess such a human and heavenly lily, ~~and wear it in my bosom~~. Heaven grant that I myself may not be symbolized by its yellow companion. Among the productions of the river's margin, I must not forget the pickerel-weed, which grows just on the edge of the water, and shoots up a long stalk, crowned with a blue spire, from among large green leaves. Both the flower and the leaves look well in a vase with pond-lilies, and relieve the unvaried whiteness of the latter; and being all alike children of the waters, they are perfectly in keeping with one another. My wife should have the credit of introducing this improvement into the arrangement of pond-lilies. She has, in perfection, the love and taste for flowers, without which a woman is a monster—and which it would be well for men to possess, if they can.

I bathe once, and often twice a day, in our river; but one dip into the salt-sea would be worth more than a whole week's soaking in such a lifeless tide. I have read of a river somewhere (whether it be in classic regions, or among our western Indians, I know not) which seemed to dissolve and steal away the vigor of those who bathed in it. Perhaps our stream will be found to have

its surface; and the fragrant white pond-lily occurs in many favored spots, generally selecting a situation just so far from the river's brink, that it cannot be grasped, except at the hazard of plunging in. But thanks be to this beautiful flower for growing at any rate. It is a marvel whence it derives its loveliness and perfume, sprouting as it does from the black mud over which the river sleeps, and from which, likewise, the yellow lily draws its unclean life and noisome perfume. So it is with many people in this world; – the same soil and circumstances may produce the good and beautiful, and the wicked and ugly; – some have the faculty of assimilating to themselves only what is evil, and so they become as noisome as the yellow water-lily. A few assimilate none but good influences; and their emblem is the spotless and fragrant pond-lily, whose very breath is a blessing to all the region roundabout. I possess such a human and heavenly lily, and ~~wear it in my bosom.~~ Heaven grant that I myself may not be symbolized by its yellow companion. Among the productions of the river's margin, I must not forget the pickerel-weed, which grows just on the edge of the water, and shoots up a long stalk, crowned with a blue spire, from among large green leaves. Both the flower and the leaves look well in a vase with pond-lilies, and relieve the unvaried whiteness of the latter; and being all alike children of the waters, they are perfectly in keeping with one another. My wife should have the credit of introducing this improvement into the arrangement of pond-lilies. She has, in perfection, the love and taste for flowers, without which a woman is a monster – and which it would be well for men to possess, if they can.

I bathe once, and often twice a day, in our river; but one dip into the salt-sea would be worth more than a whole week's soaking in such a lifeless tide. I have read of a river somewhere (whether it be in classic regions, or among our western Indians, I know not) which seemed to dissolve and steal away the vigor of those who bathed in it. Perhaps our stream will be found to have

this property. Its water, however, is pleasant in its immediate effect,
being as soft as milk, and always warmer than the air. Its hue has
a slight tinge of gold; and my limbs, when I behold them through
its medium, look tawny. I am not aware that the inhabitants
of Concord resemble their native river in any of their moral
characteristics; their forefathers, certainly, seem to have had
the energy and impetus of a mountain torrent, rather than the
torpor of this listless stream — as was proved by the blood with
which they stained their River of Peace. There are said to be plenty
of fish in it; but my most important captures have been a
mud-turtle and an enormous eel. The former made his escape to his native element — the latter we ate; and truly he
had the taste of the whole river in his flesh, with a very
prominent flavor of mud. On the whole, Concord river is no great
favorite of mine; but I am glad to have any river at all so
near at hand, being just at the bottom of our orchard. Neither
is it without a degree and kind of picturesqueness, both in
its nearness and in the distance, when a blue gleam from its
surface, among the green meadows and woods, seems like an open
eye in earth's countenance. Pleasant it is, too, to behold a
little flat-bottomed skiff gliding along its quiet bosom, which
yields lazily to the stroke of the paddle, and allows the boat
to go against its current almost as freely as with it. Pleasant
too, to watch an angler, as he strays along the margin, sometimes sheltering himself behind a tuft of bushes, and trailing his line along the water, in hopes to catch a pickerel. But, taking the river for all in all, I can find nothing
more fit to compare it with, than one of the half torpid earthworms, which I dig up for the purpose of bait. The worm
is sluggish, and so is the river — the river is muddy, and so
is the worm — you hardly know whether either of them is alive
or dead; but still, in the course of time, they both manage
to creep away. The best aspect of our river is when there is a
north-west breeze curling its surface, in a bright sunshiny
day; it then assumes a vivacity not its own. Moonlight, also,
gives it beauty — as it does to all scenery of earth or water.

this property. Its water, however, is pleasant in its immediate effect, being as soft as milk, and always warmer than the air. Its hue has a slight tinge of gold; and my limbs, when I behold them through its medium, look tawny. I am not aware that the inhabitants of Concord resemble their native river in any of their moral characteristics; their forefathers, certainly, seem to have had the energy and impetus of a mountain torrent, rather than the torpor of this listless stream – as was proved by the blood with which they stained their River of Peace. There are said to be plenty of fish in it; but my most important captures have been a mud-turtle and an enormous eel. The former made his escape to his native element – the latter we ate; and truly he had the taste of the whole river in his flesh, with a very prominent flavor of mud. On the whole, Concord river is no great favorite of mine; but I am glad to have any river at all so near at hand, being just at the bottom of our orchard. Neither is it without a degree and kind of picturesqueness, both in its nearness and in the distance, when a blue gleam from its surface, among the green meadows and woods, seems like an open eye in earth's countenance. Pleasant it is, too, to behold a little flat-bottomed skiff gliding along its quiet bosom, which yields lazily to the stroke of the paddle, and allows the boat to go against its current almost as freely as with it. Pleasant too, to watch an angler, as he strays along the margin, sometimes sheltering himself behind a tuft of bushes, and trailing his line along the water, in hopes to catch a pickerel. But, taking the river for all in all, I can find nothing more fit to compare it with, than one of the half torpid earthworms, which I dig up for the purpose of bait. The worm is sluggish, and so is the river – the river is muddy, and so is the worm – you hardly know whether either of them is alive or dead; but still, in the course of time, they both manage to creep away. The best aspect of our river is when there is a north-west breeze curling its surface, in a bright sunshiny day; it then assumes a vivacity not its own. Moonlight, also, gives it beauty – as it does to all scenery of earth or water.

August 7th. Sunday. At sunset, last evening, I ascended the hill-top opposite our house; and looking downward at a long extent of the river, it struck me that I had done it some injustice in my remarks. Perhaps, like other gentle and quiet characters, it will be better appreciated, the longer I am acquainted with it. Certainly, as I beheld it then, it was one of the loveliest features in a scene of great rural beauty. It was visible through a course of two or three miles, sweeping in a semicircle round the hill on which I stood, and being the central line of a broad vale on either side. At a distance, it looked like a strip of sky set into the earth, which it so etherealized and idealized that it seemed akin to the upper regions. Nearer the base of the hill, I could discern the shadows of every tree and rock, imaged with a distinctness that made them even more charming than the reality; because, knowing them to be unsubstantial, they assumed the ideality which the soul always craves, in the contemplation of earthly beauty. All the sky, too, and the rich clouds of sunset, were reflected in the peaceful bosom of the river; and surely, if its bosom can give such an adequate reflection of Heaven, it cannot be so gross and impure as I described it yesterday. Or, if so, it shall be a symbol to me, that even a human breast which may appear least spiritual in some aspects, may still have the capability of reflecting an infinite Heaven in its depths, and therefore of enjoying it. It is a comfortable thought, that the smallest and most turbid mud-puddle can contain its own picture of Heaven. Let us remember this, when we feel inclined to deny all spiritual life to some people, in whom, nevertheless, our Father may perhaps see the image of his face. This dull river has a deep religion of its own; so, let us trust, has the dullest human soul, perhaps unconsciously.

The scenery of Concord, as I beheld it from the summit of the hill, has no very marked characteristics, but has a

August 7th. Sunday. At sunset, last evening, I ascended the hill-top opposite our house; and looking downward at a long extent of the river, it struck me that I had done it some injustice in my remarks. Perhaps, like other gentle and quiet characters, it will be better appreciated, the longer I am acquainted with it. Certainly, as I beheld it then, it was one of the loveliest features in a scene of great rural beauty. It was visible through a course of two or three miles, sweeping in a semicircle round the hill on which I stood, and being the central line of a broad vale, on either side. At a distance, it looked like a strip of sky set into the earth, which it so etherealized and idealized that it seemed akin to the upper regions. Nearer the base of the hill, I could discern the shadows of every tree and rock, imaged with a distinctness that made them even more charming than the reality; because, knowing them to be unsubstantial, they assumed the ideality which the soul always craves, in the contemplation of earthly beauty. All the sky, too, and the rich clouds of sunset, were reflected in the peaceful bosom of the river; and surely, if its bosom can give such an adequate reflection of Heaven, it cannot be so gross and impure as I described it yesterday. Or, if so, it shall be a symbol to me, that even a human breast which may appear least spiritual in some aspects, may still have the capability of reflecting an infinite Heaven in its depths, and therefore of enjoying it. It is a comfortable thought, that the smallest and most turbid mud-puddle can contain its own picture of Heaven. Let us remember this, when we feel inclined to deny all spiritual life to some people, in whom, nevertheless, our Father may perhaps see the image of his face. This dull river has a deep religion of its own; so, let us trust, has the dullest human soul, perhaps unconsciously.

The scenery of Concord, as I beheld it from the summit of the hill, has no very marked characteristics, but has a great deal of quiet beauty, in keeping with the river. There are broad and peaceful meadows, which, I think, are among the most satisfying objects in natural scenery; the heart reposes on them, with a feeling that few things else can give, because almost all other objects are abrupt and clearly defined; but a meadow stretches out like a small infinity, yet with a secure homeliness, which we do not find either in an expanse of water or of air. The hills, which border these meadows, are broad swells of land, or long and gradual ridges, some of them densely covered with wood. The white village of Concord, at a distance on the left, appears to be embosomed among wooded hills. The verdure of the country is much more perfect than is usual at this season of the year, when the autumnal hue has generally made considerable progress over trees and grass. Last evening, after the copious showers of the preceding two days, it was worthy of early ~~Eden~~ — or, indeed, of a world just created. Had my wife been with me, I should have had a far deeper sense of beauty; for I should have looked through the medium of her spirit.

Along the horizon, there were masses of those deep clouds, ~~in~~ which the fancy may see images of all things that ever existed or were dreamed of. Over our old manse (of which I could catch but a glimpse, among its embowering trees) appeared the immensely gigantic figure of a hound, crouching down, with head erect, as if keeping watchful guard, while the master of the mansion was away. May the powers of the upper regions always keep guard over my heart's treasure, whether I am at her side, or afar off! How sweet it was to draw near my own home, after having lived so long homeless in the world; for no man can know what home is, until, as he approaches it, he feels that a wife will meet him at the threshold. With thoughts like these, I descended the hill, and clambered over the stone-wall, and crossed the road, and passed up our avenue; while the quaint old house put on an aspect of welcome.

1a

great deal of quiet beauty, in keeping with the river. There are broad and peaceful meadows, which, I think, are among the most satisfying objects in natural scenery; the heart reposes on them, with a feeling that few things else can give, because almost all other objects are abrupt and clearly defined; but a meadow stretches out like a small infinity, yet with a secure homeliness, which we do not find either in an expanse of water or of air. The hills, which border these meadows, are broad swells of land, or long and gradual ridges, some of them densely crowned with wood. The white village of Concord, at a distance on the left, appears to ↑be↓ embosomed among wooded hills. The verdure of the country is much more perfect than is usual at this season of the year, when the autumnal hue has generally made considerable progress over trees and grass. Last evening, after the copious showers of the preceding two days, it was worthy of early June – or, indeed, of a world just created. Had my wife been with me, I should have had a far deeper sense of beauty; for I should have looked through the medium of her spirit

Along the horizon, there were masses of those deep clouds in which the fancy may see images of all things that ever existed or were dreamed of. Over our old manse (of which I could catch but a glimpse, among its embowering trees) ap peared the immensely gigantic figure of a hound, crouching down, with head erect, as if keeping watchful guard, while the master of the mansion was away. May the powers of the upper regions always keep guard over my heart's treasure, whether I am at her side, or afar off! How sweet it was to draw near my own home, after having lived so long homeless in the world; for no man can know what home is, until, as he approaches it, he feels that a wife will meet him at the threshold. With thoughts like these, I descended the hill, and clambered over the stone-wall, and crossed the road, and passed up our avenue; while the quaint old house put on an aspect of welcome.

August 8th. Monday. I wish I could give a description of our house; for it really has a character of its own — which is more than can be said of most edifices in these days. It is two stories high, with a third story of attic chambers in the gable-roof. When I first visited the house, early in June, it looked pretty much as it did during the old clergyman's life-time, showing all the dust and disarray that might be supposed to have gathered about him, in the course of sixty years of occupancy. The rooms, I believe, had never been painted; at all events, the walls and panels, as well as the huge cross-beams, had a venerable and most dismal tinge of brown. The furniture consisted of high-backed, short-legged, rheumatic chairs, small old tables, bed-steads with lofty posts, stately chests of drawers, looking-glasses in antique black frames — all which were probably fashionable in the days of Dr. Ripley's predecessor. It required some energy of imagination to conceive the idea of transforming this musty edifice, where the good old minister had been writing sleepy sermons for more than half a century, into a comfortable modern residence. However, it has been successfully accomplished. The old doctor's sleeping apartment (which was the front room on the ground floor) we have converted into a parlor; and by the aid of cheerful paint and paper, a gladsome carpet, pictures and engravings, new furniture, bijouterie, and a daily supply of flowers, it has become one of the prettiest and pleasantest rooms in the whole world. The shade of our departed host will never haunt it; for its aspect has been changed as completely as the scenery of a theatre. Probably the ghost gave one peep into it, uttered a groan, and vanished forever. The opposite front-room has been metamorphosed into a store-room. Through the house, both in the first and second story, runs a spacious hall or entry, occupying more space than is ever devoted to such a purpose, in modern times. This feature contributes to give the whole house an airy, roomy, and convenient appearance; we can breathe the freer for the

August 8th. Monday. I wish I could give a description of our house; for it really has a character of its own – which is more than can be said of most edifices in these days. It is two stories high, with a third story of attic chambers in the gamble-roof. When I first visited the house, early in June, it looked pretty much as it did during the old clergyman's life-time, showing all the dust and disarray that might be supposed to have gathered about him, in the course of sixty years of occupancy. The rooms, I believe, had never been painted; at all events, the walls and panels, as well as the huge cross-beams, had a venerable and most dismal tinge of brown. The furniture consisted of high-backed, short-legged, rheumatic chairs, small old tables, bed-steads with lofty posts, stately chests of drawers, looking-glasses in antique black frames – all which were probably fashionable in the days of Dr. Ripley's predecessor. It required some energy of imagination to conceive the idea of transforming this musty edifice, where the good old minister had been writing sleepy sermons for more than half a century, into a comfortable modern residence. However, it has been successfully accomplished. The old Doctor's sleeping apartment (which was the front room on the ground floor) we have converted into a parlor; and by the aid of cheerful paint and paper, a gladsome carpet, pictures and engravings, new furniture, *bijouterie*, and a daily supply of flowers, it has become one of the prettiest and pleasantest rooms in the whole world. The shade of our departed host will never haunt it; for its aspect has been changed as completely as the scenery of a theatre. Probably the ghost gave one peep into it, uttered a groan, and vanished forever. The opposite front-room has been metamorphosed into a store-room. Through the house, both in the first and second story, runs a spacious hall or entry, occupying more space than is ever devoted to such a purpose, in modern times. This feature contributes to give the whole house an airy, roomy, and convenient appearance; we can breathe the freer for the sake of this broad passage-way. The front door of the hall looks up the stately avenue, which I have already mentioned; and the opposite door opens into the orchard, through which a path descends to the river-side. In the second story, we have fitted up three rooms, one being our own bed chamber, which I leave my wife to describe, as her taste has adorned it. The opposite room is reserved as a guest-chamber, and contains the most presentable of the old Doctor's ante-revolutionary furniture. After all, the moderns have invented nothing better, as chamber furniture, than those chests of drawers, which stand on four long, slender legs, and rear an absolute tower of mahogany to the ceiling, the whole terminating in a fantastically carved summit. Such a venerable structure adorns our guest-chamber. In the rear of the house is the little room which I call my study, and which, in its day, has witnessed the intellectual labors of better students than myself. It contains, with some additions and alterations, the furniture of my bachelor-room in Boston; but it is not difficult to detect the hand and heart of woman in many of its arrangements — for instance, in the happy disposal of the furniture, — in the little vase of flowers on one of the bookcases, and the larger bronze vase of graceful ferns, that surmounts the bureau. In size, the room is just what it ought to be; for I never could compress my thoughts sufficiently to write, in a very spacious room. It has three windows, two of which are shaded by a large and beautiful willow-tree, which sweeps against the overhanging eaves; on this side, we have a view into the orchard, and, beyond, a glimpse of the river. The other window is the one from which Mr. Emerson, the predecessor of Dr. Ripley, beheld the first fight of the Revolution — which he might well do, as the British troops were drawn up within a hundred yards of the house; and on looking forth, just now, I could still perceive the western abutment of the old bridge, the passage of which was contested. The new monument is visible from base to summit.

Notwithstanding all we have done to modernize the

sake of this broad passage-way. The front door of the hall looks up the stately avenue, which I have already mentioned; and the opposite door opens into the orchard, through which a path descends to the river-side. In the second story, we have fitted up three rooms, one being our own bed chamber, which I leave my wife to describe, as her taste has adorned it. The opposite room is reserved as a guest-chamber, and contains the most presentable of the old Doctor's ante-revolutionary furniture. After all, the moderns have invented nothing better, as chamber furniture, than those chests of drawers, which stand on four long, slender legs, and rear an absolute tower of mahogany to the cieling, the whole terminating in a fantastically carved summit. Such a venerable structure adorns our guest-chamber. In the rear of the house is the little room which I call my study, and which, in its day, has witnessed the intellectual labors of better students than myself. It contains, with some additions and alterations, the furniture of my bachelor-room in Boston; but it is not difficult to detect the hand and heart of woman in many of its arrangements – for instance, in the happy disposal of the furniture, – in the little vase of flowers on one of the bookcases, and the larger bronze vase of graceful ferns, that surmounts the bureau. In size, the room is just what it ought to be; for I never could compress my thoughts sufficiently to write, in a very spacious room. It has three windows, two of which are shaded by a large and beautiful willow-tree, which sweeps against the overhanging eaves; on this side, we have a view into the orchard, and, beyond, a glimpse of the river. The other window is the one from which Mr. Emerson, the predecessor of Dr. Ripley, beheld the first fight of the Revolution – which he might well do, as the British troops were drawn up within a hundred yards of the house; and on looking forth, just now, I could still perceive the western abutment of the old bridge, the passage of which was contested. The new monument is visible from base to summit.

Notwithstanding all we have done to modernize the

old house, we seem scarcely to have disturbed its air of antiquity. It is evident that other wedded pairs have spent their honeymoons here, though none so happily as ourselves—that children have been born here, and people have grown old and died in these rooms and chambers; although, for our behoof, the same apartments have consented to look cheerful once again. Then there are dark closets, and strange nooks and corners, where the ghosts of former occupants might hide themselves in the day time, and stalk forth, when night conceals all our sacrilegious improvement. We have seen no apparitions as yet; but we hear strange noises, especially in the kitchen; and, last night, my wife, while sitting in the parlor, heard a thumping and pounding, as of somebody at work in my study. Nay, if I mistake not (for I was half asleep when she told me) she heard a sound as of some person crumpling paper in his hand, in our very bed-chamber. This must have been old Doctor Ripley, with one of his sermons;—there is a whole chest full of them in the garret; but he need have no apprehensions of our disturbing them. I never saw the old patriarch myself;—which I regret, as I should have been glad to associate his venerable figure, at ninety years of age, with the house in which he dwelt.

Externally, the house presents the same appearance as in the Doctor's day. It had once a coat of white paint; but the storms and sunshine of many years have almost obliterated it, and produced a sober grayish hue, which entirely suits the antique form of the structure. To re-paint its venerable face would be a real sacrilege; it would look like old Doctor Ripley in a brown wig. I hardly know why it is that our cheerful and lightsome repairs and improvements, in the interior of the house, seem to be in perfectly good taste, though the heavy old beams, and high panelling of the walls, speak of ages gone by. But so it is;—the cheerful paper-hangings have the air of belonging to the old walls; and such modernisms as astral-lamps, card-vases, gilded cologne bot-

old house, we seem scarcely to have disturbed its air of antiquity. It is evident that other wedded pairs have spent their honeymoons here, though none so happily as ourselves – that children have been born here, and people have grown old and died in these rooms and chambers; although, for our behoof, the same apartments have consented to look cheerful once again. Then there are dark closets, and strange nooks and corners, where the ghosts of former occupants might hide themselves in the day time, and stalk forth, when night conceals all our sacrilegious improvements. We have seen no apparitions, as yet; but we hear strange noises, especially in the kitchen; and, last night, my wife, while sitting in the parlor, heard a thumping and pounding, as of somebody at work in my study. Nay, if I mistake not (for I was half asleep when she told me) she heard a sound as of some person crumpling paper in his hand, in our very bed-chamber. This must have been old Doctor Ripley, with one of his sermons; – there is a whole chest full of them in the garret; but he need have no apprehensions of our disturbing them. I never saw the old patriarch myself; – which I regret, as I should have been glad to associate his venerable figure, at ninety years of age, with the house in which he dwelt.

Externally, the house presents the same appearance as in the Doctor's day. It had once a coat of white paint; but the storms and sunshine of many years have almost obliterated it, and produced a sober greyish hue, which entirely suits the antique form of the structure. To re-paint its venerable face would be a real sacrilege; it would ↑look↓ like old Doctor Ripley in a brown wig. I hardly know why it is that our cheerful and lightsome repairs and improvements, in the interior of the house, seem to be in perfectly good taste, though the heavy old beams, and high panelling of the walls, speak of ages gone by. But so it is; – the cheerful paper-hangings have the air of belonging to the old walls; and such modernisms as astral-lamps, card-vases, gilded cologne bot-

tles, silver taper stands, and bronze and alabaster card-vases,
do not seem at all impertinent. It is thus that an aged man
may keep his heart warm for new things and new friends, and
often furnish himself anew with ideas, though it would not
be graceful for him to attempt to suit his exterior to the passing fashions of the day.

August 9th. Tuesday. Our orchard, in its day, has been a very
productive and profitable one; and we were told that, in one
year, it returned Dr. Ripley a hundred dollars, besides defraying
the expense of repairing the house. It is now long past its prime.
Many of the trees are moss-grown, and have dead and rotten branches intermixed among the green and fruitful ones; — and it
may well be so; for I suppose some of the trees may have
been set out by Mr. Emerson, who died in the first year of the Revolutionary war. Neither will the fruit, probably, bear comparison with the delicate productions of modern pomology. Most
of the trees seem to have abundant burthens upon them; but
they are homely russet apples, fit only for baking and
cooking. Justice Shallow's orchard, with its choice pippins and
leather-coats, was doubtless much superior. Nevertheless, it
pleases me to think of the good minister, walking in the
shadows of these old, fantastically shaped apple-trees,
here plucking some of the fruit to taste, there pruning a-
way a too luxuriant branch, and all the while computing
how many barrels will be filled, and how large a sum will
be added to his stipend, by the sale. And the same trees
offer their fruit to me, as freely as they did to him — their old
branches, like withered hands and arms, holding out apples of
the same flavor as they held out to Dr. Ripley, in his life-time.
Thus the trees, as living existences, form a peculiar link between
the dead and the living. My fancy has always found something very interesting in an orchard — especially an old orchard. Apple-trees, and all fruit-trees, have a domestic character, which brings them into relationship with man; they
have lost, in a great measure, the wild nature of the forest
tree, and have grown humanized, by receiving the care of man,

tles, silver taper-stands, and bronze and alabaster card-vases, do not seem at all impertinent. It is thus that an aged man may keep his heart warm for new things and new friends, and often furnish himself anew with ideas, though it would not be graceful for him to attempt to suit his exterior to the passing fashions of the day.

August 9th. Tuesday. Our orchard, in its day, has been a very productive and profitable one; and we were told that, in one year, it returned Dr. Ripley a hundred dollars, besides defraying the expense of repairing the house. It is now long past its prime. Many of the trees are moss-grown, and have dead and rotten branches intermixed among the green and fruitful ones; – and it may well be so; for I suppose some of the trees may have been set ↑out↓ by Mr. Emerson, who died in the first year of the Revolutionary war. Neither will the fruit, probably, bear comparison with the delicate productions of modern pomology. Most of the trees seem to have abundant burthens upon them; but they are homely russet apples, fit only for baking and cooking. Justice Shallow's orchard, with its choice pippins and leather-coats, was doubtless much superior. Nevertheless, it pleases me to think of the good minister, walking in the shadow of these old, fantastically shaped apple-trees, here plucking some of the fruit to taste, there pruning away a too luxuriant branch, and all the while computing how many barrels will be filled, and how large a sum will be added to his stipend, by the sale. And the same trees offer their fruit to me, as freely as they did to him – their old branches, like withered hands and arms, holding out apples of the same flavor as they held out to Dr. Ripley, in his life-time. Thus the trees, as living existences, form a peculiar link between the dead and the living. My fancy has always found something very interesting in an orchard – especially an old orchard. Apple-trees, and all fruit-trees, have a domestic character, which brings them into relationship with man; they have lost, in a great measure, the wild nature of the forest-tree, and have grown humanized, by receiving the care of man, and by contributing to his wants. They have become a part of the family; and their individual characters are as well understood and appreciated as those of the human members. One tree is harsh and crabbed — another mild — one is churlish and illiberal — another exhausts itself with its free-hearted bounties. Even the shapes of apple-trees have great individuality, into such strange postures do they put themselves, and thrust their contorted branches so grotesquely in all directions. And when they have stood around a house for many years, and held converse with successive dynasties of occupants, and gladdened their hearts so often in the fruitful autumn, then it would seem almost sacrilege to cut them down.

Besides the apple trees, there are various other kinds of fruit in close vicinity to the house. When we first arrived, there were several trees of ripe cherries, but so soon that we allowed them to rot upon the branches. Two long rows of currant bushes supplied us abundantly, for nearly four weeks. There is a considerable number of peach-trees, but all of an old date, their branches rotten, gummy, and mossy, and their fruit, I fear, of very inferior quality. They produce most abundantly, however — the peaches being almost as numerous as the leaves; and even the sprouts and suckers, from the roots of the old trees, have fruit upon them. Then there are pear trees of various kinds, and one or two quince trees. On the whole, these fruit-trees, and the other items and adjuncts of the place, convey a very agreeable idea of the outward comfort in which our good old Doctor must have spent his life. Everything seems to have fallen to his lot, that could possibly be supposed to render the life of a country clergyman easy and abundant. There is a barn, which probably used to be filled, annually, with his hay and other agricultural products. There are sheds, and a hen-house, and a pigeon-house, and an old stone pig-stye, the open portion of which is overgrown with tall weeds, indicating

and by contributing to his wants. They have become a part of the family; and their individual characters are as well understood and appreciated as those of the human members. One tree is harsh and crabbed – another mild – one is churlish and illiberal – another exhausts itself with its free-hearted bounties. Even the shapes of apple-trees have great individuality, into such strange postures do they put themselves, and thrust their contorted branches so grotesquely in all directions. And when they have stood around a house for many years, and held converse with successive dynasties of occupants, and gladdened their hearts so often in the fruitful autumn, then it would seem almost sacrilege to cut them down.

Besides the apple trees, there are various other kinds of fruit in close vicinity to the house. When we first arrived, there were several trees of ripe cherries, but so sour that we allowed them to rot upon the branches. Two long rows of currant bushes supplied us abundantly, for nearly four weeks. There is a considerable number of peach-trees, but all of an old date, their branches rotten, gummy, and mossy, and their fruit, I fear, of very inferior quality. They produce most abundantly, however – the peaches being almost as numerous as the leaves; and even the sprouts and suckers, from the roots of the old trees, have fruit upon them. Then there are pear trees of various kinds, and one or two quince trees. On the whole, these fruit-trees, and the other items and adjuncts of the place, convey a very agreeable idea of the outward comfort in which our good old Doctor must have spent his life. Everything seems to have fallen to his lot, that could possibly be supposed to render the life of a country clergyman easy and abundant. There is a barn, which probably used to be filled, annually, with his hay and other agricultural products. There are sheds, and a hen-house, and a pigeon-house, and an old stone pig-stye, the open portion of which is overgrown with tall weeds, indicating

that no grunter has recently occupied it. If my wife's permission
can be obtained, I have serious thoughts of inducting a new
incumbent into this part of the parsonage. It is our duty to
support a pig, even if we have no design of feasting upon his
flesh; and for my own part, I have a great sympathy and interest for the whole race of porkers, and should have much
amusement in studying the character of a pig. Perhaps I
might try to bring out his moral and intellectual nature, and
cultivate his affections. A cat, too, and perhaps a dog, would
be desirable additions to our household.

August 10th Wednesday. Yesterday was the monthlyversary
of our wedding day, & quite worthy to be so; for it
was one of the loveliest days that ever enriched the
earth. The bridal was on the 9th of July, which
dawned fair after a long season of clouds & rain
just as yesterday was born of shadows & gloom.
For it had rained nearly a week, & the sun
day and [?] shines this morning. I had been three
weeks ill, but was sure that I should be well
for such an occasion, & that the weather would
be lovely, though there was no appearance of it
the day before. I waked at light & sprang up to
hold the promise of the heavens. It was kind
though misty; but the rising sun dispersed mists,
& heavenly blue appeared. My last symptom of
illness also had gone & the Dr W. pronounced me
free from fever when he came, though my pulse
was 108. This he ascribed to approaching events.
Sarah Clarke arranged my bridal robe & dressed
my hair with pond-lilies & Cornelia braided it.
It was at half past eleven, one Saturday forenoon,
that my brother James Clarke pronounced us
husband & wife before GOD & man. There were
present besides the family, Cornelia, and Sarah &
the cook Bridget. While the ceremony was proceeding, the sun shone forth with great splendor, as

that no grunter has recently occupied it. If my wife's permission can be obtained, I have serious thoughts of inducting a new incumbent into this part of the parsonage. It is our duty to support a pig, even if we have ↑no↓ design of feasting upon his flesh; and for my own part, I have a great sympathy and interest for the whole race of porkers, and should have much amusement in studying the character of a pig. Perhaps I might try to bring out his moral and intellectual nature, and cultivate his affections. A cat, too, and perhaps a dog, would be desirable additions to our household.

August 10.th Wednesday. Yesterday was the monthlyversary of our wedding day, & quite worthy to be so, for it was one of the loveliest days that ever~~y~~ enriched the earth. The bridal was on the 9th of July, which dawned fair after a long season of clouds & rain just as yesterday was born of shadows & gloom – for it had rained nearly a week, & the sun ↑does not↓ shines ~~XXXX~~ this morning – I had been three weeks ill, but was sure that I should be well for such an occasion – & that the weather would be lovely, though there was no appearance of it the day before. I waked at light & sprang up to note the promise of the heavens. It was kind though misty; but the rising sun dispersed mists, & the heavenly blue appeared. My last symptom of illness also had gone & the Dr. W. pronounced me free from fever when he came, though my pulses were 106 – This he ascribed to approaching events. Sarah Clarke arranged my bridal robe & dressed my hair with pond lilies & Cornelia braided it. It was at half past eleven, one Saturday forenoon, that my brother James Clarke pronounced us husband & wife before GOD & Man. There were present besides the family Cornelia, and Sarah & the cook Bridget. While the ceremony was proceed ing, the sun shone forth with great splendor, as

no adventure, except that my love dropped some of his berries, because I had so carelessly fastened the string of the basket, & I threw myself upon a haystack & shocked his conscience very much. He prayed Heaven for a pitchfork to ~~put~~ it up again, but none appeared. I am very naughty. It is inexcusable for he is the loveliest being who ever breathed life. For with all his strength & spirit & power, he has the most perfect lovelinesss of nature I ever witnessed or imagined. He is a true Seraph. It was eight o'clk at our return, & we found the lamp lighted in the hall & also one pretty parlor illuminated by the good Sarah. We found we had gathered nearly two quarts of berries.

This morning my darling husband brought from the river some pond lilies, pickerel weed, cardinal flowers & one spike of arrow head, & I put them all into our alabaster fountain. One could scarcely see a fairer sight. All these are river plants & become each other wonderfully. The superb scarlet of the cardinal flower, the rich purple of the pickerel weed, & the golden stamens of the lilies make a perfect harmony set off by the broad green leaves.

August 10th. Wednesday. The natural taste of man for the original Adam's occupation is fast developing itself in me. I find that I am a good deal interested in our garden, although, as it was planted before we came here, I do not feel the same affection for the plants as if the seed had been sown by my own hands. It is something like

no adventure, except that my love dropped some of his berries, because I had so carelessly fastened the string of the basket, & I threw myself upon a haystack & shocked his conscience very much. He prayed Heaven for a pitchfork to put it up again, but none appeared. I am very naughty. It is inexcusable for he is the loveliest being who ever breathed life. Yes – with all his strength & spirit & power, he has the most perfect loveliness of nature I ever witnessed or imagined. He is a true Seraph. It was eight o'clk at our return, & we found the lamp lighted in the hall & also our pretty parlor illuminated by the good Sarah. We found we had gathered nearly two quarts of berries.

This morning my darling husband brought from the river some pond lilies, pickerel weed, cardinal flowers & one spike of arrowhead, & I put them all into our alabaster fountain. One could scarcely see a fairer sight – all these are river plants & become each other wonderfully. The superb scarlet of the cardinal flower, the rich purple of the pickerel weed, & the golden stamens of the lilies make a perfect harmony set off by the broad green leaves.

August 10th. Wednesday. The natural taste of man for the original Adam's occupation is fast developing itself in me. I find that I am a good deal interested in our garden; although, as it was planted before we came here, I do not feel the same affection for the plants as if the seed had been sown by ↑my↓ own hands. It is something like

nursing and educating another person's children. Still, it was
a very pleasant moment when I gathered the first mess of string-
beans, which were the earliest esculent that the garden contributed to our table. And I love to watch the successive development of each new vegetable, and mark their daily growth, which
always affects me with a new surprise. It is as if something
were being created under my own inspection, and partly by my
own aid. One day, perchance, I look at my bean-vines, and
see only the green leaves clambering up the poles; again, to-
morrow, I give a second glance, and there are the delicate blossoms; and a third day, on somewhat closer inspection, I discover the delicate young beans, hiding among the
depths of the foliage. Then, each morning, I watch the swelling of the pods, and calculate how soon they will be ready
to yield their treasures. All this gives a pleasure and an ideality, hitherto unthought of, to the business of providing sustenance for my family. I suppose Adam felt it in Paradise; and of merely and exclusively earthly enjoyments,
there are few purer and more harmless to be experienced.
Speaking of beans, by the way, they are a classical food, and
their culture must have been the occupation of many ancient
sages and heroes. Summer squashes are a very pleasant vegetable to be acquainted with;—they grow in the forms of
urns and vases, some shallow, others of considerable
depth, and all with a beautifully scalloped edge. Almost
any squash in our garden might be copied by a sculptor, and
would look beautifully in marble, or in china-ware; and
if I could afford it, I would have exact imitations of the
real vegetable as portions of my dining-service. They would
be very appropriate dishes for holding garden vegetables.
Besides the summer-squashes, we have the crook-necked winter squash, which I always delight to look at, when it turns
up its big belly to ripen in the autumnal sun. Except a pumpkin, there is no vegetable production that imparts such an
idea of warmth and comfort to the beholder. Our onion
crop, however, does not promise to be very abundant; for

nursing and educating another person's children. Still, it was a very pleasant moment when I gathered the first mess of string beans, which were the earliest esculents that the garden contributed to our table. And I love to watch the successive development of each new vegetable, and mark their daily growth, which always affects me with a new surprise. It is as if something were being created under my own inspection, and partly by own aid. One day, perchance, I look at my bean-vines, and see only the green leaves clambering up the poles; again, to-morrow, I give a second glance, and there are the delicate blossoms; and a third day, on somewhat closer inspection, I discover the delicate young beans, hiding among the depths of the foliage. Then, each morning, I watch the swelling of the pods, and calculate how soon they will be ready to yield their treasures. All this gives a pleasure and an ideality, hitherto unthought of, to the business of providing sustenance for my family. I suppose Adam felt ↑it↓ in Paradise; and of merely and exclusively earthly enjoyments, there are few purer and more harmless to be experienced. Speaking of beans, by the way, they are a classical food, and their culture must have been the occupation of many ancient sages and heroes. Summer squashes are a very pleasant vegetable to be acquainted with; – they grow in the forms of urns and vases, some shallow, others of considerable depth, and all with a beautifully scalloped edge. Almost any squash in our garden might be copied by a sculptor, and would look beautifully in marble, or in china-ware; and if I could afford it, I would have exact imitations of the real vegetable as portions of my dining-service. They would be very appropriate dishes for holding garden vegetables. Besides the summer-squashes, we have the crook-necked winter squash, which I always delight to look at, when it turns up its big belly to ripen in the autumnal sun. Except a pumpkin, there is no vegetable production that imparts such an idea of warmth and comfort to the beholder. Our own crop, however, does not promise to be very abundant; for

10

the leaves formed such a superfluous shade over the young blossoms, that most of the latter dropped off without producing the germ of fruit. Yesterday and to-day, I have cut off an immense number of leaves, and thus given the remaining blossoms a chance to profit by the air and sunshine; but the season is too far advanced, I am afraid, for the squashes to attain any considerable bulk, and grow yellow in the sun. We have musk-melons and water melons, which promise to supply us with as many as we can eat. After all, the greatest interest of these vegetables does not seem to consist in their being articles of food;—it is rather that we love to see something born into the world; and when a great squash or melon is produced, it is a large and tangible existence, which the imagination can seize hold of and rejoice in. I love, also, to see my own works contributing to the life and well-being of animate nature; it is pleasant to have the bees come and suck honey out of my squash-blossoms, though, when they have laden themselves, they fly away to some unknown hive, which will give me back nothing in return for what my garden has contributed. But there is so much more honey in the world; and therefore I am content.

Indian corn, in the prime and glory of its verdure, is a very beautiful vegetable, both considered in the separate plant, and in the mass of a broad field, rustling, and waving, and surging up and down in the breeze and sunshine of a summer afternoon. We have as much as fifty hills, I should think, which will give us an abundant supply. Pray Heaven we may be able to eat it all, for it is not pleasant to think that anything, which Nature has been at the pains to produce, should be thrown away. But then the hens will be glad of our superfluity; and so will the pigs—though we have neither hen nor pig of our own. But hens we must certainly keep. There is something very sociable, and quiet and soothing too, in their soliloquies and converse among themselves; and, in an idle

the leaves formed such a superfluous shade over the young blossoms, that most of the latter dropped off without producing the germ of fruit. Yesterday and to-day, I have cut off an immense number of leaves, and thus given the remaining blossoms a chance to profit by the air and sunshine; but the season is too far advanced, I am afraid, for the squashes to attain any considerable bulk, and grow yellow in the sun. We have musk-melons and water melons, which promise to supply us with as many as we can eat. After all, the greatest interest of these vegetables does not seem to consist in their being articles of food; – it is rather that we love to see something born into the world; and when a great squash or melon is produced, it is a large and tangible existence, which the imagination can seize hold of and rejoice in. I love, also, to see my own works contributing to the life and well-being of animate nature, – it is pleasant to have the bees come and suck honey out of my squash-blossoms, though, when they have laden themselves, they fly away to some unknown hive, which will give me back nothing in return for what my garden has contributed. But there is so much more honey in the world; and therefore I am content.

Indian corn, in the prime and glory of its verdure, is a very beautiful vegetable, both considered in the separate plant, and in the mass of a broad field, rustling, and waving, and surging up and down in the breeze and sunshine of a summer afternoon. We have as much as fifty hills, I should think, which will give us an abundant supply. Pray Heaven we may be able to eat it all; for it is not pleasant to think that anything, which Nature has been at the pains to produce, should be thrown away. But then the hens will be glad of our superfluity; and so will the pigs – though we have neither hen nor pig of our own. But hens we must certainly keep. There is something very sociable, and quiet and soothing too, in their soliloquies and converse among themselves; and, in an idle and half meditative mood, there is nothing pleasanter than to watch a party of hens, picking up their daily subsistence, with a gallant chanticleer in the midst of them. Milton had evidently contemplated such a picture with delight.

I find that I have not given a very complete account of our garden; although, certainly, it deserves an ample record in this chronicle; since my labors in it are the only present labor of my life. Besides what I have mentioned, we have cucumber vines, which to-day yielded us the first cucumber of the season — a bed of beets, and another of carrots, and another of parsnips and turnips — none of which promise us a very abundant harvest. In truth, the soil is worn out, and, moreover, received very little manure this season. Also, we have cabbages, in superfluous abundance, inasmuch as neither my sweetest wife nor I have the least affection for them; and it would be unreasonable to expect Sarah to eat fifty head of cabbages. Tomatoes we shall have, by and bye. At our first arrival, we found green peas ready for gathering; and these, instead of the string-beans, were the first offering of the season at our board.

August 19th. Saturday. My life, at this time, is more like that of a boy, externally, than it has been since I was really a boy. It is usually supposed that the cares of life come with matrimony; but I seem to have cast off all care, and live on with as much easy trust in Providence, as Adam could possibly have felt, before he had learned that there was a world beyond his Paradise. My chief anxiety consists in watching the prosperity of my vegetables — in observing how they are affected by the rain or sunshine — in lamenting the blight of one squash, and rejoicing at the luxurious growth of another. It is as if the original relation between Man and Nature were restored in my case, and that I were to look exclusively to her for the support of my Eve and myself — to trust to her for food and clothing, and all things needful, with the full assurance that she would not fail me. The fight with the world — the struggle

and half meditative mood, there is nothing pleasanter than to watch a party of hens, picking up their daily subsistence, with a gallant chanticleer in the midst of them. Milton had evidently contemplated such a picture with delight.

I find that I have not given a very complete ↑account↓ of our garden; although, certainly, it deserves an ample record in this chronicle; since my labors in it are the only present labor of my life. Besides what I have mentioned, we have cucumber vines, which to-day yielded us the first cucumber of the season – a bed of beets, and another of carrots, and another of parsnips and turnips – none of which promise us a very abundant harvest. In truth, the soil is worn out, and, moreover, received very little manure, this season. Also, we have cabbages, in superfluous abundance, inasmuch as neither my sweetest wife nor I have the least affection for them; and it would be unreasonable to expect Sarah to eat fifty head of cabbages. Toma tos we shall have, by and bye. At our first arrival, we found green peas ready for gathering; and these, instead of the string-beans, were the first offering of the season at our board.

August 13th. Saturday. My life, at this time, is more like that of a boy, externally, than it has been since I was really a boy. It is usually supposed that the cares of life come with matrimony; but I seem to have cast off all care, and live on with as much easy trust in Providence, as Adam could possibly have felt, before he had learned that there was a world beyond his Paradise. My chief anxiety consists in watching the prosperity of my vegetables – in observing how they are affected by the rain or sunshine – in lamenting the blight of one squash, and rejoicing at the luxurious growth of another. It is as if the original relation between Man and Nature were restored in my case, and that I were to look exclusively to her for the support of my Eve and myself – to trust to her for food and clothing, and all things needful, with the full assurance that she would not fail me. The fight with the world – the struggle of a man among men — the agony of the universal effort to wrench the means of life from a host of greedy competitors — all this seems like a dream to me. My business is merely to live and to enjoy; and whatever is essential to life and enjoyment will come as naturally as the dew from Heaven. This is — practically, at least — my faith. And so I awake in the morning with a boyish thoughtlessness as to how the outgoings of the day are to be provided for, and its incomings rendered certain. After breakfast, I go forth into my garden, and gather whatever the bountiful Mother has made fit for our present sustenance; and, of late days, she generally gives me two squashes and a cucumber, and promises me green corn and shell-beans, very soon. Then I pass down through our orchard to the river-side, and ramble along its margin, in search of flowers for my wife. Usually I discern a fragrant white lily here and there along the shore, growing, with sweet prudishness, beyond the grasp of mortal arm. But it does not escape me so. I know what is its fitting destiny, better than the silly flower knows for itself; so I wade in, heedless of wet pantaloons, and seize the shy lily by its slender stem. Thus I make prize of five or six, which are as many as usually blossom within my reach, in a single morning — some of them partially worm-eaten or blighted, like virgins of tainted fame, or with an eating sorrow at the heart; others as fair and perfect as Nature's own idea was, when she first imagined this lovely flower. A perfect pond-lily is the most satisfactory of flowers. Besides the pond-lilies, I gather whatever else of beautiful chances to be growing in the moist soil by the river-side — an amphibious tribe, yet with more richness and grace than the wild flowers of the deep and dry woodlands and hedge-rows. Sometimes the white arrow-head; always the blue spires and broad green leaves of the pickerel-flower, which contrast and harmonize so well with the white lilies. For the last two or three days, I have found scattered stalks of the cardinal-flower, the gorgeous scarlet of which it is

of a man among men – the agony of the universal effort to wrench the means of life from a host of greedy competitors – all this seems like a dream to me. My business is merely to live and to enjoy; and whatever is essential to life and enjoyment will come as naturally as the dew from Heaven. This is – practically, at least – my faith. And so I awake in the morning with a boyish thoughtlessness as to how the outgoings of the day are to be provided for, and its incomings rendered certain. After breakfast, I go forth into my garden, and gather whatever the bountiful Mother has made fit for our present sustenance; and, of late days, she generally gives me two squashes and a cucumber, and promises me green corn and shell-beans, very soon. Then I pass down through our orchard to the river-side, and ramble along its margin, in search of flowers for my wife. Usually I discern a fragrant white lily here and there along the shore, growing, with sweet prudishness, beyond the grasp of mortal arm. But it does not escape me so. I know what is its fitting destiny, better than the silly flower knows for itself; so I wade in, heedless of wet pantaloons, and seize the shy lily by its slender stem. Thus I make prize of five or six, which are as many as usually blossom within my reach, in a single morning – some of them partially worm-eaten or blighted, like virgins of tainted fame, or with an eating sorrow at the heart; others as fair and perfect as Nature's own idea was, when she first imagined this lovely flower. A perfect pond-lily is the most satisfactory of flowers. Besides the pond-lilies, I gather whatever else of beautiful chances to be growing in the moist soil by the river-side – an amphibious tribe, yet with more richness and grace than the wild flowers of the deep and dry wood lands and hedge-rows. Sometimes the white arrow-head; always the blue spires and broad green leaves of the pickerel-flower, which contrast and harmonize so well with the white lilies. For the last two or three days, I have found scattered stalks of the cardinal-flower, the gorgeous scarlet of which it is a joy even to remember. The world is made brighter and sunnier by flowers of such a hue; even perfume, which otherwise is the soul and spirit of a flower, may be spared when it arrays itself in this scarlet glory. It is a flower of thought and feeling, too; it seems to have its roots deep down in the hearts of those who gaze at it. Other bright flowers sometimes impress me as wanting sentiment; but it is not so with this. Well; having made up my bunch of flowers, I return with them to my wife, of whom what is loveliest among them are to me the imperfect emblems. My imagination twines her and the flowers into one wreath, and when I offer them to her, it seems as if I were introducing her to beings that have somewhat of her own nature in them. "My Lily, here are your sisters — cherish them!" — this is what my fancy says, while my heart smiles and rejoices at the conceit. Then my dearest wife rejoices in the flowers, and hastens to give them water, and arranges them so beautifully that they are glad to have been gathered from the muddy bottom of the river, and its wet, tangled margin — from among plants of evil smell and uncouth aspect, where the slimy eel, and the frog, and the black mud-turtle, hide themselves — glad of being rescued from such an unworthy life, and made the ornaments of our parlor. What more could the loveliest flower desire? — it is its earthly triumph, which it will remember with joy, when it blooms in the Paradise of flowers. This important affair being disposed of, I ascend to my study, and generally read, or perchance scribble in this journal, (or, possibly, sleep!) and otherwise suffer Time to loiter onward at his own pleasure, till the dinner hour. In pleasant days, the chief event of the afternoon, and the happiest one of the day, is a walk with my wife; she must describe these walks; for where she and I have enjoyed anything together, I always deem my pen unworthy and inadequate to record it. Then comes the night; and I look back upon a day spent in what the world would call idleness, and for which I can myself suggest no more appropriate epithet, and which, nevertheless, I cannot feel to have been spent amiss. True; it might be a sin and shame, in such

1a

a joy even to remember. The world is made brighter and sunnier by flowers of such a hue; even perfume, which otherwise is the soul and spirit of a flower, may be spared when it arrays itself in this scarlet glory. It is a flower of thought and feeling, too; it seems to have its roots deep down in the hearts of those who gaze ↑at↓ it. Other bright flowers sometimes impress me as wanting sentiment; but it is not so with this. Well; having made up my bunch of flowers, I return with them to my wife, of whom what is loveliest among them are to me the imperfect emblems. My imagination twines her and the flowers into one wreath; and when I offer them to her, it seems as if I were introducing her to beings that have somewhat of her own nature in them. "My Lily, here are your sisters – cherish them!" – this is what my fancy says, while my heart smiles and rejoices at the conceit. Then my dearest wife rejoices in the flowers, and hastens to give them water, and arranges them so beautifully that they are glad to have been gathered from the muddy bottom of the river, and its wet, tangled margin – from among plants of evil smell and uncouth aspect, where the slimy eel, and the frog, and the black mud-turtle, hide themselves – glad of being rescued from such an unworthy life, and made the ornaments of our parlor. What more could the loveliest flower desire? – it is its earthly triumph, which it will remember with joy, when it blooms in the Paradise of flowers. This important affair being disposed of, I ascend to my study, and generally read, or perchance scribble in this journal, (or, possibly, sleep!) and otherwise suffer Time to loiter onward at his own pleasure, till the dinner-hour. In pleasant days, the chief event of the afternoon, and the happiest one of the day, is a walk with my wife; she must describe these walks; for where she and I have enjoyed anything together, I always deem my pen unworthy and inadequate to record it. Then comes the night; and I look back upon a day spent in what the world would call idleness, and for which I can myself suggest no more appropriate epithet; and which, nevertheless, I cannot feel to have been spent amiss. True; it might be a sin and shame, in such a world as ours, to spend a lifetime in this manner; but, for a few summer weeks, it is good to live as if this world were Heaven. And so it is, and so it shall be; although, in a little while, a flitting shadow of earthly care and toil will mingle itself with our realities.

August 15th. Monday. George Hillard and his wife arrived from Boston, in the dusk of Saturday evening, to spend Sunday with us. It was a pleasant sensation when the coach rumbled up our avenue, and wheeled round at the door; for then I felt that I was regarded as a man with a wife and a household — a man having a tangible existence and locality in the world — when friends came to avail themselves of our hospitality. It was a sort of acknowledgment and reception of us into the corps of married people — a sanction by no means essential to our peace and well-being, but yet agreeable enough to receive. So my wife and I welcomed them cordially at the door, and ushered them into our parlor, and soon into the supper-room — ~~and, afterwards, we ushered them to bed. Then came my dear little wife to her husband's bosom, and slept sweetly, I trust; for she is a beloved woman; which is more than can be said of every wife in the~~ world. Pray Heaven that Mrs. Hillard had a good night's rest in our guest-chamber; but I hardly think that she slept so sweetly ~~as my lily~~. However, the night flitted over us all, and passed away, and upsose a gray and sullen morning, which would have saddened me, only that my sunny wife shone into my heart, and made it warm and bright. We had a splendid breakfast of flapjacks — (or slap-jacks, as my wife insists upon calling them) — of flap-jacks or slap-jacks, and of whortle berries, which we gathered on a neighboring hill, and of perch, bream, and pouts, which I hooked out of the river, the evening before. About nine o'clock, Hillard and I set out for a walk to Walden Pond, calling by the way at Mr. Emerson's, to obtain his guidance or directions. He, from a scruple of his external conscience, detained us till after the people had got into church, and then accompanied

a world as ours, to spend a life-time in this manner; but, for a few summer-weeks, it is good to live as ↑if↓ this world were Heaven. And so it is, and so it shall be; although, in a little while, a flitting shadow of earthly care and toil will mingle itself with our realities.

August 15th. Monday. George Hillard and his wife arrived from Boston, in the dusk of Saturday evening, to spend Sunday with us. It was a pleasant sensation when the coach rumbled up our avenue, and wheeled round at the door; for then I felt that I was regarded as a man with a wife and a household – a man having a tangible existence and locality in the world – when friends came to avail themselves of our hospitality. It was a sort of acknowledgement and reception of us into the corps of married people – a sanction by no means essential to our peace and well-being, but yet agreeable enough to receive. So my wife and I welcomed them cordially at the door, and ushered them into our parlor, and soon into the supper-room – ~~and afterwards, in due season, to bed. Then came my dear little wife to her husband's bosom, and slept sweetly, I trust; for she is a beloved woman – which is more than can be said of every wife in the world.~~ Pray Heaven that Mrs. Hillard had a good night's rest in our guest-chamber; but I hardly think that she slept so sweetly ~~as my lily.~~ However, the night flitted over us all, and passed away, and uprose a gray and sullen morning, which would have saddened me, only that my sunny wife shone into my heart, and made it warm and bright. We had a splendid breakfast of flapjacks – (or slap-jacks, as my wife insists upon calling them) – of flap-jacks or slap-jacks, and of whortle-berries, which we gathered on a neighboring hill, and of perch, bream, and pouts, which I hooked out of the river, the evening before. About nine o clock, Hillard and I set out for a walk to Walden Pond, calling by the way at Mr. Emerson's, to obtain his guidance or directions. He, from a scruple of his external conscience, detained us till after the people had got into church, and then accompanied

as in his own illustrious person. We turned aside a little from our way to visit a Mr. Edmund Hosmer, a yeoman of whose homely and self-acquired wisdom Mr. Emerson has a very high opinion. We found him walking in his fields — a short, but stalwart and sturdy personage of middle age, somewhat uncouth and ugly to look at, but with a face of shrewd and kind expression, and manners of natural courtesy. He seemed to have a very free flow of talk, and not much diffidence about his own opinions; for, with a little induction from Mr. Emerson, he began to discourse about the state of the nation, agriculture, and business in general — uttering thoughts that had come to him at the plough, and which had a sort of flavor and smell of the fresh earth about them. I was not impressed with any remarkable originality in his views; but they were sensible and characteristic, and had grown in the soil where we found them. Methought, however, the good yeoman was not quite so natural as he may have been at a former period; the simplicity of his character has probably suffered, in some degree, by his detecting the impression which he makes on those around him. There is a circle, I suppose, who look up to him as an oracle; and so he inevitably assumes the oracular manner, and speaks as if truth and wisdom were uttering themselves by his voice. Mr. Emerson has risked the doing him much mischief, by putting him in print — a trial which few persons can sustain, without losing their unconsciousness. But, after all, a man gifted with thought and expression, whatever his rank in life, and his mode of uttering himself, whether by pen or tongue, cannot be expected to go through the world, without finding himself out — and as all such self-discoveries are partial and imperfect, they do more harm than good to the character. Mr. Hosmer is more natural than ninety-nine men out of a hundred; and he is certainly a man of intellectual and moral substance, a sturdy fact, a reality, something to be felt and touched. It would be amusing to draw a parallel between him and his admirer, Mr. Emerson — the mystic, stretching his hand out of cloud-land, in vain search for something real; and the man of sturdy sense,

us in his own illustrious person. We turned aside a little from our way to visit a Mr. Edmund Hosmer, a yeoman of whose homely and self-acquired wisdom Mr. Emerson has a very high opinion. We found him walking in his fields – a short, but stalwart and sturdy personage of middle age, somewhat uncouth and ugly to look at, but with a face of shrewd and kind expression, and manners of natural courtesy. He seemed to have a very free flow of talk, and not much diffidence about his own opinions; for, with a little induction from Mr. Emerson, he began to discourse about the state of the nation, agriculture, and business in general – uttering thoughts that had come to him at the plough, and which had a sort of flavor and smell of the fresh earth about them. I was not impressed with any remarkable originality in his views; but they were sensible and characteristic, and had grown in the soil where we found them. Methought, however, the good yeoman was not quite so natural as he may have been at a former period; the simplicity of his character has probably suffered, in some degree, by his detecting the impression which he makes on those around him. There is a circle, I suppose, who look up to him as an oracle; and so he inevitably assumes the oracular manner, and speaks as if truth and wisdom were uttering themselves by his voice. Mr. Emerson has risked the doing him much mischief, by putting him in print – a trial which few persons can sustain, without losing their unconsciousness. But, after all, a man gifted with thought and expression, whatever his rank in life, and his mode of uttering himself, whether by pen or tongue, cannot be expected to go through the world, without finding himself out – and as all such self-discoveries are partial and imperfect, they do more harm than good to the character. Mr. Hosmer is more natural than ninety-nine men out of a hundred; and he is certainly a man of intellectual and moral substance, a sturdy fact, a reality, something to be felt and touched. It would be amusing to draw a parallel between him and his admirer, Mr. Emerson – the mystic, stretching his hand out of cloud-land, in vain search for something real; and the man of sturdy sense, all whose ideas seem to be dug out of his mind, hard and substantial, as he digs potatoes, beets, carrots, and turnips, out of the earth. Mr. Emerson is a great searcher for facts; but they seem to melt away and become unsubstantial in his grasp.

After leaving Mr. Hosmer, we proceeded through wood-paths to Walden Pond, picking blackberries of enormous size along the way. The pond itself was beautiful and refreshing to my soul, after such long and exclusive familiarity with our tawny and sluggish river. It lies embosomed among wooded hills, not very extensive, but large enough for waves to dance upon its surface, and to look like a piece of blue firmament earth-encircled. The shore has a narrow, pebbly strand, which it was worth a day's journey to look at, for the sake of the contrast between it and the weedy, oozy margin of the river. Farther within its depths, you perceive a bottom of pure white sand, sparkling through the transparent water, which, methought, was the very purest liquid in the world. After Mr. Emerson left us, Hillard and I bathed in the pond; and it does really seem as if not only my corporeal person, but my moral self, had received a cleansing from that bath. A good deal of mud and river-slime had accumulated on my soul; but those bright waters washed it all away.

We returned home in due season for dinner, at which my wife presided with all imaginable grace and lady-likeness. On her part, she bears testimony to my air of dignified hospitality at the other end of the table; so that there can be no reasonable doubt that we were a most accomplished host and hostess. To my misfortune, however, a box of Mediterranean wine proved to have undergone the acetous fermentation; so that the splendor of the festival suffered some diminution. Nevertheless, we ate our dinner with a good appetite, and afterwards went universally to take our several siestas. Meantime there came a needless shower, which so besprinkled the grass and shrubbery, that my wife could not ac-

all whose ideas seem to be dug out of his mind, hard and substantial, as he digs potatoes, beets, carrots, and turnips, out of the earth. Mr. Emerson is a great searcher for facts; but they seem to melt away and become unsubstantial in his grasp.

After leaving Mr. Hosmer, we proceeded through wood-paths to Walden Pond, picking blackberries of enormous size along the way. The pond itself was beautiful and refreshing to my soul, after such long and exclusive familiarity with our tawny and sluggish river. It lies embosomed among wooded hills, not very extensive, but large enough for waves to dance upon its surface, and to look like a piece of blue firmament, earth-encircled. The shore has a narrow, pebbly strand, which it was worth a day's journey to look at, for the sake of the contrast between it and the weedy, slimy, oozy margin of the river. Farther within its depths, you perceive a bottom of pure white sand, sparkling through the transparent water, which, methought, was the very purest liquid in the world. After Mr. Emerson left us, Hillard and I bathed in the pond; and it does really seem as if not only my corporeal person, but my moral self, had received a cleansing from that bath. A good deal of mud and river-slime had accumulated on my soul; but those bright waters washed it all away.

We returned home in due season for dinner, at which my wife presided with all imaginable grace and lady-likeness. On her part, she bears testimony to my air of dignified hospitality at the other end of the table; so that there can be no reasonable doubt that we were a most accomplished host and hostess. To my misfortune, however, a box of Mediterranean wine proved to have undergone the acetous fermentation; so that the splendor of the festival suffered some diminution. Nevertheless, we ate our dinner with a good appetite, and afterwards went universally to take our several siestas. Meantime there came a needless shower, which so besprinkled the grass and shrubbery, that my wife could not accompany our guests and her husband in their after-supper ramble. The chief-result of the walk was the bringing home of an immense burthen of the trailing clematis, now just in blossom, and with which all our flower-stands and vases are this morning decorated. On our return, we found my ~~[struck]~~ entertaining Mr. and Mrs. Storer and Elizabeth Hoar, who shortly took their leave; and we sat up till after ten o'clock telling ghost-stories. This morning, at seven o'clock, our friends left us; and, at the present moment, ~~being~~ I know not what hour in the forenoon, my little wife is, or ought to be, sleeping off the fatigues of her hospitality. We were both pleased with the visit; and so, I think, were our guests,—and pleased were we, likewise, as my dear wife is kind enough to say, to be left again to one another. If she want a better chronicle of yesterday's events, she must even write it herself.

August 18th. Thursday. I have been ransacking old Doctor Ripley's library, which (or, at least, a portion of it,) is deposited in one of our out-houses, where it fills two book-cases. The Doctor, of course, succeeded to the erudite tomes, as well as to the mansion and widow of the Reverend Mr. Emerson of ante-revolutionary memory; and a considerable number of the volumes ~~would~~ seem to have been transmitted to that long-ago deceased worthy from divines of a much older day. There are dark old folios, containing a thousand pages apiece, or thereabouts, some of them in Latin by Catholic authors, others demolishing Popistical doctrines with a sledge-hammer, in plain English. A dissertation on the book of Job fills, I should think, some score of small, chunky quartos, proceeding at the rate of a volume to one or two chapters. Job himself, methinks, would have found it the severest trial of his patience to read this unreasonable dissertation. Then there is a great folio Body of Divinity—too corpulent a body, I should fear, to contain much of a soul. The quarto is the most prevalent form of these ancient volumes, square, and almost as thick as they are broad and long, giving the idea of an immense number of thickly, closely-printed pages to be waded through—a hard, heavy, lumpish mass

company our guests and her husband in their after-supper ramble. The chief-result of the walk was the bringing home of an immense burthen of the trailing clematis, now just in blossom, and ↑with↓ which all our flower-stands and vases are this morning decorated. On our return, we found ~~my sweetest wife entertaining~~ Mr. and Mrs. Storer and Elizabeth Hoar, who shortly took their leave; and we sate up till after ten o clock telling ghost-stories. This morning, at seven o clock, our friends left us; and, at this present moment, being I know not what hour in the forenoon, my little wife is, or ought to be, sleeping off the fatigues of her hospitality. We were both pleased with the visit; and so, I think, were our guests, – and pleased were we, likewise, as my dear wife is kind enough to say, to be left again to one another. If she wants a better chronicle of yesterday's events, she must ever write it herself.

August 16th. Tuesday. I have been examining old Doctor Ripley's library, which (or, at least, a portion of it) is deposited in one of our out-houses, where it fills two book-cases. The Doctor, of course, succeeded to the erudite tomes, as well as to the mansion and widow of the Reverend Mr. Emerson of ante-revolutionary memory; and a considerable number of the volumes would seem to have been transmitted to that long-ago deceased worthy from divines of a much elder day. There are dark old folios, containing a thousand pages apiece, or thereabouts, some of them in Latin by Catholic authors, others demolishing Papistical doctrines with a sledge-hammer, in plain English. A dissertation on the book of Job fills, I should think, some score of small, chunky quartos, proceeding at the rate of a volume to one or two chapters. Job himself, methinks, would have found it the severest trial of his patience to read this immeasurable dissertation. Then there is a great folio Body of Divinity – too corpulent a body, I should fear, to contain much of a soul. The quarto is the most prevalent form of these ancient volumes, square, and almost as thick as they are broad and long, giving the idea of an immense number ↑of↓ sturdy, closely-printed pages to be waded through – a hard, heavy, lumpish mass

14

of learning, which it might give the intellectual stomach an indigestion even to think of. Books of this form generally date two hundred years back, or more, and are bound in black leather, very solemn, and have much such an aspect as I should attribute to books of magic. Others, of equal antiquity, are very small volumes, such as might easily have been deposited in the large waistcoat pockets of old times—small, but as black as their larger brethren, and printed in minute type, largely interfused with Latin and Greek quotations. Somehow or other these little old volumes always impress me as if they had been intended for very large ones, but had been blighted in an early stage of their growth, and so were stunted and withered. Several of the works are collections of sermons by the elder divines of New-England, once famous in their generation, but whose writings would now be found nowhere, save in a library derived, at one or two removes, from clergymen of their own epoch. In the blank leaves of many of the old books are written names of former possessors, who vacated their pulpits above a century ago—some, perhaps, who were among the early pilgrims, and others, certainly, who were born before the pilgrims had passed from their earthly labors. On some of the blank leaves, there are pages of writing in short hand, perhaps containing very deep wisdom and most important truth, but for which the world will never be the better, inasmuch as nobody can read it. Doctor Ripley's own additions to the library are not of a very interesting character. Volumes of the Christian Examiner and Liberal Preacher, modern sermons, the controversial works of Unitarian ministers, and all such trash; but which, I suppose, express fairly enough, when compared with the elder portion of the library, the difference between the cold, lifeless, vaguely liberal clergyman of our own day, and the narrow but earnest cushion-thumper of puritanical times. On the whole, I prefer the last-mentioned variety of the black-coated tribe.

In a large old leathern-covered wooden trunk, I found

of learning, which it might give the intellectual stomach an indigestion even to think of. Books of this form generally date two hundred years back, or more, and are bound in black leather, very solemn, and have much such an aspect as I should attribute to books of magic. Others, of equal antiquity, are very small volumes, such as might easily have been deposited in the large waistcoat pockets of old times – small, but as black as their larger brethren, and printed in minute type, largely interfused with Latin and Greek quotations. Somehow or other, these little old volumes always impress me as if they had been intended for very large ones, but had been blighted in an early stage of their growth, and so were stunted and withered. Several of the works are collections of sermons by the elder divines of New-England, men famous in their generation, but whose writings would now be found nowhere, save in a library derived, at one or two removes, from clergymen of their own epoch. In the blank leaves of many of the old books are written names of former possessors, who vacated their pulpits above a century ago – some, perhaps, who were among the early pilgrims, and others, certainly, who were born before the pilgrims had passed from their earthly labors. On some of the blank leaves, there are pages of writing in short hand, perhaps containing very deep wisdom and most important truth, but for which the world will never be the better, inasmuch as nobody can read it. Doctor Ripley's own additions to the library are not of a very interesting character. Volumes of the Christian Examiner and Liberal Preacher, modern sermons, the controversial works of Unitarian ministers, and all such trash; but which, I suppose, express fairly enough, when compared with the elder portion of the library, the difference between the cold, lifeless, vaguely liberal clergyman of our own day, and the narrow but earnest cushion-thumper of puritanical times. On the whole, I prefer the last-mentioned variety of the black-coated tribe.

In a large old leather-covered wooden trunk, I found

many other memorials of the venerable Doctor—such as his best beaver hat, with a brim of solemn breadth, and a silk hat in the same style, for summer wear; his study-slippers, warm and comfortable; his iron tobacco-box; a japanned tin-box for the powder-puff, wherewith his hair or wig was to be whitened, half a century ago. There are likewise two profiles, one apparently in middle life, another in his venerable age. These things are mixed up with manuscript sermons, old bundles of musty accounts, and numerous letters, some of the directions of which are in female hands. We might find something of interest in them, if my most uncompromising of wives would consent to our reading them—in defence of which much might be urged; inasmuch as we are, for the time being, the heirs of the old Doctor, and the rightful inheritors of all his history. The trunk likewise contained some books of lighter literature than the rest of his library—among them the Spiritual Quixote, [illegible], and a volume of Della Cruscan Poetry, the only one I have ever met with. Among the older volumes, I forgot to mention Sir Richard Blackmore's Alfred. Blackmore was a much admired poet in New-England, and his works constituted, probably, an important portion of the polite literature of a library, some hundred and twenty years ago.

Saturday August 20th. This week the weather has been very gloomy until yesterday. Though I think I should not have known it, had not Adam daily lamented the injury which continued dampness caused in his garden. For I care very little what guise the heavens wear, whether it be sunny or shadowy abroad, so complete & sufficient is my inward happiness, so effective a sun of my system is my dearest Lord. I have not been well in the body, so that I could not be so demonstrative as usual, but there is never any variation in my felicity, while I recognize my position, & know that I am indeed his wife

many other memorials of the venerable Doctor – such as his best beaver hat, with a brim of solemn breadth, and a silk hat in the same style, for summer wear; his study-slippers, warm and comfortable; his iron tobacco-box; a Japanned tin-box for the powder-puff, wherewith his hair or wig used to be whitened, half a century ago. There are likewise two profiles, one apparently in middle life, another in his venerable age. These things are mixed up with manuscript sermons, old bundles of musty accounts, and numerous letters, some of the directions of which are in female hands. We might find something of interest in these, if my most uncompromising of wives would consent to our reading them – in defence of which much might be urged; inasmuch as we are, for the time being, the heirs of the Old Doctor, and the rightful inheritors of all his history. The trunk likewise contained some books of lighter literature than the rest of his library – among them the Spiritual Quixote, Thaddeus of Warsaw, and a volume of Della Cruscan Poetry, the only one I have ever met with. Among the elder volumes, I forgot to mention Sir Richard Blackmore's Alfred. Blackmore was a much admired poet in New-England, and his works constituted, probably, an important portion of the polite literature of a library, some hundred and twenty years ago.

Saturday August 20th. This week the weather has been very gloomy until yesterday. Though I think I should not have known it, had not Adam daily lamented the injury which continued dampness caused in his garden. For I care very little what guise the heavens wear, whether it be sunny or shadowy abroad, so complete & sufficient is my inward happiness, so effectual a sun of my system is my dearest lord. I have not been well in the body, so that I could not be so demonstrative as usual, but there is never any variation in my felicity, while I recognize my position, & know that I am indeed his wife

for the first time since we came to 14A
Paradise. It was also the first time that
I had left my beloved in our Eden
alone, though he has often gone from
me for a season. He accompanied
me down the avenue, & along the road
a short space, but would not go with
me, because he was in undress.
Elizabeth came to the door to me, looking
very tired & worn. I never saw her so
completely weary. She was as agreeable as
she always is.

for the first time since we came to Paradise. It was also the first time that I had left my beloved in our Eden alone, though he has often gone from me for a season. He accompanied me down the avenue & along the road a short space, but would not go with me because he was in undress.

Elizabeth came to the door to me, looking very tired & worn. I never saw her so completely weary. She was as agreable as she always is.

I took a walk through the woods, yesterday afternoon, to Mr. Emerson's, with a book which Margaret Fuller had left behind her, after a call on Saturday eve. I missed the nearest way, and wandered into a very secluded portion of the forest — for forest it might justly be called, so dense and sombre was the shade of oaks and pines. Once I wandered into a tract so overgrown with bushes and underbrush that I could scarcely force a passage through. Nothing is more annoying than a walk of this kind — to be tormented to death by an innumerable host of petty impediments; it incenses and depresses me at the same time. Always when I flounder into the midst

[22 August]

I took a walk through the woods, yesterday afternoon, to Mr. Emerson's, with a book which Margaret Fuller had left behind her, after a call on Saturday eve. I missed the nearest way, and wandered into a very secluded portion of the forest – for forest it might justly be called, so dense and sombre was the shade of oaks and pines. Once I wandered into a tract so overgrown with bushes and underbrush that I could scarcely force a passage through. Nothing is more annoying than a walk of this kind – to be tormented to death by an innumerable host of petty impediments; it incenses and depresses me at the same time. Always when I flounder into the midst

15

of a tract of bushes, which cross and intertwine themselves about my legs, and brush my face, and seize hold of my clothes, with a multitudinous gripe — always, in such a difficulty, I feel as if it were almost as well to lie down and die in rage and despair, as to go one step further. It is laughable, after I have got out of the scrape, to think how miserably it affected me for the moment; but I had better learn patience betimes, for there are many such bushy tracts in this vicinity, on the margins of meadows; and my walks will often lead me into them. Escaping from the bushes, I soon came to an open space among the woods — a very lonely spot, with the tall old trees standing around, as quietly as if nobody had intruded there throughout the whole summer. A company of crows were holding their sabbath in the tops of some of the trees; apparently they felt themselves injured or insulted by my presence; for, with one consent, they began to caw — caw — caw — and launching themselves sullenly on the air, took flight to some securer solitude. Mine, probably, was the first human shape that they had seen, all day long — at least, if they had been stationary in that spot; but perhaps they had winged their way over miles and miles of country — had breakfasted on the summit of Grey Lock, and dined at the base of Wachusett, and were merely come to sup and sleep among the quiet woods of Concord. But it was my impression, at the time, that they had sat still and silent in the tops of the trees, all through the Sabbath-day; and I felt like one who should unawares disturb an assembly of worshippers. A crow, however, has no real pretensions to religion, in spite of their gravity of mien and black attire; — they are certainly thieves, and probably infidels. Nevertheless, their voices, yesterday, were in admirable accordance with the influences of the quiet, sunny, warm, yet autumnal afternoon; they were so far above my head, that their loud clamor added to the quiet of the scene, instead of disturbing it. There was no other sound, except the song of the cricket, which

of a tract of bushes, which cross and intertwine themselves about my legs, and brush my face, and seize hold of my clothes with a multitudinous gripe – always, in such a difficulty, I feel as if it were almost as well to lie down and die in rage and despair, as to go one step further. It is laughable, after I have got out of the scrape, to think how miserably it affected me for the moment; but I had better learn patience betimes; for there are many such bushy tracts in this vicinity, on the margins of meadows; and my walks will often lead me into them. Escaping from the bushes, I soon came to an open space among the woods – a very lonely spot, with the tall old trees standing around, as quietly as if nobody had intruded there throughout the whole summer. A company of crows were holding their sabbath in the tops of some of the trees; apparently they felt themselves injured or insulted by my presence; for, with one consent, they began to caw – caw – caw – and launching themselves sullenly on the air, took flight to some securer solitude. Mine, probably, was the first human shape that they had seen, all day long – at least, if they had been stationary in that spot; but perhaps they had winged their way over miles and miles of country – had breakfasted on the summit of Graylock, and dined at the base of Wachusett, and were merely come to sup and sleep among the quiet woods of Concord. But it was my impression, at the time, that they had sat still and silent in the tops of the trees, all through the Sabbath-day; and I felt like one who should unawares disturb an assembly of worshippers. A crow, however, has no real pretensions to religion, in spite of their gravity of mien and black attire; – they are certainly thieves, and probably infidels. Nevertheless, their voices, yesterday, were in admirable accordance with the influences of the quiet, sunny, warm, yet autumnal afternoon; they were so far above my head, that their loud clamor added to the quiet of the scene, instead of disturbing it. There was no other sound, except the song of the crickets, which is but an audible stillness; for though it be very loud, and heard afar, yet the mind does not take note of it as a sound, so entirely does it mingle and lose its individuality among the other characteristics of coming Autumn. Alas, for the summer! The grass is still verdant on the hills and in the valleys; the foliage of the trees is as dense as ever, and as green; the flowers are abundant along the margin of the river, and in the hedge-rows, and deep among the woods; the days, too, are as fervid as they were a month ago — and yet, in every breath of wind, and in every beam of sunshine, there is an autumnal influence. I know not how to describe it; — methinks there is a sort of coolness amid all the heat, and a mildness in the brightest of the sunshine. A breeze cannot stir, without thrilling me with the breath of autumn, and I behold its pensive glory in the far golden gleams, among the long shadows of the trees. The flowers — even the brightest of them — the Golden Rod, and the gorgeous Cardinals, all the most glorious flowers of the year, have this gentle sadness amid their pomp. Pensive Autumn is expressed in the glow of every one of them. I have felt this influence earlier in some years than in others — sometimes Autumn may be perceived even in the early days of July. There is no other feeling like what is caused by this faint, doubtful, yet real perception, or rather prophecy, of the year's decay — so deliciously sweet and sad in the same breath.

After leaving the book at Mr. Emerson's, I returned through the woods, and entering Sleepy Hollow, I perceived a lady reclining near the path which bends along its verge. It was Margaret herself. She had been there the whole afternoon, meditating or reading; for she had a book in her hand, with some strange title, which I did not understand and have forgotten. She said that nobody had broken her solitude, and was just giving utterance to a theory that no inhabitant of Concord ever visited Sleepy Hollow, when we saw a whole group of people entering the sacred precincts. Most of them followed a path that led them remote from us; but an old man passed near us, and smiled to see Margaret lying on the

is but an audible stillness; for though it be very loud, and heard afar, yet the mind does not take note of it as a sound, so entirely does it mingle and lose its individuality among the other characteristics of coming Autumn. Alas, for the summer! The grass is still verdant on the hills ↑and↓ in the vallies; the foliage of the trees is as dense as ever, and as green; the flowers are abundant along the margin of the river, and in the hedge-rows, and deep among the woods; the days, too, are as fervid as they were a month ago – and yet, in every breath of wind, and in every beam of sunshine, there is an autumnal influence. I know not how to describe it; – methinks there is a sort of coolness amid all the heat, and a mildness in the brightest of the sunshine. A breeze cannot stir, without thrilling me with the breath of autumn; and I behold its pensive glory in the far golden gleams, among the long shadows of the trees. The flowers – even the brightest of them – the Golden-Rod, and the gorgeous Cardinals, all the most glorious flowers of the year, have this gentle sadness amid their pomp. Pensive Autumn is expressed in the glow of every one of them. I have felt this influence earlier in some years than in others – sometimes Autumn may be perceived even in the early days of July. There is no other feeling like what is caused by this faint, doubtful, yet real perception, or rather prophecy, of the year's decay – so deliciously sweet and sad in the same breath.

After leaving the book at Mr. Emerson's, I returned through the woods, and entering Sleepy Hollow, I perceived a lady reclining near the path which bends along its verge. It was Margaret herself. She had been there the whole afternoon, meditating or reading; for she had a book in her hand, with some strange title, which I did not understand and have forgotten. She said that nobody had broken her solitude, and was just giving utterance to a theory that no inhabitant of Concord ever visited Sleepy Hollow, when we saw a whole group of people entering the sacred precincts. Most of them followed a path that led them remote from us; but an old man passed near us, and smiled to see Margaret lying on the ground, and we sitting by her side. He made some remark about the beauty of the afternoon, and withdrew himself into the shadow of the wood. Then we talked about Autumn—and about the pleasures of getting lost in the woods—and about the crows, whose voices Margaret had heard—and about the experiences of early childhood, whose influence remains upon the character after the recollection of them has passed away—and about the sight of mountains from a distance, and the view from their summits—and about other matters of high and low philosophy. In the midst of our talk, we heard footsteps above us, on the high bank; and while the intruder was still hidden among the trees, he called to Margaret, of whom he had gotten a glimpse. Then he emerged from the green shade; and, behold, it was Mr. Emerson, who, in spite of his clerical consecration, had found no better way of spending the Sabbath than to ramble among the woods. He appeared to have had a pleasant time; for he said that there were Muses in the woods to-day, and whispers to be heard in the breezes. It being now nearly six o'clock, we separated, Mr. Emerson and Margaret towards his house, and I towards mine, where my little wife was very busy getting tea. By the bye, Mr. Emerson gave me an invitation to dinner to-day, to be accepted or not, as might suit my convenience at the time; and it happens not to suit. He likewise communicated an invitation from Mrs. Ripley of Waltham for my wife and me to attend a party at her house, next Thursday evening—an annual party, I believe, on the evening after the Φ. B. K. celebration. If my wife chooses, she shall go, and stay all night, away from her poor desolate husband.

Last evening there was the most beautiful moonlight that ever hallowed this earthly world; and when I went to bathe in the river, which was as calm as death, it seemed like plunging down into the sky. But I had rather be on earth than even in the seventh Heaven, just now

ground, and me sitting by her side. He made some remark about the beauty of the afternoon, and withdrew himself into the shadow of the wood. Then we talked about Autumn – and about the pleasures of getting lost in the woods – and about the crows, whose voices Margaret had heard – and about the experiences of early childhood, whose influence remains upon the character after the recollection of them has passed away – and about the sight of mountains from a distance, and the view from their summits – and about other matters of high and low philosophy. In the midst of our talk, we heard footsteps above us, on the high bank; and while the intruder was still hidden among the trees, he called to Margaret, of whom he had gotten a glimpse. Then he emerged from the green shade; and, behold, it was Mr. Emerson, who, in spite of his clerical consecration, had found no better way of spending the Sabbath than to ramble among the woods. He appeared to have had a pleasant time; for he said that there were Muses in the woods to-day, and whispers to be heard in the breezes. It being now nearly six o clock, we separated, Mr. Emerson and Margaret towards his house, and I towards mine, where my little wife was very busy getting tea. By the bye, Mr. Emerson gave me an invitation to dinner to-day, to be complied with or not, as might suit my convenience at the time; and it happens not to suit. He likewise communicated an invitation from Mrs. Ripley of Waltham for my wife and me to attend a party at her house, next Thursday evening – an annual party, I believe, on the evening after the Φ. B. K. celebration. If my wife chooses, she shall go, and stay all night, away from her poor desolate husband.

Last evening there was the most beautiful moonlight that ever hallowed this earthly world; and when I went to bathe in the river, which was as calm as death, it seemed like plunging down into the sky. But I had rather be on earth than even in the seventh Heaven, just now

Wednesday 24th August. Monday morning I walked to Mrs Alcott's, two miles, to carry a letter to Mother for her to take to Boston the next day. I walked very diligently & accomplished the distance in a short time, feeling more animated every step I took & strong as a little lion. After a very pleasant call at the cottage, Mrs Alcott proposed that her brother Junius should row me home in the boat, instead of my returning through the dusty road. So Anna & Louisa & Junius & I proceeded to the river, & Mrs Alcott had a crimson cushion placed on my seat, & Mr Junius scattered twigs of trees beneath my feet to shield me from the dust or damp of the boat, & away we floated down the shining stream. It was utterly still, so that it was impossible to tell where the tangible ended & the reflected began on the margin - excepting that the reflected was far more beautiful & fresh as if bathed in [illegible]. The purple pickerel flower & the gorgeous cardinals & spirea of all colors, & arrow-head & pond lilies all seemed rejoiced to be in that fairy world beneath the earth. And the clouds of fleecy whiteness floated through the blue ether down far below us - as if, we were sailing in mid-air between two fair firmaments & all the emerald garniture of earth were poised by the power of counter-forces around us. The yellow water of the river turned all the plants that grow in its bed into pure gold. One might imagine it the golden river Pactolus & the plains beside it those of enchanting Greece. Once in a while a troop of birds flew along in the remote heaven below & vanished like spirits. Oh

Wednesday 24th August. Monday morning I walked to Mrs Alcott's, two miles, to carry a letter to mother for her to take to Boston the next day. I walked very diligently & accomplished the distance in a short time, feeling more animated every step I took & strong as a little lion. After a very pleasant call at the cottage, Mrs Alcott proposed that her brother Junius should row me home in the boat, instead of my returning through the dusty road. So Anna & Louisa & Junius & I proceeded to the river, & Mrs Alcott had a crimson cushion placed on my seat, & Mr. Junius scattered twigs of trees beneath my feet to shield me from the dust or damp of the boat, & away we floated down the shining stream. It was utterly still, so that it was impossible to tell where the tangible ended & the reflected began on the margin – excepting that the reflected was far more beautiful & fresh as if bathed in rain. The purple pickerel flower & the gorgeous cardinals & spirea of all colors, & arrowhead & pond lilies all seemed rejoiced to be in that faery world beneath the earth. And the clouds of fleecy whiteness floated through the blue ether down far below us – as if ↑we↓ were sailing in mid-air between two fair firmaments & all the emerald garniture of earth were poised by the power of counter-forces around us. The yellow water of the river turned all the plants that grow in its bed into pure gold – one might imagine it the golden river Pactolus & the plains beside it those of enchanting Greece. Once in a while a troop of birds flew along in the remote heaven below & vanished like spirits. Oh who could ever imagine that there was mud & fige & rock under one little boat instead of that rare picture! It was perfectly bewitching with one great want. My noble & kingly husband should have been sitting before me with oars in hand instead of Some Junius Alcott who had no place in my regard. Presently we anchored in a baylet & Junius sprang out & pulled up a "conclave of Cardinals" (as my dearest husband felicitously calls a group of these flowers) & presented them to me — & Louisa alcott plucked the pickerel & added them to my radiant company. But what Roman Cardinal ever wore such a cloak as these imperial yankee dignitaries? No Tyrian dye ever equalled this hue. ~~[illegible]~~ GOD paints better than man can imitate. I was landed on a rock at the foot of our orchard & arrived at dinner just after my husband & Louisa had seated themselves, feeling like a water-nymph fresh from jewelled caves & reedy depths. In the afternoon we went to our wooded hill to gather whortleberries. We first entered the pine forest till the sun should be less potent, & I laid down upon the dear old young earth & had sweet rest till I grew too cool. Then we began our labors, & most silently, like three dumb Dryads, filled our baskets. Once in a while I raised my head to take note of the progress of the sun, & called to my dear lord & Louisa to lift their eyes for one moment from the absorbing tasks. Cows were feeding beside me, breathing sweetest breath around. I very civilly accosted one, but after giving me a fashionable stare, she dodged her head & floundered

who would ever imagine that there was mud & fire & rock under our little boat instead of that rare picture? It was perfectly bewitching with one great want. My noble & kingly husband should have been sitting before me with oars in hand instead of some Junius Alcott who had no place in my regard. Presently we anchored in a baylet & Junius sprang out & pulled up a "conclave of cardinals" (as my dear husband felicitously calls a group of these flowers) & presented them to me – & Louisa ↑Alcott↓ plucked the pickerel & added them to my radiant company. But what Roman Cardinal ever wore such a cloak as these imperial yankee dignitaries? No Tyrian dye ever equalled this hue. ~~XXXXXXX~~ GOD paints better than man can imitate. I was landed on a rock at the foot of our orchard & arrived at dinner just after my husband & Louisa had seated themselves, feeling like a water -nympth fresh from jewelled caves & reedy depths. In the afternoon we went to our wooded hill to gather whortleberries. We first entered the pine forest till the sun should be less potent, & I laid down upon the dear old young Earth & had sweet rest till I grew too cool. Then we began our labors, & most silently, like three dumb Dryads, filled our baskets. Once in a while I raised my head to take note of the progress of the sun, & called to my dear lord & Luisa to lift their eyes for one moment from the absorbing task. Cows were feeding beside me, breathing sweetest breath around. I very civilly accosted one, but after giving me a fashionable stare, she dodged her head & floundered away without any grace of soul or body. There was a grand group of clouds above the sun, ready & waiting to be commuted into superb tints of purple & gold. But King Sol was sulky & would not give one particle of glory to any object near him & after delaying in vain for the expected pageant, we pettishly left his stupid majesty to enjoy his selfishness by himself. After tea, Louisa & I winnowed our berries of all unworthiness, while my beloved husband sat opposite me, shining like a star. Ah now I have thought. The sun set in his eyes & they rayed out the lost splendor upon me & into my heart. Oh sun! forgive my irreverent speech of thee. Thou art far wiser than I thought.

Yesterday, Tuesday afternoon we went to seek cardinals on the riverbanks. & we found two hundred & ninety potentates standing ankle deep in water, & pulled them out. I do not believe there was ever such a resplendent sight seen before as two hundred & ninety cardinals in a compact group, as they hung over my husband's shoulder coming home. I arranged them all in the flower table after tea in the evening.

August 24th Wednesday. I left my Sophia at five o'clock this morning, to catch some fish for dinner. On my way through the orchard, I shook our summer apple tree, and ate the golden apple which fell from it. Methinks these early apples, which come as a golden promise before the treasures of autumnal fruit, are almost delicious than anything that comes afterwards. We have but one such tree in our orchard; but it supplies us with a daily abundance, and promises to do so for at least a week to come. Meantime, other trees begin to cast their ripening windfalls upon

away without any grace of soul or body. There was a grand group of clouds above the sun, ready & waiting to be commuted into superb tints of purple & gold. But King Sol was sulky & would not give one particle of glory to any object near him & after delaying in rain for the expected pageant, we patiently left his stupid majesty to enjoy his selfishness by himself. After tea, Louisa & I winnowed our berries of all unworthiness, while my beloved husband sat opposite me, shining like a star. Ah now I have thought. The sun set in his eyes & they rayed out the lost splendor upon me & into my heart. Oh sun! forgive my irreverent speech of thee. Thou art far wiser than I thought.

Yesterday, Tuesday afternoon we went to seek Cardinals on the riverbanks – & we found two hundred & ninety potentates standing ankle deep in water, & pulled them out. I do not believe there was ever such a resplendent sight seen before as two hundred & ninety cardinals in a compact group, as they hung over my husband's shoulder coming home. I arranged them all in the flower table ~~after tea~~ in the evening.

August 24th. Wednesday. I left my Sophie~~'s arms~~ at five o clock this morning, to catch some fish for dinner. On my way through the orchard, I shook our summer apple-tree, and ate the golden apple which fell from it. Methinks these early apples, which come as a golden promise before the treasures of autumnal fruit, are almost more delicious than anything that comes afterwards. We have but one such tree in our orchard; but it supplies us with a daily abundance, and promises to do so for at least a week to come. Mean-time, other trees begin to cast their ripening windfalls upon the grass; and when I taste them, and perceive their mellowed flavor and blackening seeds, I feel somewhat overwhelmed with the impending bounties of Providence. I suppose Adam, in Paradise, did not like to see his fruits decaying on the ground, after he had watched them through the sunny days of the world's first summer. However, insects, at the worst, will hold a festival upon them; so that they will not be thrown away, in the great scheme of nature. Moreover, I have one advantage over the primeval Adam, inasmuch as there is a chance of disposing of my superfluous fruits among people who inhabit no Paradise of their own.

Passing a little way down along the river-side, I threw in my line, and soon drew out one of the smallest possible fish. It seemed to be a pretty good morning for the angler—an autumnal coolness in the air; a clear sky, but with a fog along the lowlands and on the surface of the river, which a gentle breeze sometimes condensed into wreaths. At first, I could barely discern the opposite shore of the river; but as the sun arose, the vapors gradually dispersed, till only a warm smoky tint was left along the water's surface. The farm-houses, across the river, made their appearance out of the dusky cloud;—the voices of boys were heard, shouting to the cattle as they drove them to pasture;—a mower whetted his scythe, and set to work in a neighboring meadow. Meantime, I continued to stand on the oozy margin of the stream, beguiling the little fish; and though the scaly inhabitants of our river partake somewhat of the character of their native element, and are but sluggish biters, still I continued to pull out not far from two dozen. They were all bream—a broad, flat, almost circular fish, shaped a good deal like a flounder, but swimming on their edges, instead of their flat sides. As far as mere pleasure is concerned, it is hardly worth while to fish in our river, it is so much

the grass; and when I taste them, and perceive their mellowed flavor and blackening seeds, I feel somewhat overwhelmed with the impending bounties of Providence. I suppose Adam, in Paradise, did not like to see his fruits decaying on the ground, after he had watched them through the sunny days of the world's first summer. However, insects, at the worst, will hold a festival upon them; so that they will not be thrown away, in the great scheme of nature. Moreover, I have one advantage over the primeval Adam, inasmuch as there is a chance of disposing of my superfluous fruits among people who inhabit no Paradise of their own.

Passing a little way down along the river-side, I threw in my line, and soon drew out one of the smallest possible fish. It seemed to be a pretty good morning for the angler – an autumnal coolness in the air; a clear sky, but with a fog along the lowlands and on the surface of the river, which a gentle breeze sometimes condensed into wreaths. At first, I could barely discern the opposite shore of the river; but as the sun arose, the vapors gradually dispersed, till only a warm smoky tint was left along the water's surface. The farmhouses, across the river, made their appearance out of the dusky cloud; – the voices of boys were heard, shouting to the cattle as they drove them to pasture: – a mower whetted his scythe, and set to work in a neighboring meadow. Meantime, I continued to stand on the oozy margin of the stream, beguiling the little fish; and though the scaly inhabitants of our river partake somewhat of the character of their native element, and are but sluggish biters, still I contrived to pull out not far from two dozen. They were all bream – a broad, flat, almost circular fish, shaped a good deal like a flounder, but swimming on their edges, instead of their flat sides. As far as mere pleasure is concerned, it is hardly worth while to fish in our river, it is so much like angling in a mud-puddle; and one does not attach the idea of freshness and purity to the fish, as we do to those which inhabit swift, transparent streams, or haunt the shores of the great briny deep. Standing on the weedy margin, and throwing the line over the elder-bushes that dip into the water, it seems as if we could catch nothing but frogs and mud-turtles, or reptiles akin to them; and even when a fish of reputable aspect is drawn out, you feel a shyness about touching him. As to our river, my little wife expressed its character admirably, last night; she said "it was too lazy to keep itself clean." I might write pages and pages, and only obscure the impression which this brief sentence conveys. Nevertheless, we made bold to eat some of my fish for breakfast, and found them very savory; and the rest shall meet with due entertainment at dinner, together with some shell-beans, green corn, and cucumbers from our garden; so that this day's food comes directly and entirely from beneficent Nature, without the intervention of any third person between her and us.

<u>August 27th. Saturday.</u> A peach-tree, which grows beside our house, and brushes against the kitchen window, is so burthened with fruit that I have had to prop it up. I never saw more splendid peaches in appearance—great, round, crimson-cheeked beauties, clustering all over the tree. In a week, or less, they will begin to be ripe. A pear-tree, likewise, is maturing a generous burthen of small, sweet fruit, which will require ~~to be~~ eaten about the same time as the peaches. There is something pleasantly annoying in this superfluous abundance; it is like standing under a tree of ripe apples, and giving it a shake, ~~with the~~ intention of bringing down a single one—when down come a dozen, thumping about our ears. But the idea of an infinite generosity and exhaustless bounty in our Mother Nature is well worth attaining; and I never had it so vividly as now, when I find myself, with the two or three mouths which I am to feed, the sole inheritor of the old clergyman's wealth of fruits. His children, and all his

like angling in a mud-puddle; and one does not attach the idea of freshness and purity to the fish, as we do to those which inhabit swift, transparent streams, or ↑haunt↓ the shores of the great briny deep. Standing on the weedy margin, and throwing the line over the elder-bushes that dip into the water, it seems as if we could catch nothing but frogs and mud-turtles, or reptiles akin to them; and even when a fish of reputable aspect is drawn out, you feel a shyness about touching him. As to our river, my little wife expressed its character admirably, last night; she said "it was too lazy to keep itself clean." I might write pages and pages, and only obscure the impression which this brief sentence conveys. Nevertheless, we made bold to eat some of my fish for breakfast, and found them very savory; and the rest shall meet with due entertainment at dinner, together with some shell-beans, green corn, and cucumbers from our garden; so that this day's food comes directly and entirely from beneficent Nature, without the intervention of any third person between her and us.

August 27th. Saturday. A peach-tree, which grows beside our house, and brushes against the kitchen window, is so burthened with fruit that I have had to prop it up. I never saw more splendid peaches in appearance – great, round, crimson-cheeked beauties, clustering all over the tree. In a week, or less, they will begin to be ripe. A pear-tree, likewise, is maturing a generous burthen of small, sweet fruit, which will require to be eaten about the same time as the peaches. There is something pleasantly annoying in this superfluous abundance; it is like standing under a tree of ripe apples, and giving it a shake, with the intention of bringing down a single one – when down come a dozen, thumping about our ears. But the idea of an infinite generosity and exhaustless bounty in our Mother Nature is well worth attaining; and I never had it so vividly as now, when I find myself, with the two or three mouths which I am to feed, the sole inheritor of the old clergyman's wealth of fruits. His children, and all his household, his friends in the village, and the clerical guests who came to preach in his pulpit, were all wont to eat and be filled from these trees. Now, all these hearty old people have passed away; and in their stead is a solitary pair, whose appetites are more than satisfied with the windfalls which the trees throw down at their feet. 19

Howbeit, we shall have now and then a guest to keep our peaches and pears from decaying. George Bradford, my old fellow-laborer at the Community, called on us last evening, and dined here to-day. He has been cultivating vegetables at Plymouth, this summer, and selling them in the market. What a singular mode of life for a man of education and refinement!— to spend his days in hard and earnest bodily toil, and then to convey the products of his labor, in a wheelbarrow, to the public market, and there retail them out—a peck of peas or beans, a bunch of turnips, a squash, a dozen ears of green corn. Few men, without some eccentricity of character, would have the moral strength to do this; and it is very striking to find such strength combined with the utmost gentleness, and an uncommon regularity of nature. Occasionally, he returns, for a day or two, to resume his place among scholars and idle people;—as, for instance, the present week, when he has thrown aside his spade and hoe to attend the commencement at Cambridge. He is a rare man—a perfect original, yet without any one salient point; a character to be felt and understood, but almost impossible to describe; for, should you seize upon any characteristic, it would inevitably be altered and distorted in the process of writing it down. I have invited him to become a member of my family; he is still weighing the proposition, but most probably will decline. Perhaps, with all his rare and delicate properties, which make him, in some respects, more like a shadow than a substance, it is best for us both that he should decline.

Our few remaining days of summer have been, latterly, frequently darkened with clouds. To-day, there has been a

household, his friends in the village, and the clerical guests who came to preach in his pulpit, were all wont to eat and be filled, from these trees. Now, all those hearty old people have passed away; and in their stead is a solitary pair, whose appetites are more than satisfied with the windfalls which the trees throw down at their feet.

Howbeit, we shall have now and then a guest to keep our peaches and pears from decaying. George Bradford, my old fellow-laborer at the Community, called on us last evening, and dined here to-day. He has been cultivating vegetables at Plymouth, this summer, and selling them in the market. What a singular mode of life for a man of education and refinement! – to spend his days in hard and earnest bodily toil, and then to convey the products of his labor, in a wheelbarrow, to the public market, and there retail them out – a peck of peas or beans, a bunch of turnips, a squash, a dozen ears of green corn. Few men, without some eccentricity of character, would have the moral strength to do this; and it is very striking to find such strength combined with the utmost gentleness, and an uncommon regularity of nature. Occasionally, he returns, for a day or two, to resume his place among scholars and idle people; – as, for instance, the present week, when he has thrown aside his spade and hoe to attend the Commencement at Cambridge. He is a rare man – a perfect original, yet without any one salient point: a character to be felt and understood, but almost impossible to describe; for, should you seize upon any characteristic, it would inevitably be altered and distorted in the process of writing it down. I have invited him to become an inmate of my family; he is still weighing the proposition, but most probably will decline. Perhaps, with all his rare and delicate properties, which make ↑him↓, in some respects, more like a shadow than a substance, it is best for us both that he should decline.

Our few remaining days of summer have been, latterly, grievously darkened with clouds. To-day, there has been an hour or two of hot sunshine; but the sun rose amid cloud and mist; and before he could dry up the moisture of last night's shower, upon the trees and grass, the clouds were gathered between him and us again. This afternoon, the thunder rumbles at a distance, and, I believe, a few drops of rain have fallen; but the weight of the shower has burst elsewhere, leaving us nothing but its sullen gloom. There is a muggy warmth in the atmosphere, which takes all the spring and vivacity out of mind and body.

August 28th. – Sunday. Still another rainy day – the heaviest rain, I believe, that has fallen since we came to Concord. There never was a more sombre aspect of all external nature. I gaze from the open window of my study, somewhat disconsolately, and observe the great willow-tree, that shades the house, and which has caught and retained a whole cataract of rain among its leaves and boughs; and all the fruit trees, too, are dripping continually, even in the brief intervals when the clouds give us a respite. If shaken to bring down their fruit, they will discharge a shower upon the head of him who stands beneath. The rain is warm, coming from some southern region; but the willow attests that it is an autumnal spell of weather, by scattering down an infrequent multitude of yellow leaves, which rest upon the sloping roof of the house, and strew the gravel-path and the grass. The other trees do not yet shed their leaves, though, in some of them, a lighter tint of verdure, tending towards yellow, is perceptible. All day long, we hear the water drip-drip-dripping, and splash-splash-splashing, from the eaves, and bubbling and foaming into the tubs which we have set out to receive it. The old unpainted shingles and boards of the mansion and outhouses are black with the moisture which they have imbibed. Looking at the river, we perceive that its usually smooth and mirrored surface is blurred by the infinity of rain-drops; the whole landscape, grass, trees, and houses, has a completely water-soaked aspect, as if the earth were wet through; the wooded hill, about a mile distant, whither we went to gather whortle-berries, has a mist upon its summit, as if the demon of the rain were enthroned there; and if we look to the sky, it seems as if all the water that has been poured down upon

hour or two of hot sunshine; but the sun rose amid cloud and mist; and before he could dry up the moisture of last night's shower, upon the trees and grass, the clouds have gathered between him and us again. This afternoon, the thunder rumbles at a distance, and, I believe, a few drops of rain have fallen; but the weight of the shower has burst elsewhere, leaving us nothing but its sullen gloom. There is a muggy warmth in the atmosphere, which takes all the spring and vivacity out of mind and body.

August 28th. – Sunday. Still another rainy day – the heaviest rain, I believe, that has fallen since we came to Concord. There never was a more sombre aspect of all external nature. I gaze from the open window of my study, somewhat disconsolately, and observe the great willow-tree, that shades the house, and which has caught and retained a whole cataract of rain among its leaves and boughs; and all the fruit trees, too, are dripping continually, even in the brief intervals when the clouds give us a respite. If shaken to bring down their fruit, they will discharge a shower upon the head of him who stands beneath. The rain is warm, coming from some southern region; but the willow attests that it is an autumnal spell of weather, by scattering down no infrequent multitude of yellow leaves, which rest upon the sloping roof of the house, and strew the gravel-path and the grass. The other trees do not yet shed their leaves, though, in some of them, a lighter tint of verdure, tending towards yellow, is perceptible. All day long, we hear the water drip-drip-dripping, and splash-splash-splashing, from the eaves, and bubbling and foaming into the tubs which we have set out to receive it. The old unpainted shingles and boards of the mansion and outhouses are black with the moisture which they have imbibed. Looking at the river, we perceive that its usually smooth and mirrored surface is blurred by the infinity of rain-drops; the whole landscape, grass, trees, and houses, has a completely water-soaked aspect, as if the earth were wet through; the wooded hill, about a mile distant, whither we went to gather whortle-berries, has a mist upon its summit, as if the demon of the rain were enthroned there; and if we look to the sky, it seems as if all the water that has been poured down upon as, were nothing to what is to come. Once in a while, indeed, there is a gleam of sky along the horizon, or a half sullen, half cheerful lighting up of the atmosphere; the rain-drops cease to patter down, except when the trees shake off a gentle shower; but soon we hear the broad, quiet, slow and sure recommencement of the rain. The river, if I mistake not, has risen considerably during the day, and its current will acquire some degree of energy.

In this sombre weather, when ordinary mortals almost forget that there ever was any golden sunshine, or ever will be any hereafter, my little wife seems absolutely to radiate it from her own heart and mind. The gloom cannot penetrate her; she conquers it, and drives it quite out of her sphere, and creates a moral rain-bow of hope upon the blackest cloud. As for myself, I am little other than a cloud, at such seasons; but she continues to make me a sunny one; for she gets into the remotest recesses of my heart, and shines all through me. And thus, even without the support of a stated occupation, I survive these sullen days, and am happy. This morning, my wife read us the Sermon on the Mount, most beautifully; so that methinks even the Author of it might be satisfied with such an utterance. In the course of the forenoon, the rain abated for a season; ~~and~~ I went out and gathered some corn and summer squashes for our dinner, and picked up the wind-falls of apples and pears and peaches. Wet—wet—wet—every thing was wet; the blades of the corn-stalks moistened me; the wet grass soaked my cow-hide boots quite through; the trees threw their reserved showers upon my head; and soon the remorseless rain began anew and drove me into the house. When shall we be able to walk again to the far hills, and plunge into the deep woods, and gather more cardinals along the river's margin? The track along which we trod is probably under water, now. How inhospitable Nature is, during a rain! In the fervid heat of sunny days, she still retains some degree of mercy for us;—she has shady spots, whither the sun cannot come; but she provides no shelter against

us, were nothing to what is to come. Once in a while, indeed there is a gleam of sky along the horizon, or a half sullen, half cheerful lighting up of the atmosphere; the rain-drops cease to patter down, except when the trees shake off a gentle shower; but soon we hear the broad, quiet, slow and sure recommencement of the rain. The river, if I mistake not, has risen considerably during the day, and its current will acquire some degree of energy.

In this sombre weather, when ordinary mortals almost forget that there ever was any golden sunshine, or ever will be any hereafter, my little wife seems absolutely to radiate it from her own heart and mind. The gloom cannot pervade her; she conquers it, and drives it quite out of her sphere, and creates a moral rain-bow of hope upon the blackest cloud. As for myself, I am little other than a cloud, at such seasons; but she contrives to make me a sunny one; for she gets into the remotest recesses of my heart, and shines all through me. And thus, even without the support of a stated occupation, I survive these sullen days, and am happy. This morning, my wife read us the Sermon on the Mount, most beautifully; so that methinks even the Author of it might be satisfied with such an utterance. In the course of the forenoon, the rain abated for a season; and I went out and gathered some corn and summer-squashes for our dinner, and picked up the windfalls of apples and pears, and peaches. Wet – wet – wet – every thing was wet; the blades of the corn-stalks moistened me; the wet grass soaked my cow-hide boots quite through; the trees threw their reserved showers upon my head; and soon the remorseless rain began anew and drove me into the house. When shall we ↑be↓ able to walk again to the far hills, and plunge into the deep woods, and gather more cardinals along the river's margin? The track along which we trod is probably under water, now. How inhospitable Nature is, during a rain! In the fervid heat of sunny days, she still retains some degree of mercy for us; – she has shady spots, whither the sun cannot come; but she provides no shelter against her storms. It makes one shiver to think how dripping with wet are those deep, umbrageous nooks — those over-shadowed banks — where we find such enjoyment during sultry afternoons. And what becomes of the birds, in such a soaking rain as this? Is hope, and an instinctive faith, so mixed up with their nature, that they can be cheered by the thought that the sunshine will return? — or do they think, as I almost do, that there is to be no sunshine any more? Very disconsolate must they be, among the dripping leaves; and when a single summer makes so important a portion of their lives, it seems hard that so much of it should be dissolved in rain. I, likewise, am greedy of the summer-days for my own sake; the life of man does not contain so many of them that even one can be spared without regret.

August 30th. Tuesday. My wife promised, in the midst of Sunday's rain, that yesterday should be fair; and behold! the sun came back to us, and brought one of the most perfect days that ever was made, since Adam was driven out of Paradise. By the bye, was there ever any rain in Paradise? If so, how comfortless must Eve's bower have been! — and what a wretched and rheumatic time must they have had on their bed of wet roses! It makes me shiver to think of it. Well; it seemed as if the world was newly created, yesterday morning; and I beheld its birth, for I had risen before the sun was over the hill, and had gone forth to fish. How instantaneously did all dreariness and heaviness of the earth's spirit flit away, before one smile of the beneficent sun. This proves that all gloom is but a dream and a shadow, and that cheerfulness is the real truth. It requires many clouds, long brooding over us, to make us sad; but one gleam of sunshine always suffices to cheer up the landscape. The banks of the river actually laughed, when the sunshine fell upon them; and the river itself was alive and cheerful, and, by way of fun and amusement, it had swept away many wreaths of meadow hay, and old rotten branches of trees, and all such trumpery. These matters came floating downward, whirling round and round in the

her storms. It makes one shiver to think how dripping with wet are those deep, umbrageous nooks – those over-shadowed banks – where we find such enjoyment during sultry afternoons. And what becomes of the birds, in such a soaking rain as this? Is hope, and an instinctive faith, so mixed up with their nature, that they can be cheered by the thought that the sunshine will return? – or do they think, as I almost do, that there is to be no sunshine any more? Very disconsolate must they be, among the dripping leaves; and when a single summer makes so important a portion of their lives, it seems hard that so much of it should be dissolved in rain. I, likewise, am greedy of the summer-days for my own sake; the life of man does not contain so many of them that even one can be spared without regret.

August 30th. Tuesday. My wife promised, in the midst of Sunday's rain, that yesterday should be fair; and behold! the sun came back to us, and brought one of the most perfect days that ever was made, since Adam was driven out of Paradise. By the bye, was there ever any rain in Paradise? If so, how comfortless must Eve's bower have been! – and what a wretched and rheumatic time must they have had on their bed of wet roses! It makes me shiver to think of it. Well; it seemed as if the world was newly created, yesterday morning; and I beheld its birth; for I had risen before the sun was over the hill, and had gone forth to fish. How instantaneously did all dreariness and heaviness of the earth's spirit flit away, before one smile of the beneficent sun. This proves that all gloom is but a dream and a shadow, and that cheerfulness is the real truth. It requires many clouds, long brooding over us, to make us sad; but one gleam of sunshine always suffices to cheer up the landscape. The banks of the river actually laughed, when the sunshine fell upon them; and the river itself was alive and cheerful; and, by way of fun and amusement, it had swept away many wreaths of meadow hay, and old rotten branches of trees, and all such trumpery. These matters came floating downward, whirling round and round in the eddies, or hastening onward in the main current; and many of them, before this time, have probably been carried into the Merrimack, and will be borne onward to the sea. The spots where I stood to fish, on my preceding excursion, were now under water; and the tops of many of the bushes, along the river's margin, barely emerged from the stream. Large spaces of meadow are overflowed.

There was a north-west wind throughout the day; and as many clouds, the remnants of departed gloom, were scattered about the sky, the breeze was continually blowing them across the sun. For the most part, they were gone again in a moment; but sometimes the shadow remained long enough to make me dread a relapse of sulky weather. Then would come the burst of bright sunshine, making me feel as if a rainy day were henceforth an impossibility. But let my wife describe the day; — she should be able to do it well; for she made it, or, at least, must have had something to do with its manufacture, since she prophesied it so truly.

In the afternoon, Mr. Emerson called, bringing Mr. Frost, the colleague and successor of Dr. Ripley. He is a good sort of humdrum parson enough, and well fitted to increase the stock of manuscript sermons, of which there must be a fearful quantity already in the world. I find that my respect for clerical people, as such, and my faith in the utility of their office, decreases daily. We certainly do need a new revelation — a new system — for there seems to be no life in the old one. Mr. Frost, however, is probably one of the best and most useful of his class; because no suspicion of the necessity of his profession, constituted as it now is, to mankind, and of his own usefulness and success in it, has hitherto disturbed him; and therefore he labors with faith and confidence, as ministers did a hundred years ago, when they had really something to do in the world. I do not remember any points of interest in our conversation. After the visitors were gone, I sat at the gallery window, looking

1a

eddies, or hastening onward in the main current; and many of them, before this time, have probably been carried into the Merrimack, and will be borne onward to the sea. The spots where I stood to fish, on my preceding excursion, were now under water, and the tops of many of the bushes, along the river's margin, barely emerged from the stream. Large spaces of meadow are overflowed.

There was a north-west wind throughout the day; and as many clouds, the remnants of ~~of~~ departed gloom, were scattered about the sky, the breeze was continually blowing these across the sun. For the most part, they were gone again in a moment; but sometimes the shadow remained long enough to make me dread a return of sulky weather. Then would come the burst of bright sunshine, making me feel as if a rainy day were henceforth an impossibility. But let my wife describe the day; – she should be able to do it well; for she made it, or, at least, must have had something to do with its manufacture, since she prophesied it so truly.

In the afternoon, Mr. Emerson called, bringing Mr. Frost, the colleague and successor of Dr. Ripley. He is a good sort of hum-drum parson enough, and well fitted to increase the stock of manuscript sermons, of which there must be a fearful quantity already in the world. I find that my respect for clerical people, as such, and my faith in the utility of their office, decreases daily. We certainly do need a new revelation – a new system – for there seems to be no life in the old one. Mr. Frost, however, is probably one of the best and most useful of his class; because no suspicion of the necessity of his profession, constituted as it now is, to mankind, and of his own usefulness and success in it, has hitherto disturbed him; and therefore he labors with faith and confidence, as ministers did a hundred years ago, when they had really something to do in the world. I do not remember any points of interest in our conversation. After the visitors were gone, I sat at the gallery window, looking down the avenue; and soon there appeared an elderly woman—a homely, decent old matron enough, dressed in a dark gown, and with what seemed a manuscript book under her arm. The wind sported with her gown, and blew her veil across her face, and seemed to make game of her; though, on a nearer view, she looked like a sad old creature, with a pale, thin countenance, and somewhat of a wild and wandering expression. She had a singular gait, reeling, as it were—and yet not quite reeling—from one side of the path to the other; going onward as if it were not much matter whether she went straight or crooked. Such were my observations as she approached through the scattered sunshine and shade of our long avenue, until, reaching the door, she gave a knock, and inquired for the lady of the house. That dear little personage being asleep, my sister Louisa went to inquire her business, and brought me her manuscript volume. It contained a certificate, stating that the old woman was a widow from a foreign land, who had recently lost her son, and was now utterly destitute of friends and kindred, and without means of support. Appended to the certificate, there was a list of names of people who had bestowed charity on her, with the amounts of their several donations—none, as I recollect, higher than twenty-five cents. Here is a strange life, and a character fit for romance and poetry. All the early part of her life, I suppose, and much of her widowhood, were spent in the quiet of a home, with kinsfolks about her, and children, and the life-long gossiping acquaintances that women always create around them. But in her decline, she has wandered away from all these, and from her native country itself, and is a vagrant, yet with something of the homeliness and decency of aspect belonging to one that has been a wife and mother, and has had a roof of her own above her head—yet with all this, a wildness proper to her present life. I have a liking for vagrants of all sort, and never, that I know of, refused my mite to a wandering beggar, when I had anything in my own pocket. There is so much want and wretchedness

down the avenue; and soon there appeared an elderly woman – a homely, decent old matron enough, dressed in a dark gown, and with what seemed a manuscript book under her arm. The wind sported with her gown, and blew her veil across her face, and seemed to make game of her; though, on a nearer view, she looked like a sad old creature, with a pale, thin countenance, and somewhat of a wild and wandering expression. She had a singular gait, reeling, as it were – and yet not quite reeling – from one side of the path to the other; going onward as if it were not much matter whether she went straight or crooked. Such were my observations as she approached through the scattered sunshine and shade of our long avenue, until, reaching the door, she gave a knock, and inquired for the lady of the house. That dear little personage being asleep, my sister Louisa went to inquire her business, and brought me her manuscript volume. It contained a certificate, stating ↑that↓ the old woman was a widow from a foreign land, who had recently lost her son, and was now utterly destitute of friends and kindred, and without means of support. Appended to the certificate, there was a list of names of people who had bestowed charity on her, with the amounts of their several donations – none, as I recollect, higher than twenty-five cents. Here is a strange life, and a character fit for romance and poetry. All the early part of her life, I suppose, and much of her widowhood, were spent in the quiet of a home, with kinsfolks about her, and children, and the life-long gossiping acquaintances that women always create around them. But in her decline, she has wandered away from all these, and from her native country itself; and is a vagrant, yet with something of the homeliness and decency of aspect, belonging to one that has been a wife and mother, and has had a roof of her own above her head – yet with all this, a wildness proper to her present life. I have a liking for vagrants of all sorts, and never, that I know of, refused my mite to a wandering beggar, when I had anything in my own pocket. There is so much want and wretchedness in the world,—but we may safely take the word of any mortal, when they say that they need our assistance; and even should we be deceived, still the good to ourselves, resulting from a kind act, is worth more than the trifle by which we purchase it. It is desirable, I think, that such persons should be permitted to roam through our land of plenty, scattering the seeds of tenderness and charity—as birds of passage bear the seeds of precious plants from land to land, without even dreaming of the office which they perform.

Sept 1st Thursday. Mr. Thorow dined with us yesterday. He is a singular character—a young man with much of wild original nature still remaining in him; and so far as he is sophisticated, it is in a way and method of his own. He is as ugly as sin, long-nosed, queer-mouthed, and with uncouth and somewhat rustic, although courteous manners, corresponding very well with such an exterior. But his ugliness is of an honest and agreeable fashion, and becomes him much better than beauty. He was educated, I believe, at Cambridge, and formerly kept school in this town; but for two or three years back, he has repudiated all regular modes of getting a living, and seems inclined to lead a sort of Indian life among civilized men—an Indian life, I mean, as respects the absence of any systematic effort for a livelihood. He has been for some time an inmate of Mr. Emerson's family; and, in requital, he labors in the garden, and performs such other offices as may suit him—being entertained by Mr. Emerson for the sake of what true manhood there is in him. Mr. Thorow is a keen and delicate observer of nature—a genuine observer, which, I suspect, is almost as rare a character as even an original poet; and Nature, in return for his love, seems to adopt him as her especial child, and shows him secrets which few others are allowed to witness. He is familiar with beast, fish, fowl, and reptile, and has strange stories to tell of adventures and friendly passages with these lower brethren of mortality. Herb and flower, likewise, wherever they grow, whether in garden or wild wood, are his familiar friends. He is also

in the world, that we may safely take the word of any mortal, when they say that they need our assistance; and even should we be deceived, still the good to ourselves, resulting from a kind act, is worth more than the trifle by which we purchase it. It is desirable, I think, that such persons should be permitted to roam through our land of plenty, scattering the seeds of tenderness and charity – as birds of passage bear the seeds of precious plants from land to land, without ever dreaming of the office which they perform.

September 1st. Thursday. Mr. Thorow dined with us yesterday. He is a singular character – a young man with much of wild original nature still remaining in him; and so far as he is sophisticated, it is in a way and method of his own. He is as ugly as sin, long-nosed, queer-mouthed, and with uncouth and somewhat rustic, although courteous manners, corresponding very well with such an exterior. But his ugliness is of an honest and agreeable fashion, and becomes him much better than beauty. He was educated, I believe, at Cambridge, and formerly kept school in this town; but for two or three years back, he has repudiated all regular modes of getting a living, and seems inclined to lead a sort of Indian life among civilized men – an Indian life, I mean, as respects the absence of any systematic effort for a livelihood. He has been for sometime an inmate of Mr. Emerson's family; and, in requital, he labors in the garden, and performs such other offices as may suit him – being entertained by Mr. Emerson for the sake of what true manhood there is in him. Mr. Thorow is a keen and delicate observer of nature – a genuine observer, which, I suspect, is almost as rare a character as even an original poet; and Nature, in return for his love, seems to adopt him as her especial child, and shows him secrets which few others are allowed to witness. He is familiar with beast, fish, fowl, and reptile, and has strange stories to tell of adventures, and friendly passages with these lower brethren of mortality. Herb and flower, likewise, wherever they grow, whether in garden or wild wood, are his familiar friends. He is also on intimate terms with the clouds, and can tell the portents of storms. It is a characteristic trait, that he has a great regard for the memory of the Indian tribes, whose wild life would have suited him so well; and strange to say, he seldom walks over a ploughed field without picking up an arrow-point, a spear-head, or other relic of the red men—as if their spirits willed him to be the inheritor of their simple wealth.

With all this he has more than a tincture of literature—a deep and true taste for poetry, especially the elder poets, although more exclusive than is desirable, like all other Transcendentalists, so far as I am acquainted with them. He is a good writer—at least, he has written one good article, a rambling disquisition on Natural History in the last Dial,—which, he says, was chiefly made up from journals of his own observations. Methinks this article paints a very fair image of his mind and character—so true, minute, and literal in observation, yet giving the spirit as well as letter of what he sees, even as a lake reflects its wooded banks, showing every leaf, yet giving the wild beauty of the whole scene;—then there are passages in the article of cloudy and dreamy metaphysics, partly affected, and partly the natural exhalations of his intellect;—and also passages where his thoughts seem to measure and attune themselves into spontaneous verse, as they rightfully may, since there is real poetry in him. There is a basis of good sense and moral truth, too, throughout the article, which also is a reflection of his character; for he is not unwise to think and feel, however imperfect in his own mode of action. On the whole, I find him a healthy and wholesome man to know.

After dinner (at which we cut the first water-melon and musk melon that our garden has ripened) Mr. Thorow and I walked up the bank of the river; and, at a certain point, he shouted for his boat. Forthwith, a young man paddled it across the river, and Mr. Thorow and I voyaged further up the stream, which soon became more beautiful than any picture, with its dark and quiet sheet of water, half shaded, half sunny, between high and wooded banks. The late

on intimate terms with the clouds, and can tell the portents of storms. It is a characteristic trait, that he has a great regard for the memory of the Indian tribes, whose wild life would have suited him so well; and strange to say, he seldom walks over a ploughed field without picking up an arrow-point, a spear-head, or other relic of the red men – as if their spirits willed him to be the inheritor of their simple wealth.

With all this he has more than a tincture of literature – a deep and true taste for poetry, especially the elder poets, although more exclusive than is desirable, like all other Transcendentalists, so far as I am acquainted with them. He is a good writer – at least, he has written one good article, a rambling disquisition on Natural History in the last Dial, – which, he says, was chiefly made up from journals of his own observations. Methinks this article gives a very fair image of his mind and character – so true, minute, and literal in observation, yet giving the spirit as well as letter of what he sees, even as a lake reflects its wooded banks, showing every leaf, yet giving the wild beauty of the whole scene; – then there are passages in the article of cloudy and dreamy metaphysics, partly affected, and partly the natural exhalations of his intellect; – and also passages where his thoughts seem to measure and attune themselves into spontaneous verse, as they rightfully may, since there is real poetry in him. There is a basis of good sense and moral truth, too, throughout the article, which also is a reflection of his character; for he is not unwise to think and feel, however imperfect in his own mode of action. On the whole, I find him a healthy and wholesome man to know.

After dinner (at which we cut the first water-melon and musk melon that our garden has ripened) Mr. Thorow and I walked up the bank of the river; and, at a certain point, he shouted for his boat. Forthwith, a young man paddled it across the river, and Mr. Thorow and I voyaged further up the stream, which soon became more beautiful than any picture, with its dark and quiet sheet of water, half shaded, half sunny, between high and wooded banks. The late rains have swollen the stream so much, that many trees are standing up to their knees, as it were, in the water; and boughs, which lately swung high in air, now dip and drink deep of the passing wave. As to the poor cardinals, which glowed upon the bank, a few days since, I could see only a few of their scarlet caps, peeping above the water. Mr. Thoreau managed the boat so perfectly, either with two paddles or with one, that it seemed instinct with his own will, and to require no physical effort to guide it. He said that, when some Indians visited Concord a few years since, he found that he had acquired, without a teacher, their precise method of propelling and steering a canoe. Nevertheless, being in want of money, the poor fellow was desirous of selling the boat, of which he is so fit a pilot, and which was built by his own hands; so I agreed to give him his price (only seven dollars) and accordingly became possessor of the Musketaquid. I wish I could acquire the aquatic skill of its original owner at as a reasonable a rate.

Sept 2d Friday. Yesterday afternoon, while my wife, and Louisa and I were gathering the windfallen apples in our orchard, Mr. Thoreau arrived with the boat. The adjacent meadow being overflowed by the rise of the stream, he had rowed directly to the foot of the orchard, and landed at the bars, after floating over forty or fifty yards of water, where people were making hay, a week or two since. I entered the boat with him, in order to have the benefit of a lesson in rowing and paddling. My little wife, who was looking on, cannot feel very proud of her husband's proficiency. I managed, indeed, to propel the boat by rowing with two oars; but the use of the single paddle is quite beyond my present skill. Mr. Thoreau had assured me that it was only necessary to will the boat to go in any particular direction, and she would immediately take that course, as if imbued with the spirit of the steersman. It may be so with him, but certainly not with me; the boat seemed to be bewitched, and turned its head to every point of the compass except the right one. He

rains have swollen the stream so much, that many trees are standing up to their knees, as it were, in the water; and boughs, which lately swung high in air, now dip and drink deep of the passing wave. As to the poor cardinals, which glowed upon the bank, a few days since, I could see only a few of their scarlet caps, peeping above the water. Mr. Thorow managed the boat so perfectly, either with two paddles or with one, that it seemed instinct with his own will, and to require no physical effort to guide it. He said that, when some Indians visited Concord a few years since, he found that he had acquired, without a teacher, their precise method of propelling and steering a canoe. Nevertheless, being in want of money, the poor fellow was desirous of selling the boat, of which he is so fit a pilot, and which was built by his own hands; so I agreed to give him his price (only seven dollars) and accordingly became possessor of the Musketaquid. I wish I could acquire the aquatic skill of its original owner at as a reasonable a rate.

September 2d Friday. Yesterday afternoon, while my wife, and Louisa, and I, were gathering the windfallen apples in our orchard, Mr. Thorow arrived with the boat. The adjacent meadow being overflowed by the rise of the stream, he had rowed directly to the foot of the orchard, and landed at the bars, after floating over forty or fifty yards of water, where people were making hay, a week or two since. I entered the boat with him, in order to have the benefit of a lesson in rowing and paddling. My little wife, who was looking on, cannot feel very proud of her husband's proficiency. I managed, indeed, to propel the boat by rowing with two oars; but the use of the single paddle is quite beyond my present skill. Mr. Thorow had assured me that it was only necessary to will the boat to go in any particular direction, and she would immediately take that course, as if imbued with the spirit of the steersman. It may be so with him, but certainly not with me; the boat seemed to be bewitched, and turned its head to every point of the compass except the right one. He then took the paddle himself, and though I could observe nothing peculiar in his management of it, the Musketaquid immediately became as docile as a trained steed. I suspect that she has not yet transferred her affections from her old master to her new one. By and bye, when we are better acquainted, she will grow more tractable; especially after the ~~[illegible]~~ has had the honor of bearing my little wife, who is loved by all things, living or inanimate. We propose to change her name from Musketaquid (the Indian name of Concord river, meaning the river of meadows) to the Pond Lily—which will be very beautiful and appropriate, as, during the summer season, she will bring home many a cargo of pond lilies from along the river's weedy shore. It is not very likely that I shall make such long voyages in her as Mr. Thoreau has. He once followed our river down to the Merrimack, and thence, I believe, to Newburyport—a voyage of about eighty miles, in this little vessel.

In the evening, Ellery Channing called to see us, wishing to talk with me about the Boston Miscellany, of which he had heard that I was to be editor, and to which he desired to contribute. He is one of those queer and clever young men whom Mr. Emerson (that everlasting rejecter of all that is, and seeker for he knows not what) is continually picking up by way of a genius. There is nothing very peculiar about him—some originality and self-inspiration in his character, but none, or very little, in his intellect. Nevertheless, the lad himself seems to feel as if he were a genius; and, ridiculously enough, looks upon his own verses as too sacred to be sold for money. Prose he will sell to the highest bidder; but measured feet and jingling lines are not to be exchanged for gold—which, indeed, is not very likely to be offered for them. I like him well enough, however; but after all, these originals in a small way, after one has seen a few of them, become more dull and common-place than even those who keep the ordinary pathway of life. They have a rule and a routine, which they follow with as little variety as other people do their rule and routine; and when once we have fathomed their mystery, nothing can be more

then took the paddle himself, and though I could observe nothing peculiar in his management of it, the Musketaquid immediately became as docile as a trained steed. I suspect that she has not yet transferred her affections from her old master to her new one. By and bye, when we are better acquainted, she will grow more tractable; especially after she shall have had the honor of bearing my little wife, who is loved by all things, living or inanimate. We propose to change her name from Musketaquid (the Indian name of Concord river, meaning the river of meadows) to the Pond Lily – which will be very beautiful and appropriate, as, during the summer season, she will bring home many a cargo of pond lilies from along the river's weedy shore. It is not very likely that I shall make such long voyages in her as Mr. Thorow has. He once followed our river down to the Merrimack, and thence, I believe, to Newburyport – a voyage of about eighty miles, in this little vessel.

In the evening, Ellery Channing called to see us, wishing to talk with me about the Boston Miscellany, of which he had heard that I was to be Editor, and to which he desired to contribute. He is one of those queer and clever young men whom Mr. Emerson (that everlasting rejecter of all that is, and seeker for x he knows not what) is continually picking up by way of a genius. There is nothing very peculiar about him – some originality and self-inspiration in his character, but none, or very little, in his intellect. Nevertheless, the lad himself seems to feel as if he were a genius; and, ridiculously enough, looks upon his own x verses as too sacred to be sold for money. Prose he will sell to the highest bidder; but measured feet and jingling lines are not to be exchanged for gold – which, indeed, is not very likely to be offered for them. x I like him well enough, however; but after all, these originals in a small way, after one has seen a few of them, become more dull and common-place than even those who keep the ordinary pathway of life. They have a rule and a routine, which they follow with as little variety as other people do their rule and routine; and when once we have fathomed their mystery, nothing can be more

24

wearisome. An innate perception and reflection of truth gives the only sort of originality that does not finally grow intolerable.

Septr 4th. Sunday. I made a voyage in the Pond Lily all by myself, yesterday morning, and was much encouraged by my success in causing the boat to go whither I would. I have always liked to be afloat, but I think I have never adequately conceived of the enjoyment till now, when I begin to feel a power over that which supports me. I suppose I must have felt something like this sense of triumph, long years ago, when I first learned to swim; but I have forgotten it. Oh that I could run wild!— that is, that I could put myself into a true relation with nature, and be on friendly terms with all congenial elements.

We had a thunder-storm last evening; and to-day has been a cool, breezy, north-west, autumnal day, such as my soul and body love. My wife went to church in the forenoon— but not so her husband. He loves the Sabbath, however, though he has no set way of observing of it; but it seldom comes and goes without — but here are some visitors; so this disquisition must rest among the things that never will be written. They are Miss Fuller and Mr. Sam Ward, I believe.

Thursday Septr 8th. My dearest husband has gone to sail on the river, & it is quite early. The sun has not risen above our opposite hill & I think I will record a little of my beautiful life, my happiest, most enchanting life. (Little Kit sits on the opposite page of this book, purring very contentedly— & now & then putting her paw very gently on my pen.) Those visitors who interrupted my dear husband in the above sentence, (O that they had come later) were Margaret & Mr Sam Ward. We had an exceedingly pleasant visit from them. Mr Ward was greatly delighted with the house & its environs. He seemed to think Boston could not afford so charming a drawing room as our quaint old parlor

wearisome. An innate perception and reflection of truth gives the only sort of originality that does not finally grow intolerable.

Septr 4th. Sunday. I made a voyage in the Pond Lily all by myself, yesterday morning, and was much encouraged by my success in causing the boat to go whither I would. I have always liked to be afloat; but I think I have never adequately conceived of the enjoyment till now, when I begin to feel a power over that which supports me. I suppose I must have felt something like this sense of triumph, long years ago, when I first learned to swim; but I have forgotten it. Oh that I could run wild! – that is, that I could put myself into a true relation with nature, and be on friendly terms with all congenial elements.

We had a thunder-storm, last evening; and to-day has been a cool, breezy, north-west, autumnal day, such as my soul and body love. My wife went to church in the forenoon; – but not so her husband. He loves the Sabbath, however, though he has no set way of observing of it; but it seldom comes and goes without – but here are some visitors; so this disquisition must rest among the things that never will be written. They are Miss Fuller and Mr. Sam Ward, I believe.

Thursday Septr 8th. My dearest husband has gone to sail on the river, & it is quite early. The sun has not risen above our opposite hill & I think I will record a little of my beautiful life, my happiest, most enchanting life. (Little Kit sits on the opposite page of this book, purring very contentedly – & now & then putting her paw very gently on my pen) Those visitors who interrupted my dear husband in the above sentence, (O that they had come later) were Margaret & Mr Sam Ward. We had an exceedingly pleasant visit from them. Mr Ward was greatly delighted with the house & its environs He seemed to think Boston could not afford so charming a drawing room as our quaint old parlor

& that it could not be persuaded to imitate it in
its present degenerate taste. We went down the
orchard to the river's banks, & my husband & Mr W.
laid down upon the grass while Margaret & I
sat on rocks. Margaret was very brilliant & while
she talked to my husband, Mr Ward addressed
himself to me, whom he apparently thought a
kind of enchanted mortal, in an earthly Elysium
He wanted to know what we did, & I told him
we did nothing to describe, yet very much in
reality- that we did not intend to accomplish
any thing that could be told of, these lovely
summer days. He said he was idle two months
after his marriage, but had not had ten days of
leisure since, & he seemed to think we must
begin to work now, as our two months had passed
He said the honey moon never would end, which I
could have assured him of. Margaret at last
invited me to take him into the house, & shew
him the outlined furniture, while she remained
with my dearest husband. He was delighted with
our gallery, & thought the furniture beautiful,
& also the view from the windows of our
chamber. In short he was entirely pleased & I
imagine he thought my husband was a kingly
man, far surpassing all he had anticipated,
for who can prefigure him? I cannot even,
from day to day. Tuesday the day dawned
lustrously without a cloud. Our sister Louisa
went away in the stage at 1/2 past six. I like
Louisa very much, she is so sincere & true &
disinterested, & I am glad she has been to
see us, because I wanted her to know that her
worshipped brother is not very miserable with me,
& that he lives in a sweet retirement. I shall not
blame her if she thinks his wife by no means worthy

& that it could not be persuaded to imitate it in its present degenerate taste. We went down the orchard to the river's banks, & my husband & Mr W. laid down upon the grass while Margaret & I sat on rocks. Margaret was very brilliant & while she talked to my husband, Mr Ward addressed himself to me, whom he apparently thought a kind of enchanted mortal, in an earthly Elysium He wanted to know what we did, & I told him we did nothing to describe, yet very much in reality – that we did not intend to accomplish any thing that could be told of, these lovely summer days. He said he was idle two months after his marriage, but had not had ten days of leisure since, & he seemed to think we must begin to work now, as our two months had passed He said the honeymoon never would end, which I could have assured him of – Margaret at last invited me to take him into the house, & shew him the outhired furniture, while she remained with my dearest husband. He was delighted with our gallery, & thought the furniture beautiful, & also the views from the windows of our chamber. In short he was entirely pleased & I imagine he thought my husband was a kingly man far surpassing all he had anticipated, for who can prefigure him? I cannot even, from day to day. Tuesday the day dawned lustrously without a cloud. Our sister Louisa went away in the stage at ½ past six. I like Louisa very much, she is so sincere & true & disinterested, & I am glad she has been to see us, because I wanted her to know that her worshipped brother is not very miserable with me, & that he lives in a sweet retirement. I shall not blame her if she thinks his wife by no means worthy

dim smile through a tear-cloud. The earth, however looked fresh & green & autumn had hung out one or two gorgeous banners as a token. We soon descended the hill & then outshone the unaccommodating sun, illuminating the fields & river & woods with a gold light beneath a stern blue sky. The river was perfectly still & soft, taking all the trees & that heavens captive in its depths, where we decided that they were more real than those we could look & see above; at least as real — why not?
All men seemed asleep, except in a neighbouring farm-yard, but at a ~~great~~ distance, we discerned good Mr. Jack Pratt with two shining tin-pails, about to milk his cows. ~~[illegible]~~ We left the river & wended through a short lane, in which grew the blue gentian with closed bells or soapwort, & my dearest love gathered all there was. It is very beautiful to see him plucking flowers with so much interest. It adds such a grace to his kingliness.

Sept 18th. Sunday. How the summer time flits away — even while it seems to be loitering onward, arm in arm with autumn! Of late, I have walked but little over the hills and through the woods — my leisure being chiefly occupied with my boat, which I have now learned to manage with tolerable skill. Yesterday afternoon (my dearest wife having gone to Mr. Emerson's with her mother) I made a voyage alone up the North Branch of Concord River. There was a strong north-west wind blowing dead against me, which, together with the current, increased by the height of the water, made the first part of the passage pretty toilsome. The black river was all dimpled over with little eddies and whirl-pools; and

dim smile through a drear cloud. The earth, however looked fresh & green & autumn had hung out one or two gorgeous banners as a token. We soon descended the hill & then outshone the unaccommodating sun, illum -inating the fields & river & woods with a gold light beneath a stern, blue sky. The river was perfectly still & soft, taking all the trees & the heavens captive in its depths, where we decided that they were more real than those we could touch & see above; at least as real – why not? All men seemed asleep, except in a neighboring farmyard, but at a ~~good~~ distance, we discerned good Mr Jack Flint with two shining tin-pails, about to milk his cows. ~~in his barn yard~~. We left the river & wended through a short lane, in which grow the blue gentian with closed bells – or soapwort, & my dearest love gathered all there was. It is very beautiful to see him plucking flowers with so much interest. It adds such a grace to his kingliness.

Septr 18th. – Sunday. How the summer-time flits away – even while it seems to be loitering onward, arm in arm with autumn! Of late, I have walked but little over the hills and through the woods, – my leisure being chiefly occupied with my boat, which I have now learned to manage with tolerable skill. Yesterday afternoon (my dearest wife having gone to Mr. Emerson's with her mother) I made a voyage alone up the North Branch of Concord river. There was a strong north-west wind blowing dead against me, which, together with the current, increased by the height of the water, made the first part of the passage pretty toilsome. The black river was all dimpled over with little eddies and whirl-pools; and the breeze, moreover, caused the billows to beat against the bow of the boat, with a sound like the flapping of a birds' wing. The water-weeds, where they were discernible through the tawny water, were straight outstretched by the force of the current, looking as if they were forced to hold on to their roots with all their might. If, for a moment, I desisted from paddling, the head of the boat was swept round by the combined might of wind and tide. However, I toiled onward stoutly, and, entering the North Branch, soon found myself floating quietly along a tranquil stream, sheltered from the breeze by the woods and a lofty hill. The current, likewise, lingered along so gently, that it was merely a pleasure to propel the boat against it. I never could have conceived that there was so beautiful a river-scene in Concord, as this of the North Branch. The stream ~~stream~~ flows through the midmost privacy and deepest heart of a wood, which, as if but half satisfied with its intrusion, calm, gentle, and unobtrusive as it is, seems to crowd upon it, and barely to allow it passage; for the trees are rooted on the very verge of the water, and dip their pendent branches into it. On ~~on~~ one side, there is a high bank, forming the side of a hill, the Indian name of which I have forgotten, though Mr. Thoreau told it to me; and here, in some instances, the trees seem ready to precipitate themselves down, and stand leaning over the river, stretching out their arms, as if about to plunge headlong in. On the other side, the bank is almost on a level with the water; and here the quiet congregation of trees stand with their feet in the flood, and fringed with foliage down to its very surface. Vines here and there twine themselves about birches, or aspens, or alder trees, and hang their clusters, (though scanty and infrequent, this season) over the water, so that I can reach them from my boat. I scarcely remember a scene of more complete and lovely seclusion than the passage of the river through this wood; even an Indian canoe, in olden times, could ^not^ have floated onward in more com-

the breeze, moreover, caused the billows to beat against the bow of the boat, with a sound like the flapping of a bird's wing. The water-weeds, where they were discernible through the tawny water, were straight outstretched by the force of the current, looking as if they were forced to hold on to their roots with all their might. If, for a moment, I desisted from paddling, the head of the boat was swept round by the combined might of wind and tide. However, I toiled onward stoutly, and, entering the North Branch, soon found myself floating quietly along a tranquil stream, sheltered from the breeze by the woods and a lofty hill. The current, likewise, lingered along so gently, that it was merely a pleasure to propel the boat against it. I never could have conceived that there was so beautiful a river-scene in Concord, as this of the North Branch. The stream ~~stream~~ flows through the midmost privacy and deepest heart of a wood, which, as if but half satisfied with its intrusion, calm, gentle, and unobtrusive as it is, seems to crowd upon it, and barely to allow it passage; for the trees are rooted on the very verge of the water, and dip their pendent branches into it. On ~~on~~ one side, there is a high bank, forming the side of a hill, the Indian name of which I have forgotten, though Mr. Thorow told it to me; and here, in some instances, the trees seem ready to precipitate themselves down, and stand leaning over the river, stretching out their arms, as if about to plunge headlong in. On the other side, the bank is almost on a level with the water; and here the quiet congregation of trees stand with their feet in the flood, and fringed with foliage down to its very surface. Vines here and there twine themselves about birches, or aspens, or elder-trees, and hang their clusters, (though scanty and infrequent, this season) over the water, so that I can reach them from my boat. I scarcely remember a scene of more complete and lovely seclusion than the passage of the river through this wood; even an Indian canoe, in olden times, could ↑not↓ have floated onward in more com-

26

plete solitude than mine did. I have never elsewhere had such an opportunity to observe how much more beautiful reflection is than what we call reality. The sky, and the clustering foliage on either hand, and the effect of sunlight as it found its way through the shade, giving lightsome hues in contrast with the quiet depth of the prevailing tints — all these seemed unsurpassably beautiful, when beheld in upper air. But, on gazing downward, there they were, the same even to the minutest particular, yet arrayed in ideal beauty, which satisfied the spirit incomparably more than the actual scene. I am half convinced that the reflection is indeed the reality — the real thing which Nature imperfectly images to our grosser sense. At all events, the disembodied shadow is nearest to the soul.

There were many tokens of autumn in this beautiful scene. Two or three of the trees were actually arrayed in their coats of many colors, the real scarlet and gold which they wear before they put on mourning. These stood on low, marshy spots, where a frost has probably touched them already. Others were of a light, fresh green, resembling the hues of Spring, though this, likewise, is a token of decay. The great mass of the foliage, however, appears unchanged; but ever and anon, down came a yellow leaf, half flitting upon the air, half falling through it, and finally settling upon the water. A multitude of these were floating here and there along the river, many of them curling upward, so as to form little boats, fit for fairies to voyage in. They looked strangely pretty, and yet a melancholy prettiness, as they floated down the stream. The general aspect of the river, however, differed but little from what it is in summer; at least, the difference defies expression; — it is more in the character of the rich yellow sunlight, than in aught else. The water of the stream has now a chill of autumnal coolness; yet, whenever a broad gleam fell across it, through an interstice

plete solitude than mine did. I have never elsewhere had such an opportunity to observe how much more beautiful reflection is than what we call reality. The sky, and the clustering foliage on either hand, and the effect of sunlight as it found its way through the shade, giving lightsome hues in contrast with the quiet depth of the prevailing tints – all these seemed unsurpassably beautiful, when beheld in upper air. But, on gazing downward, there they were, the same even to the minutest particular, yet arrayed in ideal beauty, which satisfied the spirit incomparably more than the actual scene. I am half convinced that the reflection is indeed the reality – the real thing which Nature imperfectly images to our grosser sense. At all events, the disembodied shadow is nearest to the soul.

There were many tokens of autumn in this beautiful scene. Two or three of the trees were actually arrayed in their coats of many colors, the real scarlet and gold which they wear before they put on mourning. These stood on low, marshy spots, where a frost has probably touched them already. Others were of a light, fresh green, resembling the hues of spring, though this, likewise, is a token of decay. The great mass of the foliage, however, appears unchanged; but ever and anon, down came a yellow leaf, half flitting upon the air, half falling through it, and finally settled upon the water. A multitude of these were floating here and there along the river, many of them curling upward, so as to form little boats, fit for fairies to voyage in. They looked strangely pretty, and yet a melancholy prettiness, as they floated down the stream. The general aspect of the river, however, differed but little from what it is in summer; at least, the difference defies expression; – it is more in the character of the rich yellow sunlight, than in aught else. The water of the stream has now a thrill of autumnal coolness; yet, wherever a broad gleam fell across it, through an interstice of the foliage, multitudes of insects were darting to and fro upon its surface. The sunshine, thus falling across the dark river, has a most beautiful effect; it brightens it, as it were, and yet leaves it as dark as ever.

On my return, I suffered the boat to float almost of its own will down the stream, and caught fish enough for this morning's breakfast. But, partly from a qualm of conscience, and partly, I believe, because I eschewed the trouble of cleaning them, I finally put them all into the water again, and saw them swim away as if nothing had happened.

October 10th. Monday. A long while, indeed, since my last date. But the weather has generally been sunny and pleasant, though often very cold; and I cannot endure to waste anything so precious as autumnal sunshine by staying in the house. So I have spent almost all the daylight hours in the open air. My chief amusement has been boating up and down the river. A week or two ago (September 27th and 28th) I went on a pedestrian excursion with Mr. Emerson, and was gone two days and one night — it being the first and only night that I slept away from my belovedest wife. We spent the night at the village of Harvard, and the next morning walked three miles farther, to the Shaker village, where we breakfasted. Mr. Emerson held a theological discussion with two of the Shaker brethren; but the particulars of it have faded from my memory; and all the other adventures of the tour have now so lost their freshness that I cannot adequately recall them. Therefore let them rest untold. I recollect nothing so well as the aspect of some fringed gentians, which we saw growing by the roadside, and which were so beautiful that I longed to turn back, and bring them to my little wife. After our arduous journey, we arrived safe home in the afternoon of the second day — the first time that I ever came home in my life; for I never had a home before. On Saturday of the same week, my friend David Roberts came to see us, and stayed till Tuesday morning. My wife shall describe him. On Wed-

of the foliage, multitudes of insects were darting to-and-fro upon its surface. The sunshine, thus falling across the dark river, has a most beautiful effect; it burnishes it, as it were, and yet leaves it as dark as ever.

On my return, I suffered the boat to float almost at its own will down the stream, and caught fish enough for this morning's breakfast. But, partly from a qualm of conscience, and partly, I believe, because I eschewed the trouble of cleaning them, I finally put them all into the water again, and saw them swim away as if nothing had happened.

October 10th. Monday. A long while, indeed, since my last date. But the weather has generally been sunny and pleasant; though often very cold; and I cannot endure to waste anything so precious as autumnal sunshine by staying in the house. So I have spent almost all the daylight hours in the open air. My chief amusement has been boating up and down the river. A week or two ago (September 27th and 28th) I went on a pedestrian excursion with Mr. Emerson, and was gone two days and one night – it being the first and only night that I slept away from my belovedest wife. We spent the night at the village of Harvard, and the next morning walked three miles further, to the Shaker village, where we breakfasted. Mr. Emerson held a theological discussion with two of the Shaker brethren; but the particulars of it have faded from my memory; and all the other adventures of the tour have now so lost their freshness that I cannot adequately recall them. Wherefore let them rest untold. I recollect nothing so well as the aspect of some fringed gentians, which we saw growing by the roadside, and which were so beautiful that I longed to turn back, and bring them to my little wife. After our arduous journey, we arrived safe home in the afternoon of the second day – the first time that I ever came home in my life; for I never had a home before. On Saturday of the same week, my friend David Roberts came to see us, and staid till Tuesday morning. My wife shall describe him. On Wed-

27

unless there was a little stream in the village that I would make a description of, if it had possessed any picturesque points. The foregoing are the chief outward events of our life.

In the meantime, autumn has been advancing, and is said to be a month earlier than usual. We had frosts, sufficient to kill the beans and squash vines, more than a fortnight ago; but there has since been some of the most delicious Indian-summer weather that I ever experienced — mild, sweet, perfect days, in which the warm sunshine seemed to embrace the earth, and all earth's children, with love and tenderness. Generally, however, the bright days have been vexed with winds from the north-west, somewhat too keen and high for comfort. These winds have strewn our avenue with withered leaves, although the trees still retain a considerable density of foliage, which is now embrowned or otherwise variegated by autumn. Our apples, too, have been falling, falling, falling; and we have picked the fairest of them from the dewy grass, and put them in our store-room and elsewhere. On Thursday, [illegible] & Dick began to gather those which remained on the trees; and I suppose they will amount to nearly twenty barrels, or perhaps more. As usual, when I have anything to sell, apples are very low indeed, and will not fetch me more than a dollar a barrel. I have sold my share of the potatoe field for twenty dollars, and ten bushels for my own use. This may suffice for the economical history of our recent life.

12 o'clock A.M. Just now, I heard a sharp tapping at the window of my study, and looking up from my book (a volume of Rabelais), behold the head of a little bird, who seemed to demand admittance! He was probably attempting to get a fly, which was on the pane of glass against which he rapped; and on my first motion, the feathered visitor took wing. This incident had a curious effect on me; it impressed me as if the bird had been a spiritual visitant — so strange was it that this little wild thing should seem to ask our hospitality.

nesday there was a Cattle Show in the village, which I would make a description of, if it had possessed any picturesque points. The foregoing are the chief outward events of our life.

In the meantime, autumn has been advancing, and is said to be a month earlier than usual. We had frosts, sufficient to kill the bean and squash vines, more than a fortnight ago; but there has since been some of the most delicious Indian-summer weather that I ever experienced – mild, sweet, perfect days, in which the warm sunshine seemed to embrace the earth, and all earth's children, with love and tenderness. Generally, however, the bright days have been vexed with winds from the north-west, somewhat too keen and high for comfort. These winds have strewn our avenue with withered leaves, although the trees still retain a considerable density of foliage, which is now embrowned or otherwise variegated by autumn. Our apples, too, have been falling, falling, falling; and we have picked the fairest of them from the dewy grass, and put them in our store-room and elsewhere. On Thursday, John Flint began to gather those which remained on the trees; and I suppose they will amount to nearly twenty-barrels, or perhaps more. As usual, when I have anything to sell, apples are very low indeed, and will not fetch me more than a dollar a barrel. I have sold my share of the potatoe field for twenty-dollars, and ten bushels for my own use. This may suffice for the economical history of our recent life.

12 o clock. A.M. Just now, I heard a sharp tapping at the window of my study; and looking up from my book (a volume of Rabelais) beheld the head of a little bird, who seemed to demand admittance! He was probably attempting to get a fly, which was on the pane of glass against which he rapped; and on my first motion, the feathered visitor took wing. This incident had a curious effect on me; it impressed me as if the bird had been a spiritual visitant – so strange was it that this little wild thing should seem to ask our hospitality.

November 8th. Tuesday. I am sorry that our journal has fallen so into neglect; but unless my naughty little wife will take the matter in hand, I see no chance of amendment. All my scribbling propensities will be far more than gratified in writing nonsense for the press; so that any gratuitous labor of the pen becomes peculiarly distasteful. Since the last date, we have paid a visit of nine days to Boston and Salem, whence we returned a week ago yesterday. Thus we lost above a week of delicious autumnal weather, which should have been spent in the woods, or upon the river. Ever since our return, however, until to-day, there has been a succession of genuine Indian summer days, with gentle winds, or none at all, and a misty atmosphere, which idealizes all nature, and a mild, beneficent sunshine, inviting one to lie down in a nook and forget all earthly care. To-day, the sky is dark and lowering, and occasionally lets fall a few sullen tears. I suppose we must bid farewell to Indian summer, now, and expect no more love and tenderness from Mother Nature till next spring be well advanced. She has already made herself as unlovely, in outward aspect, as can well be. My wife and I took a walk to Sleepy Hollow yesterday, and beheld scarcely a green thing — except the everlasting verdure of the family of pines; which, indeed, are trees to thank God for, at this season. A range of young birches had retained a pretty liberal covering of yellow or tawny leaves, which became very cheerful in the sunshine. There were one or two oak-trees whose foliage still retained a deep, dusky red, which looked rich and warm; but most of the oaks had reached the last stage of autumnal decay — the dusky brown hue. Millions of their leaves strew the woods and rustle underneath the foot; but enough remain upon the trees to make a melancholy harping, when the wind sweeps through them. We found some fringed gentians in the meadow; most of them blighted and withered; but a few were quite perfect. The other day, since our return from Salem, I found a violet; yet it was so cold, that day, that I found

November 8th. Tuesday. I am sorry that our journal has fallen so into neglect; but unless my naughty little wife will take the matter in hand, I see no chance of amendment. All my scribbling propensities will be far more than gratified in writing nonsense for the press; so that any gratuitous labor of the pen becomes peculiarly distasteful. Since the last date, we have paid a visit of nine days to Boston and Salem, whence we returned a week ago yesterday. Thus we lost above a week of delicious autumnal weather, which should have been spent in the woods, or upon the river. Ever since our return, however, until to-day, there has been a succession of genuine Indian summer days, with gentle winds, or none at all, and a misty atmosphere, which idealizes all nature, and a mild, beneficent sunshine, inviting one to lie down in a nook and forget all earthly care. To-day, the sky is dark and lowering, and occasionally lets fall a few sullen tears. I suppose we must bid farewell to Indian summer, now, and expect no more love and tenderness from Mother Nature till next spring be well advanced. She has already made herself as unlovely, in outward aspect, as can well be. My wife and I took a walk to Sleepy Hollow yesterday, and beheld scarcely a green thing – except the everlasting verdure of the family of pines; which, indeed, are trees to thank God for, at this season. A range of young birches had retained a pretty liberal covering of yellow or tawny leaves, which became very cheerful in the sunshine. There were one or two oak-trees whose foliage still retained a deep, dusky red, which looked rich and warm; but most of the oaks had reached the last stage of autumnal decay – the dusky brown hue. Millions of their leaves strew the woods and rustle underneath the foot; but enough remain upon the trees to make a melancholy harping, when the wind sweeps through them. We found some fringed gentians in our meadow – most of them blighted and withered; but a few were quite perfect. The other day, since our return from Salem, I found a violet; yet it was so cold, that day, that I found

28

a large pool of water, under the shadow of some trees, which had remained frozen from morning till afternoon. The ice was so thick as not to be broken by some sticks and small stones, which I threw upon it. But ice, and snow too, will soon be no extraordinary matters with us.

During the last week, we have had three stoves put up, and henceforth no light of a cheerful fire will gladden us at eventide. Stoves are detestable in every respect, except that they keep us perfectly comfortable.

Nov. 24th. Thursday. This is Thanksgiving Day — a good old festival; and my wife and I have kept it with our hearts, and besides have made good cheer upon our turkey, and puddings, and pies, and custards, although none sat at our board but our two selves. There was a new and livelier sense, I think, that we have at last found a home, and that a new family has been gathered since the last Thanksgiving Day.

There have been many bright, cold days, latterly — so cold that it has required a pretty rapid pace to keep one warm in walking. Day before yesterday, I saw a party of boys skating on a pond of water that has overflowed a neighboring meadow. Running water has not yet frozen. Vegetation has quite come to a stand, except in a few sheltered spots. In a deep ditch, my wife and I found a tall plant of the freshest and healthiest green, which looked as if it must have grown within the last few weeks. We wander among the wood-paths, which are very pleasant in the sunshine of the afternoons — the trees looking rich and warm, such of them, I mean, as have retained their russet leaves; and where the leaves are strewn along the paths, or heaped plentifully in some hollow of the hills, the effect is not without a charm. To-day, the morning rose with rain, which has since changed to snow and sleet; and now the landscape is as dreary as can well be imagined — white, with the brown ops of the soil and withered grass every where peeping out. The swollen river, of a leaden hue, drags itself sluggishly along; and this may be termed the first winter's day.

a large pool of water, under the shadow of some trees, which had remained frozen from morning till afternoon. The ice was so thick as not to be broken by some sticks and small stones, which I threw upon it. But ice, and snow too, will soon be no extraordinary matters with us.

During the last week, we have had three stoves put up; and henceforth, no light of a cheerful fire will gladden us at even tide. Stoves are detestable in every respect, except that they keep us perfectly comfortable

<u>Nov[r] 24th. Thursday</u>. This is Thanksgiving Day – a good old festival; and my wife and I have kept ↑it↓ with our hearts, and besides have made good cheer upon our turkey, and pudding, and pies, and custards, although none sat at our board but our two selves. There was a new and livelier sense, I think, that we have at last found a home, and that a new family has been gathered since the last Thanksgiving Day.

There have been many bright, cold days, latterly – so cold that it has required a pretty rapid pace to keep one warm in walking. Day before yesterday, I saw a party of boys skating on a pond of water that has overflowned a neighboring meadow. Running water has not yet frozen. Vegetation has quite come to a stand, except in a few sheltered spots. In a deep ditch, my wife and I found a tall plant of the freshest and healthiest green, which looked as if it must have grown within the last few weeks. We wander among the wood-paths, which are very pleasant in the sunshine of the afternoons – the trees looking rich and warm, such of them, I mean, as have retained their russet leaves; and where the leaves are strewn along the paths, or heaped plentifully into some hollow of the hills, the effect is not without a charm. To-day, the morning rose with rain, which has since changed to snow and sleet; and now the landscape is as dreary as can well be imagined – white, with the brownness of the soil and withered grass every where peeping out. The swollen river, of a leaden hue, drags itself sullenly along; and this may be termed the first winter's day.

1842

December 11th Sunday morning. It is nearly three months since I have recorded my life & love in this journal. We have had many visitors, & have been to Boston & Salem meanwhile & various things have prevented my writing here. Last week we took our first walk together since the snow fell. The afternoon commenced with being rather dim, with pale blue sky beautified with very soft delicate clouds of faint purple. This dimness was to me very beautiful, but my dearest husband said he preferred broad sunshine. We went towards Peter's lane, but finding an inland sea that covers a meadow (for the nonce) quite frozen over, & boys skating upon it, we concluded to walk across it. This was very pleasant. Little islands of trees & bushes were scattered about in the icy arms of the tiny sea, clasped with immitigable force. The surface was very rough, but the boys did not mind it, & one long, ugly urchin kept rushing near us as if to show his wonderful skill & grace, when lo! he made himself a spectacle of awkwardness—

"Oh that some power the gift would gie us
To see oursels as others see us!"

as sung the fiery Burns. We soon crossed the frozen lake & then the snow was not hard enough to uphold us and nearly every step an evil 'jinnee' seemed to pull our heels down as if to weary us out; but we did not heed it & proceeded on over another meadow & entered Sleepy Hollow by a very pretty winding ascent between the trees. On the summit my dear lord threw himself down on the fair snow & I, quite breathless with climbing with unmanageable

1842

December 11th Sunday morning – It is nearly three months since I have recorded my life & love in this journal. We have had many visitors, & have been to Boston & Salem meanwhile & various things have prevented my writing here. Last week we took our first walk together since the snow fell. The afternoon commenced with being rather dim, with pale blue sky beautified with very soft delicate clouds of faint purple. This dimness was to me very beautiful, but my dearest husband said he preferred broad sunshine. We went towards Peter's lane; but finding an inland sea that covers a meadow (for the nonce) quite frozen over, & boys skating upon it, we concluded to walk across it. This was very pleasant. Little islands of trees & bushes were scattered about in the icy arms of the tiny sea, clasped with immitigable force. The surface was very rough, but the boys did not mind it, & one long, ugly urchin kept rushing near us as if to show his wonderful skill & grace, when lo! he made himself a spectacle of awkwardness –

"Oh that some power the gift would gie us
To see oursels as others see us!"

as sung the fiery Burns. We soon crossed the frozen lake & then the snow was not hard enough to uphold us & at nearly every step an evil 'jinnee' seemed to pull our heels down as if to weary us out; but we did not heed it & proceeded on over another meadow & entered Sleepy Hollow by a very pretty winding ascent between the trees. On the summit my dear lord threw himself down on the fair snow & I, quite breathless with climbing with unmanageable

~~every day but XXXXXXXXXXXXXX that I XXX within XXXXXXXXXXXXXXX, I left off, both because it [hurt] my eyes & was painful to [stoop] & XXXXXXX~~ In the evening my

to him ... Friday afternoon ... my dearest husband,

March 31st 1843. Friday. The first month of Spring is already gone, and still the snow lies deep on hill and valley; and the river is still frozen from bank to bank; although a late rain has caused pools of water to stand on the surface of the ice, and the

March 31st. 1843. Friday. The first month of Spring is already gone; and still the snow lies deep on hill and valley; and the river is still frozen from bank to bank; although a late rain has caused pools of water to stand on the surface of the ice, and the meadows are overflowed into broad lakes. Such a protracted winter has not been known for twenty years at least. I have almost forgotten the wood-paths and shady places, which I used to know so well, last summer; and my views are so much confined to the interior of our home, that sometimes, looking out of the window, I am surprised to catch a glimpse of houses at no great distance, which had quite passed out of my recollection. From present appearances, another month may scarcely suffice to wash away all the snow from the open country; and in the woods and hollows, it may linger yet longer. The winter will not have been a day less than five months long; and it would not be unfair to call it seven. A great space, indeed, to miss the smile of Nature, in a single year of human life. Even out of the midst of happiness, I have sometimes sighed and groaned; for I love the sunshine and the green woods, and the sparkling blue water; and it seems as if the picture of our inward bliss should be set in a beautiful frame of outward nature. My dear little wife bears it infinitely better than I; and except on my account, I do believe that she has not once wished for summer. But she is sunshine, and delicate Spring and delightful Summer, in her own person; else the winter would have been dreary indeed. One grief we have had nearly a month, which has been recorded in the preceding pages; all else has been happiness. Nor did this grief penetrate to the reality of our life. We do not feel as if our promised child were taken from us forever; but only as if his coming had been delayed for a season; and that, by and bye, we shall welcome that very same little stranger, whom we had expected to gladden our home at an earlier period. The longer we live together — the deeper we penetrate into one another, and become mutually interfused — the happier we are. God will surely crown our union with children, because it fulfils the highest conditions of marriage.

As to the daily course of our life, I have written with pretty commendable diligence, averaging from two to four hours a day; and the result is seen in various Magazines,

x

meadows are overflowed into broad lakes. Such a protracted winter has not been known for twenty years at least. I have almost forgotten the wood-paths and shady places, which I used to know so well, last summer; and my views are so much confined to the interior of our home, that sometimes, looking out of the window, I am surprised to catch a glimpse of houses at no great distance, which had quite passed out of my recollection. From present appearances, another month may scarcely suffice to wash away all the snow from the open country; and in the woods and hollows, it may linger yet longer. The winter will not have been a day less than five months long; and it would not be unfair to call it seven. A great space, indeed, to miss the smile of Nature, in a single year of human life. Even out of the midst of happiness, I have sometimes sighed and groaned; for I love the sunshine and the green woods, and the sparkling blue water; and it seems as if the picture of our inward bliss should be set in a beautiful frame of outward nature. My dear little wife bears it infinitely better than I; and except on my account, I do believe that she has not once wished for summer. But she is sunshine, and delicate Spring and delightful Summer, in her own person; else the winter would have been dreary indeed. ~~One grief we have had – that which she herself has recorded in the preceding pages;~~ all else has been happiness. Nor did the grief penetrate to the reality of our life. ~~We do not feel as if our promised child were taken from us forever; but only as if his coming had been delayed for a season; and that, by-and-by, we shall welcome that very same little stranger, whom we had expected to gladden our home at an earlier period.~~ The longer we live together – the deeper we penetrate into one another, and become mutually interfused – the happier we are. God will surely crown our union with children, because it fulfils the highest conditions of marriage.

As to the daily course of our life, I have written with pretty commendable diligence, averaging from two to four hours a day; and the result is seen in various Magazines.

I might have written more, if it had seemed worth while; but I was content to earn only so much gold as might suffice for our immediate wants, having prospect of official station and emolument, which would do away the necessity of writing for bread. Those prospects have not yet had their fulfilment; and we are well content to wait; because an office would inevitably remove us from our present happy home — at least from our outward home; for there is an inner one that will accompany us wherever we go. Meantime, the Magazine people do not pay their debts; so that we taste some of the inconveniences of poverty, and the mortification — only temporary, however — of owing money, with empty pockets. It is an annoyance; not a trouble.

Every day, I trudge through snow and slosh to the village, look into the Post Office, and spend an hour at the reading-room; and then return home, generally without having spoken a word to any human being. My wife is, in the strictest sense, my sole companion; and I need no other — there is no vacancy in my mind, any more than in my heart. In truth, I have spent so many years in total seclusion from all human society, that it is no wonder if I now feel all my desires satisfied by this sole intercourse. But my Dove has come to me from the midst of many friends, and a large circle of acquaintance; yet she lives from day to day in this solitude, seeing nobody but myself and our Molly, while the snow of our avenue is untrodden for weeks by any footstep save mine; yet she is always cheerful, and far more than cheerful. Thank God that I suffice for her boundless heart!

In the way of exercise, I saw and split wood; and physically I never was in so good condition as now. This is chiefly owing, doubtless, to a satisfied heart, — in aid of which comes the exercise above-mentioned, and about a fair proportion of intellectual labor, and a diet in which apples form a considerable part; though not to the exclusion of more substantial viands.

On the 9th of this month, we left home on a visit to

I might have written more, if it had seemed worth while; but I was content to earn only so much gold as might suffice for our immediate wants, having prospects of official station and emolument, which would do away the necessity of writing for bread. Those prospects have not yet had their fulfilment; and we are well content to wait; because an office would inevitably remove us from our present happy home – at least from an outward home; for there is an inner one that will accompany us wherever we go. Meantime, the Magazine people do not pay their debts; so that we taste some of the inconveniences of poverty, and the mortification – only temporary, however – of owing money, with empty pockets. It is an annoyance; not a trouble.

Every day, I trudge through snow and slosh to the village, look into the Post Office, and spend an hour at the reading-room; and then return home, generally without having spoken a word to any human being. My wife is, in the strictest sense, my sole companion; and I need no other – there is no vacancy in my mind, any more than in my heart. In truth, I have spent so many years in total seclusion from all human society, that it is no wonder if I now feel all my desires satisfied by this sole intercourse. But my Dove has come to me from the midst of many friends, and a large circle of acquaintance; yet she lives from day-to-day in this solitude, seeing nobody but myself and our Molly, while the snow of our avenue is untrodden for weeks by any footstep save mine; yet she is always cheerful, and far more than cheerful. Thank God that I suffice for her boundless heart!

In the way of exercise, I saw and split wood; and physically I never was in so good condition as now. This is chiefly owing, doubtless, to a satisfied heart, – in aid of which comes the exercise above-mentioned, and about a fair proportion of intellectual labor, and a diet in which apples form a considerable part; though not to the exclusion of more substantial viands.

On the 9th of this month, we left home on a visit to

Boston and Salem — at least, my wife stopt at the former place, and I went to the latter, where I resumed all my bachelor habits for nearly a fortnight, leading the same life in which ten years of my youth flitted away like a dream. But how much changed was I! — at last, I had caught hold of a reality, which never could be taken from me. It was good thus to get apart from my happiness, for the sake of contemplating it. On the 22d, I returned to Boston, and went out to Cambridge to dine with Longfellow, whom I had not seen since his return from Europe. The next day, we came back to our old house, which had been deserted all this time; for our Molly Bryan had gone with us to Boston.

April 7th. Friday. My belovedest wife has deserted her poor husband; she has this day gone to Boston to see her sister Mary, who is to marry Mr. Mann in two or three weeks, and then immediately to visit Europe for six months. A wagon came at about eleven o'clock to carry my Dove to the stage-house. I helped her in, and stood watching her, on the door-step, till she was out of sight. Then I betook myself to sawing and splitting wood; there being an inward inquietude, which demanded active exercise; and I sawed, I think, more briskly than ever before. When I re-entered the house, it was with somewhat of a desolate feeling; yet not without an intermingled pleasure, as being the more conscious that all separation was temporary, and scarcely real even for the little time that it may last. After my solitary dinner, I lay down, with the Dial in my hand, and attempted to sleep; but sleep would not come, — for the sufficient reason, perhaps, that my little wife was at that very moment jolting most uncomfortably over a rough road. So I arose, and began this record in the Journal, almost at the commencement of which I was interrupted by a visit from Mr. Thoreau, who came to return a book, and to announce his purpose of going to reside at Staten Island, as private tutor in the family of

Boston and Salem – at least, my wife stopt at the former place, and I went to the latter, where I resumed all my bachelor habits for nearly a fortnight, leading the same life in which ten years of my youth flitted away like a dream. But how much changed was I! – at last, I had caught hold of a reality, which never could be taken from me. It was good thus to get apart from my happiness, for the sake of contemplating it. On the 21st, I returned to Boston, and went out to Cambridge to dine with Longfellow, whom I had not seen since his return from Europe. The next day, we came back to our old house, which had been deserted all this time; for our Molly Bryan had gone with us to Boston.

April 7th. Friday. My belo↑ve↓dest wife has deserted her poor husband; she has this day gone to Boston to see her sister Mary, who is to marry Mr. Mann in two or three weeks, and then immediately to visit Europe for six months. A wagon came at about eleven o clock to carry my Dove to the stage-house. I helped her in, and stood watching her, on the door-step, till she was out of sight. Then I betook myself to sawing and splitting wood; there being an inward inquietness, which demanded active exercise; and I sawed, I think, more briskly than ever before. When I re-entered the house, it was with somewhat of a desolate feeling; yet not without an intermingled pleasure, as being the more conscious that all separation was temporary, and scarcely real even for the little time that it may last. After my solitary dinner, I lay down, with the Dial in my hand, and attempted to sleep; but sleep would not come, – for the sufficient reason, perhaps, that my little wife was at that very moment jolting most uncomfortably over a rough road. So I arose, and began this record in the Journal, almost at the commencement of which I was interrupted by a visit from Mr. Thoreau, who came to return a book, and to announce his purpose of going to reside at Staten Island, as private tutor in the family of

Mr. Emerson's brother. We had some conversation upon this subject, and upon the spiritual advantages of change of place, and upon the Dial, and upon Mr. Alcott, and other kindred or concatenated subjects. I am glad, on Mr. Thoreau's own account, that he is going away; as he is physically out of health, and, morally and intellectually, seems not to have found exactly the guiding clue; and in all these respects, he may be benefitted by his removal;—also, it is one step towards a circumstantial position in the world. On my account, I should like to have him remain here; he being one of the few persons, I think, with whom to hold intercourse is like hearing the wind among the boughs of a forest-tree; and with all this wild freedom, there is high and classic cultivation in him too. He says that Ellery Channing is coming back to Concord, and that he (Mr. Thoreau) has concluded a bargain, in his behalf, for the hire of a small house, with land attached, at $55 per year. I am rather glad than otherwise; but Ellery, so far as he has been developed to my observation, is but a poor substitute for Mr. Thoreau.

I had a purpose, if circumstances would permit, of passing the whole term of my wife's absence without speaking a word to any human being; but now my Pythagorean vow has been broken, within three or four hours after my departure—*her* departure, I should have said; but *my* will do as well.

April 8th. Saturday. After journalizing yesterday afternoon, I went out and sawed and split wood, till supper-time; then studied German, (translating Lenore,) with an occasional glance at a beautiful sunset, which I could not enjoy sufficiently, by myself, to induce me to lay aside the book. After lamp-light, finished Lenore, and drowsed over Voltaire's Candide, occasionally refreshing myself with a tune from Mr. Thoreau's musical-box, which he had left in my keeping. The evening was but a dull one. How much more spiritual than lamp-light or fire-light in the presence of my

Mr. Emerson's brother. We had some conversation upon this subject, and upon the spiritual advantages of change of place, and upon the Dial, and upon Mr. Alcott, and other kindred or concatenated subjects. I am glad, on Mr. Thoreau's own account, that he is going away; as he is physically out of health, and, morally and intellectually, seems not to have found exactly the guiding clue; and in all these respects, he may be benefitted by his removal; – also, it is one step towards a circumstantial position in the world. On my account, I should like to have him remain here; he being one of the few persons, I think, with whom to hold intercourse is like hearing the wind among the boughs of a forest-tree; and with all this wild freedom, there is high and classic cultivation in him too. He says that Ellery Channing is coming back to Concord, and that he (Mr. Thoreau) has concluded a bargain, in his behalf, for the hire of a small house, with land attached, at $55 per year. I am rather glad than otherwise; but Ellery, so far as he has been developed to my observation, is but a poor substitute for Mr. Thoreau.

I had a purpose, if circumstances would permit, of passing the whole term of my wife's absence without speaking a word to any human being; but now my Pythagorean vow has been broken, within three or four hours after my departure – *her* departure, I should have said; but *my* will do as well.

April 8th. Saturday. After journalizing yesterday afternoon, I went out and sawed and split wood, till supper-time; then studied German, (translating Lenore,) with an occasional glance at a beautiful sunset, which I could not enjoy sufficiently, by myself, to induce me to lay aside the book. After lamp-light, finished Lenore, and drowsed over Voltaire's Candide, occasionally refreshing myself with a tune from Mr. Thoreau's musical-box, which he had left in my keeping. The evening was but a dull one. How much more essential than lamp-light or fire-light is the presence of my

33

brightest little wife! I bathed and went to bed, soon after nine. ~~Where was my little wife then?~~ I felt some apprehension that the old Doctor's ghost would take this opportunity to visit me; but I rather think his former visitations have been intended for my wife, and that I am not sufficiently spiritual for ghostly communication. At all events, I met with no disturbance of the kind, and slept soundly enough till six o'clock, or thereabouts. Before nine, there being nothing to detain me in bed, I arose. The forenoon was spent with the pen in my hand; and sometimes I had the glimmering of an idea, and endeavored to materialize it in words; but, on the whole, my mind was idly vagrant, and refused to work to any systematic purpose. Between eleven and twelve, I went to the Post-Office, but found no letter; then spent above an hour, reading at the Athenæum. On my way home, I encountered Gaffer Flint, for the first time these many weeks, although Gaffer is our next neighbor, in one direction. I inquired of Gaffer if he could sell us some potatoes; and he promised to send half-a-bushel for trial; also, encouraged me to hope that he might buy a barrel of our apples. After my encounter with Gaffer, I returned to our lonely old abbey, opened the door with no such heart-spring as if I were to be welcomed by my wife's loving smile, ascended to my study, and began to read a tale of Tieck. Slow work, and dull work too! Anon, Molly rang the bell for dinner — a sumptuous banquet of stewed veal and maccaroni, to which I sat down in solitary state. My appetite served me sufficiently to eat with, but not for enjoyment; nothing has a zest, in my present widowed state. (Thus far I had written when Mr Emerson called.) After dinner, I lay down on the couch, with the Dial as a soporific, and had a short nap; then began to journalize.

Mr. Emerson came, with a sunbeam in his face; and we had as good a talk as ~~as~~ I ever remember experiencing with him. My little wife, I know, will demand to know every word that was spoken; but she knows me too

brightest little wife! I bathed and went to bed, soon after nine. ~~Where was my little wife then?~~ I felt some apprehension that the old Doctor's ghost would take this opportunity to visit me; but I rather think his former visitations have been intended for my wife, and that I am not sufficiently spiritual for ghostly communication. At all events, I met with no disturbance of the kind, and slept soundly enough till six o clock, or thereabouts. Before seven, there being nothing to detain me in bed, I arose. The forenoon was spent with the pen in my hand; and sometimes I had the glimmering of an idea, and endeavored to materialize it in words; but, on the whole, my mind was idly vagrant, and refused to work to any systematic purpose. Between eleven and twelve, I went to the Post-Office, but found no letter; then spent above an hour, reading at the Athenaeum. On my way home, I encountered Gaffer Flint, for the first time these many weeks, although Gaffer is our next neighbor, in one direction. I inquired of Gaffer if he could sell us some potatoes; and he promised to send half-a-bushel for trial; also, encouraged me to hope that he might buy a barrel of our apples. After my encounter with Gaffer, I returned to our lonely old abbey, opened the door with no such heart-spring as if I were to be welcomed by my wife's loving smile, ascended to my study, and began to read a tale of Tieck. Slow work, and dull work too! Anon, Molly rang the bell for dinner – a sumptuous banquet of stewed veal and maccaroni, to which I sat down in solitary state. My appetite served me sufficiently to eat with, but not for enjoyment; nothing has a zest, in my present widowed state. (Thus far I had written when Mr. Emerson called.) After dinner, I lay down on the couch, with the Dial as a soporific, and had a short nap; then began to journalize.

Mr. Emerson came, with a sunbeam in his face; and we had as good a talk as ~~if~~ I ever remember experiencing with him. My little wife, I know, will demand to know every word that was spoken; but she knows me too to anticipate anything of the kind. He seemed fullest of Margaret Fuller, who, he says, has risen perceptibly into a higher state, since their last meeting. He apotheosized her as the greatest woman, I believe, of ancient or modern times, and the one figure in the world worth considering. (There rings the supper-bell.) Then we spoke of Ellery Channing, a volume of whose poems is to be immediately published, with revisions by Mr. Emerson himself, and Mr. Sam Ward. He seems to anticipate no very wide reception for them; he calls them "poetry for poets;" and thinks that perhaps a hundred persons may admire them very much, while, to the rest of the world, they will be little or nothing. Next Mr. Thoreau was discussed, and his approaching departure; in respect to which we agreed pretty well; but Mr. Emerson appears to have suffered some inconveniency from his experience of Mr. Thoreau as an inmate. It may well be that such a sturdy and uncompromising person is fitter to meet occasionally in the open air, than to have as a permanent guest at table and fireside. We talked of Brook Farm, and the singular moral aspects which it presents, and the great desirability that its progress and developements should be observed, and its history written. We talked of Charles Newcomb, who, it appears, is now passing through a new moral phasis; he is silent, inexpressive, talks little or none, and listens without response except a sardonic laugh; and some of his friends think that he is passing into permanent eclipse. Various other matters were discussed or glanced at; and finally, between five and six o'clock, Mr. Emerson took his leave, threatening to come again, unless I call on him very soon. I then went out to chop wood, my allotted space for which had been very much abridged by his visit; but on the whole, I was not sorry. I went on with the Journal for a few minutes before supper, and have finished the present record in the setting sunshine and gathering dusk. I would like to see my wife!

1a

to anticipate anything of the kind. He seemed fullest of Margaret Fuller, who, he says, has risen perceptibly into a higher state, since their last meeting. He apotheosized her as the greatest woman, I believe, of ancient or modern times, and the one figure in the world worth considering. (There rings the supper-bell.) Then we spoke of Ellery Channing, a volume of whose poems is to be immediately published, with revisions by Mr. Emerson himself, and Mr. Sam Ward. He seems to anticipate no very wide reception for them; he calls them "poetry for poets," and thinks that perhaps a hundred persons may admire them very much; while, to the rest of the world, they will be little or nothing. Next Mr. Thoreau was discussed, and his approaching departure; in respect to which we agreed pretty well; but Mr. x Emerson appears to have suffered some inconveniency from his experience of Mr. Thoreau as an inmate. It may well be that such a sturdy and uncompromising person is fitter to meet occasionally in the open air, than to have as a permanent guest at table and fireside. We talked of Brook Farm, and the singular moral aspects which it presents, and the great desirability that its progress and developements should be observed, and its history written. We talked of Charles Newcomb, who, it appears, is now passing through a new moral phasis; he is silent, inexpressive, talks little or none, and listens without response except a sardonic laugh; and some of his friends think that he is passing into permanent eclipse. Various other matters were discussed or glanced at; and finally, between five and six o clock, Mr. Emerson took his leave, threatening to come again, unless I call on him very soon. I then went out to chop wood, my allotted space for which had been very much abridged by his visit; but, on the whole, I was not sorry. I went on with the journal for a few minutes before supper; and have finished the present record in the setting sunshine and gathering dusk. I would like to see my wife!

34

April 9th. Sunday. Dear little wife, after finishing my record in the Journal, I sat a long time in Grandmother's chair, thinking of many things; but the thought of thee—the great thought of thee—was among all other thoughts, like the pervading sunshine falling through the branches and boughs of a tree, and tinging every separate leaf. Not that I was very cheerful either; my spirits were at a lower ebb than they ever descend to, while thou art present; nevertheless, neither was I absolutely sad. Many times I wound and re-wound Mr. Thoreau's little musical-box; but certainly its peculiar sweetness has evaporated, and I am pretty sure that I should throw it out of the window, were I doomed to hear it long and often. It has not an infinite soul. When it was almost as dark as the moonlight would let it be, I lighted the lamp, and went on with Tieck's tale, slowly and painfully, and often wishing for thy bright little wits to help me out of my difficulties. At last, I determined to learn a little about pronouns and verbs, before proceeding further, and so took up the Phrase Book, with which I was commendably busy, when, at about a quarter of nine, came a knock to my study-door; and behold there was Molly with thy letter! How she came by it, I did not ask, being content to suppose that it was brought by a heavenly messenger. Dearest wife, I had not expected a letter; and thou canst not imagine what a comfort it was to me in my loneliness and dreariness; even though its contents did somewhat disturb me, to think that thou shouldst have sitten an hour-and-a-half in that tobacco-smoky tavern, with those ugly people—whom, nevertheless, God made, though of course thou wilt deny it. I called Molly to take her letter, which she received with a face of delight as broad and bright as the kitchen-fire. Then I read, and re-read, and re-re-read, and quadruply, quintuply, and sextuply re-read thy dearest epistle, until I had it all by heart; and then continued to re-read it for the sake of looking at thy fairy penmanship. Then I took up the Phrase Book again; but could not study; and

April 9th. Sunday. Dear little Wife, after finishing my record in the Journal, I sat a long time in Grandmother's Chair, thinking of many things; but the thought of thee – the great thought of thee – was among all other thoughts, like the pervading sunshine falling through the branches and boughs of a tree, and tinging every separate leaf. Not that I was very cheerful either; my spirits were at a lower ebb than they ever descend to, while thou art present; nevertheless, neither was I absolutely sad. Many times I wound and re-wound Mr. Thoreau's little musical-box; but certainly its peculiar sweetness has evaporated, and I am pretty sure that I should throw it out of the window, were I doomed to hear it long and often. It has not an infinite soul. When it was almost as dark as the moonlight would let it be, I lighted the lamp, and went on with Tieck's tale, slowly and painfully, and often wishing for thy bright little wits to help me out of my difficulties. At last, I determined to learn a little about pronouns and verbs, before proceeding further, and so took up the Phrase Book, with which I was commendably busy, when, at about a quarter of nine, came a knock to my study-door; and behold there was Molly with thy letter! How she came by it I did not ask; being content to suppose that it w[as] brought by a heavenly messenger. Dearest wife, I had not expected a letter; and thou canst not imagine what a comfort it was to me in my loneliness and sombreness; even though its contents did somewhat disturb me, to think that thou shouldst have sitten an hour-and-a half in that tobacco-smoky tavern, with those ugly people – whom, nevertheless, god made, though of course thou wilt deny it. I called Molly to take her letter, which she received with a face of delight as broad and bright as the kitchen-fire. Then I read, and re-read, and re-re-read, and quadruply, quintuply, and sextuply re-read, thy dearest epistle, until I had it all by heart; and then continued to re-read it for the sake of looking at thy fairy penmanship. Then I took up the Phrase Book again; but could not study; and so bathed and went to bed; it being now not far from ten o'clock. I lay awake a good deal in the night, but saw no ghost.

I arose about seven, and found that the upper part of my nose, and the region roundabout, was grievously discolored; and at the angle of the left eye, there is a great spot of almost black purple, and a broad streak of the same hue ~~semi-cir~~circling beneath either eye; while green, yellow, and orange, overspread the circum-jacent country. It looks not unlike a gorgeous sunset, throwing its splendor over the heaven of thy husband's countenance. It will behove me to show myself as little as possible during thy absence; else people will think that we have fought a pitched battle together, and that thou hast fled the field; though, from my battered aspect, there would appear to be more cause for me to flee than for thee. The devil take the stick of wood! What had I done, that it should bemaul me so? However, there is no pain, though, I think, a very slight affection of the eyes.

This forenoon, I began to write, and caught an idea by the tail, which I intend to hold fast, though it struggles to get free. As it was not ready to be put on paper, however, I took up the Dial, and finished the article on Mr. Alcott. It is not very satisfactory, and has not taught me much. Then I read Margaret's article on Canova, which is good. About this time, the dinner-bell rang; and I went down without much alacrity, though with a good appetite enough. But I shall not digest my food well, until thou comest back. After dinner, I began this letter ~~to my sweetest little dove (that ought to be always, but is not now)~~ whom may God bless forever and ever;— and this is praying for myself as well as thee. Thy truest Husband.

P.S. It was in the angle of my right eye, not my left, that the blackest purple was collected. But they both look like the very devil.

Half past 5 o'clock. After writing the above letter to my dearest Spouse, I again set to work on Tieck's tale, and worried through

so bathed and went to bed; it being now not far from ten o clock. I lay awake a good deal in the night, but saw no ghost.

I arose about seven, and found that the upper part of my nose, and the region roundabout, was grievously discolored; and at the angle of the left eye, there is a great spot of almost black purple, and a broad streak of the same hue semi-circling beneath either eye; while green, yellow, and orange, overspread the circum-jacent country. It looks not unlike a gorgeous sunset, throwing its splendor over the heaven of thy husband's countenance. It will behove me to show myself as little as possible during thy absence; else people will think that we have fought a pitched battle together, and that thou hast fled the field; though, from my battered aspect, there would appear to be more cause for me to flee than ↑for↓ thee. The devil take the stick of wood! What had I done, that it should bemaul me so? However, there is no pain, though, I think, a very slight affection of the eyes.

This forenoon, I began to write, and caught an idea by the tail, which I intend to hold fast, though it struggles to get free. As it was not ready to be put on paper, however, I took up the Dial, and finished the article on Mr. Alcott. It is not very satisfactory, and has not taught me much. Then I read Margaret's article on Canova, which is good. About this time, the dinner-bell rang; and I went down without much alacrity, though with a good appetite enough. But I shall not digest my food well, until thou comest back. After dinner, I began this letter ~~to my sweetest little bedfellow, (that ought to be always, but is not now)~~ whom may God bless forever and ever; – and this is praying for myself as well as thee. Thy truest Husband. P.S. It was in the angle of my right eye, not my left, that the blackest purple was collected. But they both look like the very Devil.

Half past 5 o clock. After writing the above letter ~~to my dearest spouse,~~ I again set to work on Tieck's tale, and worried through

36

sealed pages; and then, at half past four, threw open one of the western windows of my study, and sallied forth to take the sunshine. I went down through the orchard to the river-side. The orchard-path is still deeply covered with snow, and so is the whole visible universe except in streaks upon the hill-sides and spots in the sunny hollows, where the brown earth peeps through. The river, which a few days ago was entirely imprisoned, has now broken its fetters; but a tract of ice extended across from near the foot of the monument to the abutment of the old bridge, and looked so solid that I supposed it would yet remain for a day or two. Large cakes and masses of ice came floating down the current, which, though not very violent, hurried along at a much swifter pace than the ordinary one of our sluggish river-god. These ice-masses, when they struck the barrier of ice above-mentioned, acted upon it like a battering-ram, and were themselves forced high out of the water, or sometimes carried beneath the main sheet of ice. At last, down the stream came an immense mass of ice, and striking the barrier about at its centre, it gave way, and the whole was swept onward together, leaving the river entirely free, with only here and there a cake of ice floating quietly along. The great accumulation, in its downward course, hit against a tree that stood in mid-current, and caused it to quiver like a reed; and it swept quite over the shrubbery that bordered what, in summer-time, is the river's bank, but which is now nearly the centre of the stream. Our river, in its present state, has quite a noble breadth. The little hillock, which formed the abutment of the old bridge, is now an island with its tuft of trees. Along the hither shore, a row of trees stand up to their knees, and the smaller ones up to their middles, in the water; and afar off on the surface of the stream, we see tufts of bushes emerging, thrusting up their heads, as it were, to breathe. The water comes over the stone-wall, and encroaches several yards on the boundaries of our

several pages; and then, at half past four, threw open one of the western windows of my study, and sallied forth to take the sunshine. I went down through the orchard to the river-side. The orchard-path is still deeply covered with snow; and so is the whole visible universe, ↑except↓ in streaks upon the hill-sides, and spots in the sunny hollows, where the brown earth peeps through. The river, which a few days ago was entirely imprisoned, has now broken its fetters; but a tract of ice extended across from near the foot of the monument to the abutment of the old bridge, and looked so solid that I supposed it would yet remain for a day or two. Large cakes and masses of ice came floating down the current, which, though not very violent, hurried along at a much swifter pace than the ordinary one of our sluggish river-god. These ice-masses, when they struck the barrier of ice above-mentioned, acted upon it like a battering-ram, and were themselves forced high out of the water, or sometimes carried beneath the main sheet of ice. At last, down the stream came an immense mass of ice, and striking the barrier about at its centre, it gave way; and the whole was swept onward together, leaving the river entirely free, with only here and there a cake of ice floating quietly along. The great accumulation, in its down-ward course, hit against a tree that stood in mid-current, and caused it to quiver like a reed; and it swept quite over the shrubbery that bordered what, in summer-time, is the river's bank, but which is now nearly the centre of the stream. Our river, in its present state, has quite a noble breadth. The little hillock, which formed the abutment of the old bridge, is now an island with its tuft of trees. Along the hither shore, a row of trees stand up to their knees, and the smaller ones up to their middles, in the water; and afar off on the surface of the stream, we see tufts of bushes emerging, thrusting up their heads, as it were, to breathe. The water comes over the stone-wall, and encroaches several yards on the boundaries of our orchard. (Here the supper-bell rang.) If our boat were in good order, I should now set forth on voyages of discovery, and visit nooks on the borders of the meadows, which, by-and-by, will be a mile or two from the water's edge. But she is in very bad condition, full of water and doubtless as leaky as a sieve.

On coming from supper, I found that little Puss had established herself in the study, probably with intent to pass the night here. She now lies on the footstool, between my legs, purring most obstreperously. The day of my wife's departure, she came to me, talking with the greatest earnestness; but whether it was to condole with me on my loss, or to demand my redoubled care for herself, I could not well make out. As Puss now constitutes a third part of the family, this mention of her will not appear amiss. How Molly employs herself, I know not. Once in a while, I hear a door slam like a thunder-clap; but she never shows her face, nor speaks a word, unless to announce a visitor or deliver a letter. This day, on my part, will have been spent without exchanging a syllable with any human being; unless something unforeseen should yet call for the exercise of speech, before bed-time.

April 10th. Monday. I sat till eight o'clock, meditating upon this world and the next, and my dear little wife, as connected with both; and sometimes dimly shaping out scenes of a tale. Then lighted the lamp, and betook myself to the German Phrase-Book. Ah, dearest, these are but dreary evenings. The lamp would not brighten my spirits, though Molly had duly filled it. Nevertheless, lacking energy to bathe, I deferred that duty later than usual, and did not get to bed till ten o'clock. What is the use of going to bed at all, in solitude? I dreamed a good deal, but to no good purpose; for all the characters and incidents have vanished. At half-past three, I awoke, and did not fall asleep again till daylight; then slept till after six, and arose at seven.— Dearest wife, what a good husband thou hast, to be so minute in the record of his sleepings and wakings! I would

orchard. (Here the supper-bell rang.) If our boat were in good order, I should now set forth on voyages of discovery, and visit nooks on the borders of the meadows, which, by-and-by, will be a mile or two from the water's edge. But she is in very bad condition, full of water, and doubtless as leaky as a sieve.

On coming from supper, I found that little Puss had established herself in the study, probably with intent to pass the night here. She now lies on the footstool, between my legs, purring most obstreperously. The day of my wife's departure, she came to me, talking with the greatest earnestness; but whether it was to condole with me on my loss, or to demand my redoubled care for herself, I could not well make out. As Puss now constitutes a third part of the family, this mention of her will not appear amiss. How Molly employs herself, I know not. Once in a while, I hear a door slam~~m~~ like a thunder-clap; but she never shows her face, nor speaks a word, unless to announce a visiter or deliver a letter. This day, on my part, will have been spent without exchanging a syllable with any human being; unless something unforeseen should yet call for the exercise of speech, before bed-time.

April 10th. Monday. I sat till eight o clock, meditating upon this world and the next, and my dear little wife, as connected with both; and sometimes dimly shaping out scenes of a tale. Then lighted the lamp, and betook myself to the German Phrase Book. Ah, dearest, these are but dreary evenings. The lamp could not brighten my spirits, though Molly had duly filled it. Nevertheless, lacking energy to bathe, I deferred that duty later than usual, and did not get to bed till ten o clock. ~~What is the use of going to bed at all, in solitude?~~ I dreamed a good deal, but to no good purpose; for all the characters and incidents have vanished. At half-past-three, I awoke, and did not fall asleep again till daylight; then slept till after six, and arose at seven. – Dearest wife, what a good husband thou hast, to be so minute in the record of his sleepings and wakings! I would

36

like to have thee know my life, during our separation, as circumstantially as if thou hadst been all the time by my side. The forenoon was spent in scribbling, by no means to my satisfaction, until past eleven, when I went to the village. Nothing in our box at the Post Office. I read during the customary hour, or more, at the Atheneum, and returned without saying a word to mortal. I gathered from some conversation that I overheard, that a son of Adam is to be buried this afternoon, from the meeting-house; but the name of the deceased escaped me. It is no great matter, so it be but written in the Book of Life. Since my return, I have made this important entry in the journal; and now, with some impatience, await the dinner-bell.

My variegated face looks somewhat more human, to-day; though I was unaffectedly ashamed to meet my landlady's gaze, and therefore turned my back, or my shoulder, as much as possible, upon the world.

At dinner, behold an immense joint of roast veal! Dearest love, thou art not mighty in the capacity of trencher-woman; yet I would willingly have had thy assistance, small as it might be, in the discussion of this great piece of calf. I am ashamed to eat alone; it becomes the mere gratification of animal appetite—the tribute which we are compelled to pay to our grosser nature; whereas, in thy company, it is refined, and moralized, and spiritualized; and over our earthly victuals (or rather vittles, for the former is a very foolish mode of spelling) over our earthly vittles is diffused a sauce of lofty and gentle thoughts; and tough meat is mollified with tender feelings. But, Oh, these solitary meals are the dismallest part of my present experience. When the company rose from table, they all, in the single person of thy husband, ascended to the study, and employed themselves in reading the article on Oregon, in the Democratic Review. Then they plodded onward into the rugged and bewildering depths of Tieck's tale, until five o'clock; when, with one accord, they went out to split wood. This has been a gray day, with

like to have thee know my life, during our separation, as circumstantially as if thou hadst been all the time by my side. The forenoon was spent in scribbling, by no means to my satisfaction, until past eleven, when I went to the village. Nothing in our box at the Post Office. I read during the customary hour, or more, at the Athenaeum; and returned without saying a word to mortal. I gathered from some conversation that I overheard, that a son of Adam is to be buried, this afternoon, from the meeting-house; but the name of the deceased escaped me. It is no great matter, so it be but written in the Book of Life. Since my return, I have made this important entry in the Journal; and now, with some impatience, await the dinner-bell.

My variegated face looks somewhat more human, to-day; though I was unaffectedly ashamed to meet anybody's gaze, and therefore turned my back, or my shoulder, as much as possible, upon the world.

At dinner, behold an immense joint of roast veal! Dearest love, thou art not mighty in the capacity of trencher-woman; yet I would willingly have had thy assistance, small as it might be, in the discussion of this great piece of calf. I am ashamed to eat alone; it becomes the mere gratification of animal appetite – the tribute which we are compelled to pay to our grosser nature; whereas, in thy company, it is refined, and moralized, and spiritualized; and over our earthly victuals (or rather vittles; for the former is a very foolish mode of spelling) over our earthly vittles is diffused a sauce of lofty and gentle thoughts; and tough meat is mollified with tender feelings. But, Oh, these solitary meals are the dismallest part of my present experience. When the company rose from table, they all, in the single person of thy husband, ascended to the study, and employed themselves in reading the article on Oregon, in the Democratic Review. Then they plodded onward into the rugged and bewildering depths of Tieck's tale, until five o clock, when, with one accord, they went out to split wood. This has been a gray day, with now and then a sprinkling of snow-flakes through the air. Surely, thou shouldst not have deserted me without manufacturing a sufficient quantity of sunshine to last till thy return! Art thou not ashamed?

To-day, no more than yesterday, have I spoken a word to mortal. ~~Come home soon, little Dove, or thy husband will have forgotten the use of speech.~~ It is now sunset; and I must meditate till dark.

April 11th 1843. I meditated, accordingly, but without any very wonderful result. Then, at eight o'clock, lighted the lamp, and bothered myself till after nine with this eternal tale of Tieck. Bath and bed at about ten. Terrible late hours, my Dove! ~~My greatest enjoyment in bed is to extend myself cross-wise, diagonally, semicircularly, & in all other postures that would be incompatible with a bedfellow. I believe, too, that, during my sleep, I seek thee throughout the empty width of our couch;~~ for I found myself, when I awoke, in quite a different region than I had occupied in the early part of the night. I arose before seven o'clock. Was not that good? The forenoon was spent in scribbling; but, at eleven o'clock, my thoughts ceased to flow—indeed, their current had been woefully interrupted, all along—so I threw down my pen, and set out on the daily journey to the village. Horrible walking! There was nothing at the Post Office; so I wasted the customary hour at the Athenaeum, and returned home—if home it may be called, where thou art not.—Till dinner time, I labored on Tieck's tale, and resumed that agreeable employment after the banquet. It is my purpose, poor little wife, that thou, the very morning after thy return, shalt take up this awful business, and finish the tale, and then lead thy husband through its bewilderments, perfectly at his ease.

Just when I was at the point of choking with a huge German word, Molly announced Mr. Thoreau. He wanted to take a row in the boat, for the last time, perhaps, before he leaves Concord. So we emptied the water out of

now and then a sprinkling of snow-flakes through the air. Surely, thou shouldst not have deserted me without manufacturing a sufficient quantity of sunshine to last till thy return! Art thou not ashamed?

To-day, no more than yesterday, have I spoken a word to mortal. ~~Come home soon, little Dove, or thy husband will have forgotten the use of speech.~~ It is now sunset; and I must meditate till dark.

April 11th 1843. I meditated, accordingly, but without any very wonderful result. Then, at eight o clock, lighted the lamp, and bothered myself till after nine with this eternal tale of Tieck. Bath and bed at about ten. Terrible late hours, my Dove! ~~My greatest enjoyment in bed is to extend myself cross-wise, diagonally, semi-circularly, and in all other postures that would be incompatible with a bed-fellow. I believe, too, that, during my sleep, I seek thee throughout the empty vastitude of our couch; for~~ I found myself, when I awoke, in quite a different region than I had occupied in the early part of the night. I arose before seven o clock. Was not that good? The forenoon was spent in scribbling; but, at eleven o clock, my thoughts ceased to flow – indeed, their current had been woefully interrupted, all along – so I threw down my pen, and set out on the daily journey to the village. Horrible walking! There was nothing at the Post Office; so I wasted the customary hour at the Athenaeum, and returned home – if home it may be called, where thou art not. – Till dinner time, I labored on Tieck's tale, and resumed that agreeable employment after the banquet. It is my purpose, poor little wife, that thou, the very morning after thy return, shall take up this awful business, and finish the tale, and then lead thy husband through its bewilderments, perfectly at his ease.

Just when I was at the point of choking with a huge German word, Molly announced Mr. Thoreau. He wanted to take a row in the boat, for the last time, perhaps, before he leaves Concord. So we emptied the water out of

37

her, and set forth on our voyage. She leaks, but not more than she did in the autumn. We rowed to the foot of the hill which borders the north-branch, and there landed, and climbed the moist and mossy hill-side, for the sake of the prospect. Looking down the river, it might well have been mistaken for an arm of the sea, so broad is now its swollen tide; and I could have fancied that, beyond one other headland, the mighty ocean would outspread itself before the eye. On our return, we boarded a large cake of ice, which was floating down the river, and were borne by it directly to our own landing-place, with the boat towing behind.

Parting with Mr. Thoreau, I spent half an hour in chopping wood; when Molly informed me that Mr. Emerson wished to see me. He had brought a letter of Ellery Channing's, written in a style of very pleasant humor. This being read and discussed, together with a few other matters, he took his leave; since which, I have been attending to my journalizing duty — and thus the record is brought down to the present moment; ten minutes past six. To-night — to-night — yes, within an hour — this Eden, which is no Eden to a solitary Adam, will regain its Eve.

her, and set forth on our voyage. She leaks; but not more than she did in the autumn. We rowed to the foot of the hill which borders the north-branch, and there landed, and climbed the moist and snowy hillside, for the sake of the prospect. Looking down the river, it might well have been mistaken for an arm of the sea, so broad is now its swollen tide; and I could have fancied that, beyond one other headland, the mighty ocean would outspread itself before the eye. On our return, we boarded a large cake of ice, which was floating down the river, and were borne by it directly to our own landing-place, with the boat towing behind.

Parting with Mr. Thoreau, I spent half an hour in chopping wood; when Molly informed me that Mr. Emerson wished to see me. He had brought a letter of Ellery Channing's, written in a style of very pleasant humor. This being read, and discussed, together with a few other matters, he took his leave; since which, I have been attending to my journalizing duty – and thus the record is brought down to the present moment; ten minutes past six. To-night – to-night – yes, within an hour – this Eden, which is no Eden to a solitary Adam, will regain its Eve.

& are truly perfect soul in every fibre. It is the
inward thought alone that renders the body
either material or angelical. "Are ye not the
temple of the living GOD?" says the apostle.
Ah yes – also I suppose some persons are the
den of the ~~fallen~~ archfiend; & through such
has this miraculous form come into disrepute.
Before our marriage I knew nothing of its capacities
& the truly married alone can know what a wondrous
instrument it is for the purposes of the heart.
Those who are wedded for convenience or
whim forever exclude themselves from the
most distant imagination of what it is meant
to express. The unholiness of a union on any other
ground than entire oneness of spirit, immediately
& eternally causes the sword of the flaming
Cherubim to wave before this tree of life.
The profane never can taste the joys of Elysium
because it is a spiritual joy, & they cannot perceive
it.

For several days I felt in a sleepy state. I do not

[April 11th or April 12th–April 22?]

& are truly perfect soul in every fibre. It is the inward thought alone that renders the body either material or angelical. "Are ye not the temple of the living GOD?" says the apostle. Ah yes – also I suppose some persons are the den of the ~~fallen~~ archfiend, & through such has this miraculous form come into disrepute. Before our marriage I knew nothing of its capacities & the truly married alone can know what a wondrous instrument it is for the purposes of the heart. Those who are wedded for convenience or whim forever exclude themselves from the most distant imagination of what it is meant to express. The unholiness of a union on any other ground than entire oneness of spirit, immediately & eternally causes the sword of the flaming Cherubim to wave before this tree of life. The profane never can taste the joys of Elysium – because it is a spiritual joy, & they cannot percieve it.

For several days I felt in a sleepy state. I do not

fear of more cold & frost I presume, for how 29
can the birds be mistaken? They hold the
most animated conversation till after sunset
from earliest dawn. It seems as if they were discus-
-sing important measures for their summer
residences. They have no time now to sit on a
twig & pour forth overtures, operas, symphonies
& waltzes. Anxious questions are asked — & only
by accident, as from pure ecstasy — once in a
while a rich warble rolls its tiny waves
of gold sound through the atmosphere.
Their little forms are as busy as their voices
They are in a constant flutter & restlessness.
Even when three or four retreat to a
treetop to hold council, they wag their
tails & heads all the time instead of
sitting still. Once I saw two robins springing
from the ground into the air exactly as
chickens when they are angry; but I presume
it was a strife of love & not of hate with the
robins. On Thursday (8th) my darling husband took
me out in the boat. It was charming to be
again on the water. We went to the red
bridge, but the tide was so high & the
stream so rapid beneath it, that we could
not go under. The counter currents held
our waterlily almost still, but finally we
turned & gave it to the care of the
downward flow without using the paddle
much. We floated over the meadows where
in summer we walk upon the grass, &
the trees seemed growing directly from the
river's depths. It was the first time I had taken
the fresh since I came back, & it was very
reviving. We seemed on a small sea, so
much has the river risen.

fear of more cold & frost I presume, for how can the birds be mistaken? They hold the most animated conversation till after sunset from earliest dawn. It seems as if they were discussing important measures for their summer residences. They have no time now to sit on a twig & pour forth overtures, operas, symphonies & waltzes – anxious questions are asked – & only by accident, as from pure ecstasy – once in a while a rich warble rolls its tiny waves of gold sound through the atmosphere. Their little forms are as busy as their voices. They are in a constant flutter & restlessness. Even when three or four retreat to a treetop to hold council, they wag their tails & heads all the time instead of sitting still. Once I saw two robins springing from the ground into the air exactly as chickens when they are angry; but I presume it was a strife of love & not of hate with the robins. On Thursday (13th my darling husband took me out in the boat. It was charming to be again on the water. We went to the red bridge, but the tide was so high & the stream so rapid beneath it, that we could not go under. The counter currents held our water lily almost still, but finally we turned & gave it to the care of the downward flow without using the paddle much. We floated over the meadows where in the summer we walk upon the grass, & the trees seemed growing directly from the river's depths. It was the first time I had taken the fresh since I came back, & it was very reviving. We seemed on a small sea, so much has the river risen.

I never was in the country before at the opening of Spring that I recollect. At any rate I never observed it before—I never felt it before. This sense of new-coming life from sympathy with the deliverance of earth from winter is a novel experience. My soul is a mighty river also, breaking free from frost & ice—no—not frost & ice neither, for I have been free & unshackled all through the cold weather, in the heavenly summer of my husband's heart—but still it breaks forth. I have a new hope, partly from the sun of joy in my dear love's eyes, for he has sighed much for warm days & flowers & green grass, & now he is very glad—& partly I suppose from involuntary response to the budding trees & rushing waters & birds' wings & voices. But I could not be satisfied in feeling this mighty springing upwards & forwards unless I were in love. I am thankful that I first knew Spring after I am married. My heart is so full—it rises to so high a mark—it overflows so bountifully, that were there not another heart to receive my boundless love, I should feel sad & aimless. Oh Father GOD! I thank thee that I can rush on to him ~~sweet~~ husband with all my many waters & ring & thunder with all my waves in the vast expanse of his comprehensive bosom. How I exult there—how I foam & sparkle in the sea of his love—how I wish for no broader region, because I have as yet found no limit to this. I myself am Spring with all its birds, its rivers, its buds, singing, rushing, blooming into his arms. I feel new as the Earth which is just born again. I rejoice that I am, because I am his, wholly & unreservedly his. Therefore is my

I never was in the country before at the opening of Spring that I recollect. At any rate I never observed it before. I never felt it before. This sense of new coming life from sympathy with the deliverance of earth from winter is a novel experience. My soul is a mighty river also, breaking free from frost & ice – no – not frost & ice neither; for I have been free & unshackled all through the cold weather, in the heavenly summer of my husband's heart – but still it breaks forth. I have a new hope, partly from the sun of joy in my dear love's eyes, for he has sighed much for warm days & flowers & green grass, & now he is very glad – & partly I suppose from involuntary response to the budding trees & rushing waters & birds' wings & voices. But I could not be satisfied in feeling this mighty springing upwards & forwards unless I were in love. I am thankful that I first know Spring after I am married. My heart is so full – it rises to so high a mark – it overflows so bountifully, that were there not another heart to receive my boundless love, I should feel sad & aimless. Oh lovely GOD! I thank thee that I can rush into my ~~sweet~~ husband with all my many waters, & sing & thunder with all my waves in the vast expanse of his comprehensive ~~bosom.~~ How I exult there – how I foam & sparkle in the Sun of his love – how I wish for no broader region, because I have as yet found no limit to this. I myself am Spring with all its birds, its rivers, its buds, singing, rushing, blooming ~~in his arms.~~ I feel new as the Earth which is just born again. I rejoice that I am, because I am his, ~~wholly, unreservedly his.~~ Therefore is my

be beautiful & gracious—therefore is the word pleasant as roses. ~~[illegible]~~

April 23d Sunday. It is far different today from last Sunday. Then it was soft & sunny after a misty dawn, & the birds sang on every twig. They sang without an end—I felt inclined to respond "Yes, yes, yes—I know it I know it! there never was such a sun such an air, such a sky, such a GOD! I know it, dear little fellow worshippers!" My heart said this but they were not content to stop. Today it is rainy & chilly & scarcely a bird is heard. Last Sunday evening Ellery Channing made us his first visit. He looked brighter & was more sociable than he used to be last summer. I think perhaps he will prove more worthy & interesting a companion than thou supposest, dearest husband. He has to me a pleasanter way of saying things than Mr Thoreau, because so wholly without the air of saying any thing of consequence. Monday he dined & took tea with us & I enjoyed his visit better than any from him before. His complexion seems several shades lighter & he smiles oftener.—[Ah I must hear the meadow lark, swinging its little sign on its gold-hinges. The rain does not discourage him. He knows the sun shines above the clouds—] Ellery came again this week & went out in the boat & took tea on the

life beautiful & gracious. Therefore is the world pleasant as roses. ~~XXXXXXXXXXXXXXXXX XXXXXXXXXXXXXXXXXXXXXXXXXXX XXXXXXXXXXXXXXXXXXXXXXXXXXX XXXXXXX a Spring with the XXXX indeed XXXX Eternity XXXXXXXXXXXXXXXXXXX; XXXXXXXXXXXXXXXXXXXXXXXXXXX shall we not XXXXXXX forever also?~~

April 23d. Sunday. It is far different today from last Sunday. Then it was soft & sunny after a misty dawn, & the birds sang on every twig. They sang without an end – I felt inclined to respond "Yes, yes, yes – I know it I know it! There never was such a sun, such an air, such a sky, such a GOD! I know it, dear little fellow worshippers!" My heart said this but they were not content to stop. Today it is rainy & chilly & scarcely a bird is heard. Last Sunday evening Ellery Channing made us his first visit. He looked brighter & was more sociable than he used to be last summer. I think perhaps he will prove more worthy & interesting a companion than thou supposest, dearest husband. He has to me a pleasanter way of saying things than Mr Thoreau, because so wholly without the air of saying any thing of consequence. Monday he dined & took tea with us & I enjoyed his visit better than any from him before. His complexion seems several shades lighter & he smiles oftener. — (Ah now I hear the meadow lark, swinging its little sign on its gold-hinges. The rain does not discourage him. He knows the sun shines above the clouds —) Ellery came again this week & went out in the boat & took tea on his

to him. Friday afternoon my dearest husband took me out in the boat. We went aground on the meadows, were nearly upset in a maelstrom beneath the red bridge, beating up against the rocks, & upon attempting to go ashore at the foot of the orchard, were stuck fast between the stones of the wall & narrowly escaped destruction! My sweetest love seemed discouraged at once before all these mishaps & obstacles, while I could only laugh; for I cannot feel fear & danger. I do not mind with him: but I found out a solution of this mystery when we were landed. Thou wert discouraged for my sake only, thou kindest hero. Alone thou never feelest alarm. Can I love or admire thee most?

I called at Mrs Bosworth's after we came back & found only the blooming Miss Abba blooming & stalwart. But I must not forget to mention that we floated on the river by a small snake, who evidently had set sail by accident & was vainly attempting to keep his head & white throat above the water. My husband tried to lift him out on his paddle, but he wriggled off, not knowing friends from enemies. We passed an even row of young willows upon which were many chattering blackbirds with agitated tails. I think they are probably the gossips & scandal mongers among birds & also contrivers of mischief & therefore wear the livery of his sable majesty. Across the river we saw the greenest slope which yet had refreshed our eyes. Why should some spots be greener than others, dearest husband?

return. Friday afternoon my dearest husband took me out in the boat. We went aground on the meadows, were nearly upset in a maelstrom beneath the red bridge, beating up against the rocks, & upon attempting to go ashore at the foot of the orchard, were stuck fast between the stones of the wall & narrowly escaped destruction! My sweetest love seemed discouraged at once before all these mishaps & obstacles, while I could only laugh; for I cannot feel fear; & danger I do not mind with him: but I found out a solution of this mystery when we were landed. Thou wast discouraged for my sake only, thou tender hero. Alone thou never feelest alarm. Can I love or admire thee most? I called at Mrs Prescott's after we came back & found only the blooming Miss Abba – blooming & stalwart. But I must not forget to mention that we floated on the river by a small snake, who evidently set sail by accident & was vainly attempting to keep his head & white throat above the water. My husband tried to lift him out on his paddle, but he wriggled off, not knowing friends from enemies. We passed an even row of young willows upon which were many chattering blackbirds with agitated tails. I think they are probably the gossips & scandal mongers among the birds & also contrivers of mischief & therefore wear the livery of his sable majesty Across the river we saw the greenest slope which yet had refreshed our eyes. Why should some spots be greener than others, dearest husband?

38

I had a nice pleasure last week in raking up dry leaves & twigs in the avenue. It was small calisthenics. It was a rich delight for not only I was making the avenue nice, but I was giving the new grass air & light, & was myself breathing pure nectar & tides of music from birds above & around sweetly made, with rapture-quakers gently shocked the air.

April 25th. Tuesday. Spring is advancing, sometimes with sunny days, and sometimes—as is the case now—with chill, moist, sullen ones. There is an influence in the season that makes it almost impossible for me to bring my mind down to literary employment—perhaps because several months' pretty constant work has exhausted that species of energy—perhaps because, in spring, it is more natural to labor actively than to think. But my impulse is to be idle altogether;—to lie in the sun, or wander about and look at the revival of Nature from her death-like slumber;—or to be borne down the current of the river in my boat. If I had wings I would gladly fly; yet would prefer to be wafted along by a breeze, sometimes alighting on a patch of green grass, then gently whirled away to a still sunnier spot. But here I linger upon earth, very happy, it is true, at bottom, but a good deal troubled with the sense of imbecility—one of the discomfortablest sensations, methinks, that mortal can experience—the consciousness of a blunted pen, benumbed fingers, and a mind no longer capable of a vigorous grasp. My torpidity of intellect makes me irritable.

Oh, how blest should I be, were there nothing to do! Then I would watch every inch and hair's breadth of the progress of the season, and not a leaf should put itself forth, in the vicinity of our old mansion, without my noting it. But now, with the burthen of a continual task upon me, I have not freedom of mind to

I had a new pleasure last week in raking up dry leaves & twigs in the avenue. It was rural calisthenics. It was a rich delight for not only I was making the avenue nice, but I was giving the new grass air & light, & was myself breathing pure nectar & tides of music from birds above & around sweetly mad, with rapture – quakes gently shocked the air.

April 25th. Tuesday. Spring is advancing, sometimes with sunny days, and sometimes – as is the case now – with chill, moist, sullen ones. There is an influence in the season that makes it almost impossible for me to bring my mind down to literary employment – perhaps because several months' pretty constant work has exhausted that species of energy – perhaps because, in Spring, it is more natural to labor actively than to think. But my impulse is to be idle altogether; – to lie in the sun, or wander about and look at the revival of Nature from her death-like slumber; – or to be borne down the current of the river in my boat. If I had wings I would gladly fly; yet would prefer to be wafted along by a breeze, sometimes alighting on a patch of green grass, then gently whirled away to a still sunnier spot. But here I linger upon earth, very happy, it is true, at bottom, but a good deal troubled with the sense of imbecility – one of the dismallest sensations, methinks, that mortal can experience – the consciousness of a blunted pen, benumbed fingers, and a mind no longer capable of a vigorous grasp. My torpidity of intellect makes me irritable.

Oh, how blest should I be, were there nothing to do! Then I would ↑watch↓ every inch and hair's breadth of the progress of the season; and not a leaf should put itself forth, in the vicinity of our old mansion, without my noting it. But now, with the burthen of a continual task upon me, I have not freedom of mind to make such observations. I merely see what is going on, in a very general way. The snow, which, two or three weeks ago, covered hill and valley, is now diminished to one or two solitary specks, in the visible landscape; though, doubtless, there are still heaps of it in the shady places of the woods. There have been no violent rains to carry it off; it has diminished gradually, inch by inch, and day after day; and I observed, along the roadside, that the green blades of grass had sometimes sprouted on the very edge of the snow drift, the moment that the earth was uncovered. The pastures and grass-fields have not yet a general effect of green; nor have they that cheerless brown tint, which they wear in latter autumn, when vegetation has entirely ceased. There is now a suspicion of verdure — the faint shadow of it — but not the warm reality. Some tracts, in a happy exposure — there is one such tract across the river; the carefully cultivated mowing-field in front of an old red homestead — such patches of land wear a beautiful and tender green, which no other season will equal; because, let the grass be green as it may hereafter, it will not be so set off by surrounding barrenness. The trees, in our orchard and elsewhere, have as yet no leaves; yet, to the most careless eye, they appear full of life and vegetable blood. It seems as if, by one magic touch, they might instantaneously put forth all their foliage, and that the wind, which now sighs through their naked branches, might all at once find itself impeded by innumerable leaves. This sudden development would be scarcely more wonderful than the gleam of verdure which often brightens in a moment, as it were, along the slope of a bank, or roadside; it is like a gleam of sunlight. A moment ago, it was brown, like the rest of the scenery; look again, and there is an apparition of green grass. The Spring, no doubt, comes onward with fleeter footsteps, because Winter has lingered so long, that, at best, she can hardly retrieve half the allotted term of her reign.

The river, this season, has encroached farther on the land than it has been known to do for twenty years past. It has formed, along its course, a succession of lakes, with a cur-

make such observations. I merely see what is going on, in a very general way. The snow, which, two or three weeks ago, covered hill and valley, is now diminished to one or two solitary specks, in the visible landscape; though, doubtless, there ↑are↓ still heaps of it in the shady places of the woods. There have been no violent rains to carry it off; it has diminished gradually, inch by inch, and day after day; and I observed, along the roadside, that the green blades of grass had sometimes sprouted on the very edge of the snow drift, the moment that the earth was uncovered. The pastures and grass-fields have not yet a general effect of green; nor have they that cheerless brown tint, which they wear in latter autumn, when vegetation has entirely ceased. There is now a suspicion of verdure – the faint shadow of it – but not the warm reality. Some tracts, in a happy exposure – there is one such tract across the river; the carefully cultivated mowing-field in front of an old red homestead – such patches of land wear a beautiful and tender green, which no other season will equal; because, let the grass be green as it may hereafter, it will not be so set off by surrounding barrenness. The trees, in our orchard and elsewhere, have as yet no leaves; yet, to the most careless eye, they appear full of life and vegetable blood. It seems as if, by one magic touch, they might instantaneously put forth all their foliage, and that the wind, which now sighs through their naked branches, might all at once find itself impeded by innumerable leaves. This sudden development would be scarcely more wonderful than the gleam of verdure which often brightens in a moment, as it were, along the slope of a bank, or roadside; it is like a gleam of sunlight. A moment ago, it was brown, like the rest of the scenery; look again, and there is an apparition of green grass. The Spring, no doubt, comes onward with fleeter footsteps, because Winter has lingered so long, that, at best, she can hardly retrieve half the allotted term of her reign.

The river, this season, has encroached farther on the land than it has been known to do for twenty years past. It has formed, along its course, a succession of lakes, with a cur-

39

out through the midst. My boat has lain at the bottom of the orchard, in very convenient proximity to the house. It has borne me over stone-fences; and a few days ago, Ellery Channing and I passed through a pair of bars into the great northern road, along which we paddled a considerable distance. The trees have a singular appearance in the midst of waters; the curtailment of their trunks quite destroys the proportions of the whole tree; and we become conscious of a regularity and propriety in the forms of Nature, by the effect of this abbreviation. The waters are now subsiding, but gradually; — islands become annexed to the mainland, and other islands emerge from the flood, and will soon, likewise, be connected with the continent. We have seen, on a small scale, the process of the deluge, and can now witness that of the reappearance of the earth.

Crows visited us, long before the snow was off; they seem mostly to have departed now; or else to have betaken themselves to remote depths of the woods, which they haunt all summer long. Ducks have come in considerable numbers, and many sportsmen went in pursuit of them, along the river; but they also have now made themselves scarce. Gulls come up from seaward, and soar high overhead, flapping their broad wings in the upper sunshine. They are among the most picturesque birds that I am acquainted with — indeed, quite the most so — because the manner of their flight makes them almost stationary parts of a landscape; the imagination has time to rest upon them — they have not flitted away in a moment. You go up among the clouds, and lay hold of these soaring gulls, and repose with them upon the sustaining atmosphere. The smaller birds — the birds that build their nests in our trees, and sing for us at morning-red, — I leave to my wife to describe. She is bird-like in many things, and loves them as if they were her own kindred. But I must mention the great companies of blackbirds — more than the famous "four and twenty", who were baked in a pie — that congregate in the tops of contiguous trees, and vociferate with all the

rent through the midst. My boat has lain at the bottom of the orchard, in very convenient proximity to the house. It has borne me over stone-fences; and a few days ago, Ellery Channing and I passed through a pair of bars into the great northern road, along which we paddled a considerable distance. The trees have a singular appearance in the midst of waters; the curtailment of their trunks quite destroys the proportions of the whole tree; and we become conscious of a regularity and propriety in the forms of Nature, by the effect of this abbreviation. The waters are now subsiding, but gradually; – islands become annexed to the mainland, and other islands emerge from the flood, and will soon, likewise, be connected with the continent. We have seen, on a small scale, the process of the deluge, and can now witness that of the reappearance of the earth.

Crows visited us, long before the snow was off; they seem mostly to have departed now; or else to have betaken themselves to remote depths of the woods, which they haunt all summer long. Ducks have come in considerable numbers, and many sportsmen wait in pursuit of them, along the river; but they also have now made themselves scarce. Gulls come up from seaward, and soar high overhead, flapping their broad wings in the upper sunshine. They are among the most picturesque birds that I am acquainted with – indeed, quite the most so – because the manner of their flight makes them almost stationary parts of a landscape; the imagination has time to rest upon them – they have not flitted away in a moment. You go up among the clouds, and lay hold of these soaring gulls, and repose with them upon the sustaining atmosphere. The smaller birds – the birds that build their nests in our trees, and sing for us at morning-red- I leave to my wife to describe. She is birdlike in many things, and loves them as if they were her own kindred. But I must mention the great companies of blackbirds – more than the famous 'four-and twenty', who were baked in a pie – that congregate in the tops of contiguous trees, and vociferate with all the clamor of a turbulent political meeting. Politics must certainly be the occasion of such a tumultuous debate; but still there is a melody in each individual utterance, and a harmony in the general effect. Mr. Thoreau tells me that these noisy assemblages consist of three different species of black-birds — one of them the cow-blackbird — but I forget the other two. Robins have been long among us; and swallows have more recently arrived.

April 26th Wednesday. Here is another misty day, muffling the sun. The lilac-shrubs, under my study-window, are almost in leaf; in two or three days more, I may put forth my hand and pluck a green bough. These lilacs appear to be very aged, and have lost the luxuriant foliage of their prime. Old age has a singular aspect in lilacs, rose-bushes, and other ornamental shrubs; it seems as if such things, as they grow only for beauty, ought to flourish in immortal youth, or, at least, to die before their decrepitude. They are trees of Paradise, and therefore not naturally subject to decay, but have lost their birthright by being transplanted hither. But there is a kind of ludicrous unfitness in the idea of a venerable rose-bush; and there is something analogous to this in human life. Persons who can only be graceful and ornamental — who can give the world nothing but flowers — should die young, and never be seen with grey hair and wrinkles, any more than the flower-shrubs with mossy bark and scanty foliage, like the lilacs under my window. Not that beauty is not worthy of immortality — nothing else, indeed, is worthy of it — and thence, perhaps, the sense of impropriety, when we see it triumphed over by time. Apple-trees, on the other hand, grow old without reproach; let them live as long as they may, and contort themselves in whatever fashion they please, they are still respectable, even if they afford us only an apple or two in a season, or none at all. Human flower-shrubs, if they will grow old on earth, should, beside their lovely blossoms, bear some kind of fruit that will satisfy earthly appetites; else men will not be satisfied that the moss should gather on them.

Winter and Spring are now struggling for the mastery in my study; and I yield somewhat to each, and wholly to neither. The

clamor of a turbulent political meeting. Politics must certainly be the occasion of such a tumultuous debate; but still there is a melody in each individual utterance, and a harmony in the general effect. Mr. Thoreau tells me that these noisy assemblages consist of three different species of black-birds – one of them the crow-blackbird – but I forget the other two. Robins have been long among us; and swallows have more recently arrived.

April 26th Wednesday. Here is another misty day, muffling the sun. The lilac-shrubs, under my study-window, are almost in leaf; in two or three days more, I may put forth my hand and pluck a green bough. These lilacs appear to be very aged, and have lost the luxuriant foliage of their prime. Old age has a singular aspect in lilacs, rose-bushes, and other ornamental shrubs; it seems as if such things, as they grow only for beauty, ought to flourish in immortal youth, or, at least, to die before their decrepitude. They are trees of Paradise, and therefore not naturally subject to decay, but have lost their birthright by being transplanted hither. But there is a kind of ludicrous unfitness in the idea of a venerable rose-bush; and there is something analogous to this in human life. Persons who can only be graceful and ornamental – who can give the world nothing but flowers – should die young, and never be seen with grey hairs and wrinkles, any more than the flower-shrubs with mossy bark and scanty foliage, like the lilacs under my window. Not that beauty is not worthy of immortality – nothing else, indeed, is worthy of it – and thence, perhaps, the sense of impropriety, when we see it triumphed over by time. Apple-trees, on the other hand, grow old without reproach; let them live as long as they may, and contort themselves in whatever fashion they please, they are still respectable, even if they afford us only an apple or two in a season, or none at all. Human flower-shrubs, if they will grow old on earth, should, beside their lovely blossoms, bear some kind of fruit that will satisfy earthly appetites; else men will not be satisfied that the moss should gather on them.

Winter and spring are now struggling for the mastery in my study; and I yield somewhat to each, and wholly to neither. The window is open; and there is a fire in the stove. The day when the window is first thrown open should be an epoch in the year; but I have forgotten to record it. Seventy or eighty springs have visited this old house; and sixty of them found old Dr. Ripley here—not always old, it is true, but gradually getting wrinkles and gray hairs, and looking more and more like the picture of winter; but he was no flower-shrub, but one of those fruit-trees, or timber-trees, that acquire a grace with their old age. Last Spring found the house solitary, for the first time since it was built; and now again she peeps into our open windows, and finds new faces here. Methinks my little wife is twin-sister of the Spring; so they should greet one another tenderly; for they both are fresh and dewy, both full of hope and cheerfulness, both have bird-voices always singing out of their hearts, both are sometimes overcast with flitting mists, which only make the flowers bloom brighter; and both have a power to renew and re-create the weary spirit. I have married the Spring!—I am husband to the month of May!

It is remarkable how much uncleanness Winter brings with it, or leaves behind it. My dearest wife has almost toiled herself to death with endeavors to purify her empire within the house; and the yard, garden, and avenue, which should be my department, require a still greater amount of labor. The avenue is strewn with withered leaves—the whole crop, apparently, of last year, some of which my wife has raked into heaps, intending to make a bonfire of them. I wonder what becomes of them, when there is no "neat-handed Phillis" to sweep them away. There are quantities of decayed branches, which one tempest after another has flung down, black and rotten. In the garden are the old cabbages, which we did not think worth gathering, last autumn; and the dry bean-vines, and the withered stalks of the asparagus bed;—in short, all the wrecks of the departed year—her mouldering relics—her dry bones. It is a pity that the world cannot be really made over anew, every Spring. Then in the yard, there are the piles of fire-wood, which I ought to have sawed and

window is open; and there is a fire in the stove. The day when the window is first thrown open should be an epoch in the year; but I have forgotten to record it. Seventy or eighty springs have visited this old house; and sixty of them found old Dr. Ripley here – not always old, it is true, but gradually getting wrinkles and gray hairs, and looking more and more the picture of winter; but he was no flower-shrub, but one of those fruit trees, or timber trees, that acquire a grace with their old age. Last Spring found the house solitary, for the first time since it was built; and now again she peeps into our open windows, and finds new faces here. Methinks my little wife is twin-sister of the Spring; so they should greet one another tenderly; for they both are fresh and dewy, both full of hope and cheerfulness, both have bird-voices always singing out of their hearts, both are sometimes overcast with flitting mists, which only make the flowers bloom brighter; and both have a power to renew and re-create the weary spirit. I have married the Spring! – I am husband to the month of May!

It is remarkable how much uncleanness Winter brings with it, or leaves behind it. My dearest wife has almost toiled herself to death with endeavors to purify her empire within the house; and the yard, garden, and avenue, which should be my department, require a still greater amount of labor. The avenue is strewed with withered leaves – the whole crop, apparently, of last year, some of which my wife has raked into heaps, intending to make a bonfire of them. I wonder what becomes of them, when there is no 'neat-handed Phillis' to sweep them away. There are quantities of decayed branches, which one tempest after another has flung down, black and rotten. In the garden, are the old cabbages, which we did not think worth gathering, last Autumn; and the dry bean-vines, and the withered stalks of the asparagus bed; – in short, all the wrecks of the departed year – her mouldering relics – her dry bones. It is a pity that the world cannot be really made over anew, every spring. Then in the yard, there are the piles of fire-wood, which I ought to have sawed and thrown into the shed, long since, but which will cumber the earth, I fear, till June at least. Quantities of chips are strewn about, and on removing them, we find the yellow stalks of grass sprouting underneath. Nature does her best to beautify this disarray. The grass springs up most industriously, especially in sheltered and sunny angles of the buildings, or round the door-steps—a locality which seems particularly favorable to its growth; for it is already high enough to bend over, and wave in the wind. I was surprised to observe that some weeds—especially a plant that stains the fingers with its yellow juice—had lived, and retained their freshness and sap as perfectly as in summer—through all the frosts and snows of last winter. I saw them, the last green thing in the Autumn, and here they are again, the first in the spring.

April 27th. Thursday. I took a walk into the fields, and round our opposite hill, yesterday noon, but made no very remarkable observations. The frogs have begun their concerts, though not as yet with a full choir. I found no violets nor anemones, nor anything in the likeness of a flower, though I looked carefully along the shelter of the stone-walls, and in all spots apparently propitious. I ascended the hill, and had a wide prospect of the swollen river, extending around me in a semicircle of three or four miles, and rendering the view much finer than in summer, had there only been foliage. It seemed like the formation of a new world; for islands were everywhere emerging, and capes extending forth into the flood; and these tracts, which were thus won from the watery empire, were among the greenest in the landscape. The moment the deluge leaves them, Nature asserts them as her property by covering them with verdure; or perhaps the grass had been growing under the water. On the hill-top, where I stood, the grass had scarcely begun to sprout; and I observed that even those tracts, which looked greenest at a distance, were but scantily grass-covered when I actually reached them. It was hope that painted them so bright.

Last evening, we saw a bright light on the river, betokening that a boat's party were engaged in spearing fish. It looked like a descended star—like red Mars—and as the water was per-

thrown into the shed, long since, but which will cumber the earth, I fear, till June at least. Quantities of chips are strewn about; and on removing them, we find the yellow stalks of grass sprouting underneath. Nature does her best to beautify this disarray. The grass springs up most industriously, especially in sheltered and sunny angles of the buildings, or round the door-steps – a locality which seems particularly favorable to its growth; for it is already high enough to bend over, and wave in the wind. I was surprised to observe that some weeds – especially a plant that stains the fingers with its yellow juice – had lived, and retained their freshness and sap as perfectly as in summer – through all the frosts and snows of last winter. I saw them, the last green thing in the Autumn, and here they are again, the first in the spring.

April 27th. Thursday. I took a walk into the fields, and round our opposite hill, yesterday noon, but made no very remarkable observations. The frogs have begun their concerts, though not as yet with a full choir. I found no violets nor anemones, nor anything in the likeness of a flower, though I looked carefully along the shelter of the stone-walls, and in all spots apparently propitious. I ascended the hill, and had a wide prospect of the swollen river, extending around me in a semicircle of three or four miles, and rendering the view much finer than in summer, had there only been foliage. It seemed like the formation of a new world; for islands were everywhere emerging, and capes extending forth into the flood; and these tracts, which were thus won from the watery empire, were among the greenest in the landscape. The moment the deluge leaves them, Nature asserts them as her property by covering them with verdure; or perhaps the grass had been growing under the water. On the hill-top, where I stood, the grass had scarcely begun to sprout; and I observed that even those tracts, which looked greenest at a distance, were but scantily grass-covered when I actually reached them. It was hope that painted them so bright.

Last evening, we saw a bright light on the river, betokening that a boat's party were engaged in spearing a fish. It looked like a descended star – like red Mars – and as the water was per-

41

fectly smooth, its gleam was reflected downward into the depths. It is a very picturesque sight. After we went to bed, in the deep quiet of the night, we suddenly heard the light and lively note of a bird, from a neighboring tree—a real song, such as those which greet the purple dawn, or mingle with the yellow sunshine. What could the little bird mean by pouring it forth at midnight? Probably the note gushed out from the midst of a dream in which he fancied himself in Paradise with his mate; and suddenly awaking, he found himself on a cold, leafless bough, with a New-England mist penetrating through his feathers. That was a sad exchange of imagination for reality; but if he found his mate beside him, all was well.

This is another misty morning, ungenial in aspect, but kinder than it looks; for it paints the hills and valleys with a richer brush than the sunshine could. There is more verdure now than when I looked out of the window an hour ago. The willow tree, opposite my study window, is ready to put forth its leaves. There are some objections to willows; it is not a dry and cleanly tree—it impresses me with an association of sliminess; and no trees, I think, are perfectly satisfactory which have not a firm and hard texture of trunk and branches. But the willow is almost the earliest to put forth its leaves, and the last to scatter them on the ground; and during the whole winter its yellow twigs give it a sunny aspect, which is not without a cheering influence, in a proper point of view. Our old house would lose much, were the willow to be cut down, with its golden crown over the roof in winter, and its heap of summer verdure. The present Mr Ripley planted it, fifty years ago, or thereabouts.

I bought a load of manure, yesterday, for six dollars, and shall soon begin gardening. There is, besides, an abominable quantity of labor to be done, or which ought to be done—principally in clearing away the last year's rubbish from the garden, yard, and orchard. I hate all labor, but less that of the hands than of the head.

fectly smooth, its gleam was reflected downward into the depths. It is a very picturesque sight. After we went to bed, in the deep quiet of the night, we suddenly heard the light and lively note of a bird, from a neighboring tree – a real song, such as those which greet the purple dawn, or mingle with the yellow sunshine. What could the little bird mean by pouring it forth at midnight? Probably the note gushed out from the midst of a dream, in which he fancied himself in Paradise with his mate; and suddenly awaking, he found himself on a cold, leafless bough, with a New-England mist penetrating through his feathers. That was a sad exchange of imagination for reality; but if he found his mate beside him, all was well.

This is another misty morning, ungenial in aspect, but kinder than it looks; for it paints the hills and valleys with a richer brush than the sunshine could. There is more verdure now than when I looked out of the window an hour ago. The willow-tree, opposite my study-window, is ready to put forth its leaves. There are some objections to willows; it is not a dry and cleanly tree – it impresses me with an association of sliminess; and no trees, I think, are perfectly satisfactory which have not a firm and hard texture of trunk and branches. But the willow is almost the earliest to put forth its leaves, and the last to scatter them on the ground; and during the whole winter its yellow twigs give it a sunny aspect, which is not without a cheering influence, in a proper point of view. Our old house would lose much, were this willow to be cut down, with its golden crown over the roof in winter, and its heap of summer verdure. The present Mr. Ripley planted it, fifty years ago, or thereabouts.

I bought a load of manure, yesterday, for six dollars, and shall soon begin gardening. There is, besides, an abominable quantity of labor to be done, or which ought to be done – principally in clearing away the last year's rubbish from the garden, yard, and orchard. I hate all labor, but less that of the hands than of the head.

May 9th Tuesday. Dearest husband, thou shouldst not have to labour, especially with the hands, & thou hatest it rightfully. Thou art a seraph come to observe Nature & men in a still repose, without being obliged to exert thyself in reproduction or in clearing away old rubbish. Apollo among his herds could not have looked so out of place as thou with saw & axe & rake in hand. The flower of Time should only unfold. It should be put to no use. I wish I could be Midas long enough to turn into sufficient gold for thy life's sustenance & embellishment, whatever I touch. But wae's me! I do nothing but love thee. This thou couldst not do without, but I wish more could be added.

Last Thursday 4th I took the first walk into the woods with my Phoebus Apollo. There was no sunshine & the wind was determinately east & strong so that we were chilled to our hearts, but not through those warm tropics of love; for no wind could chill the airs there. We walked along Peter's path & found no flowers. We visited the ruined cottage & moralized a little over its hearth stone & then descended into a vale by the water, entirely overgrown with skunk cabbages, a disgusting vegetable. We wound along an uncleared path for some distance & then found we must return upon our steps. We continued to follow the woodland aisle & I was very much attracted by the pale green moss that hung from the trees like long hoary hair. It was beautiful to examine, like the sea moss & I gathered some to make a wreath. The ground was flaked with the white everlasting, springing up in great abundance

May 9th. Tuesday. Dearest husband, thou shouldst not have to labour, especially with the hands, & thou hatest it rightfully. Thou art a seraph come to observe Nature & men in a still repose, without being *obliged* to exert thyself in reproduction or in clearing away old rubbish. Apollo among his herds could not have looked so out of place as thou with saw & axe & rake in hand. The Flower of Time should only unfold. It should be put to no Use. I wish I could be Midas long enough to turn into sufficient gold for thy life's sustenance & embellishment, whatever I touch. But waes me! I do nothing but love thee. This thou couldst not do without, but I wish more could be added.

Last Thursday 4.th I took the first walk into the woods with my Phoebus Apollo. There was no sunshine & the wind was determinately east & strong so that we were chilled *to* our hearts, but not *through* those warm tropics of love; for no wind could chill the airs there.

We walked along Peter's path & found no flowers. We visited the ruined cottage & moralized a little over its hearthstone & then descended into a vale by the water, entirely overgrown with skunk cabbages, a disgusting vegetable. We wound along an uncleared path for some distance & then found we must return upon our steps. We continued to follow the woodland aisle & I was very much attracted by the pale green moss that hung from the trees like long hoary hair. It was beautiful to examine, like the sea moss – & I gathered some to make a wreath. The ground was flaked with the white everlasting, springing up in great abundance every where as if to write Immortality all over the earth. My darling husband finally saw a cliff in the wood & we went in & climbed it, & there we found were many columbine plants, but no sign yet of a flower. The maple trees were in bloom, showing that beautiful scarlet blossom before the leaf comes. Coming home we were arrested by an orchestra of blackbirds upon a leafless tree. My opinion of these birds has changed very much upon farther acquaintance. They have evidently settled all their domestic & political affairs & left off gossip, & now in bands of forties & fifties they perform wonderful symphonies. One might shut his eyes & dream he had caught the music of the spheres in his ear, or that through the gate of Heaven careless-ly left open, a mingled strain of sackbut psaltery, dulcimer & harp touched by angels, had strayed to Earth to reclaim man to harmony. The swallows seemed to have arrived that day, for just beyond the swan-necked elms there were multitudes swooping through the air with marvellous velocity – almost too rapid their motion is for perfect grace, but they appear to be made to remain on the wing & never to alight. Once in a while, when one cleaves the air without fluttering its wings, it is eminently beautiful, & one of these reposeful individuals moved directly over our heads & very low down, so that we could see it to great advantage. In their aerial dance they passed & repassed each other in endless mazes, but never touched or became entangled any more.

every where as if to write Immortality all over the earth. My darling husband finally saw a cliff in the wood & we went in & climbed it, & there we found were many columbine plants, but no sign yet of a flower. The maple trees were in bloom, showing that beautiful scarlet blossom before the leaf comes. Coming home we were arrested by an orchestra of blackbirds upon a leafless tree. My opinion of these birds has changed very much upon farther acquaintance. They have evidently settled all their domestic & political affairs & left off gossip, & now in bands of forties & fifties they perform wonderful symphonies. One might shut his eyes & dream he had caught the music of the spheres in his ear, or that through the gate of Heaven – careless-ly left open, a mingled strain of sackbut, psaltery, dulcimer & harp touched by angels, had strayed to Earth to reclaim man to harmony. The swallows seemed to have arrived that day; for just beyond the swan-necked elms there were multitudes swooping through the air with marvelous velocity – almost too rapid their motion is for perfect grace, but they appear to be made to remain on the wing & never to alight. Once in a while, when one cleaves the air without fluttering its wings, it is eminently beautiful, & one of these reposeful individuals moved directly over our heads & very low down, so that we could see it to great advantage. In their aerial dance they passed & repassed each other in endless mazes, but never touched or became entangled any more

than the planets in their orbits.
The next afternoon 5th May, Friday we walked to the wood crowned hill. Barrett's Hill. We as yet had seen no flowers, but I felt sure that some lowly violets were blooming on that sunny declivity. So as we strayed along earnestly looking, I finally caught the blue eye of the first violet!! I threw myself down & kissed the precious little stranger. A few others grew around. Then we climbed the hill & sat quietly beneath the pine trees a short time. Descending again what should I behold beneath some bushes but a fair white anemone, bending its lily head like an ivory bell. I shouted aloud & we found more & more till finally we gathered a very large bunch of these most graceful of flowers. So we returned very rich that memorable day.
On Saturday 6th we went to Sleepy Hollow by the way of the village & by Cesar's castle. On a hill at the right entering the Hollow we found a few of the first Pedate violets, tall & paler than the others. But after leaving Sleepy Hollow, & crossing a narrow brook, thousands of wood anemones greeted our vision on the bank, & the white violet in purple brocade. I sat down & gathered as many as I could hold. Miss Martha Prescott & her lover Mr John Keyes sat on the hill-top meanwhile. On this day we had a visit from Ellery Channing who had arrived to take up his residence in Concord.
On Saturday 7th Mr Lane & Mr Saml Larned called to see us. I liked Mr Lane very much. He was very genial & agreeable & full of

than the planets in their orbits.

The next afternoon 5th May, Friday we walked to the wood crowned hill, Barrett's Hill. We as yet had seen no flower, but I felt sure that some lowly violets were blooming on that sunny declivity. So as we strayed along earnestly looking, I finally caught the blue eye of the first violet! I threw myself down & kissed the precious little stranger. A few others grew around. Then we climbed the hill & sat quietly beneath the pine trees a short time. Descending again what should I behold beneath some bushes but a fair white anemone, bending its lily head like an ivory bell. I shouted aloud & we found more & more till finally we gathered as very large bunch of these most graceful of flowers. So we returned very rich that memorable day.

On Saturday 6th. we went to Sleepy Hollow by the way of the village & by Cesar's castle. On a hill at the right entering the Hollow we found a few of the first Pedate violets, tall & paler than the others. But after leaving Sleepy Hollow, & crossing a narrow brook, thousands of wood anemones greeted our vision on the bank, & the white violet in purple brocade. I sat down & gathered as many as I could hold. Miss Martha Prescott & her lover Mr John Keyes sat on the hill-top meanwhile. On this day we had a visit from Ellery Channing who had arrived to take up his residence in Concord.

On Saturday 7.th. Mr Lane & Mr Samuel Larned called to see us. I liked Mr Lane very much. He was very genial & agreable & full of

45

seate, & decidedly Scotty in countenance - very much altered since I saw him last autumn. Mr L. I thought very handsome, of the picturesque, tropical beauty. Ellery came to tea in the afternoon, to escape a great talk at Mr Emerson's between a Mr Bennett Mr Lane &c. And in the evening we were delighted to receive George Bradford, as pure a spirit as God ever made. The next morning he called again to take a letter for me to Mother. That evening 8th Monday Father arrived, his first visit to us since our marriage. He stayed till Saturday morning 13th. We did not walk while he was here, because I did not like to leave him, but Saturday afternoon we went to a rocky field on the banks of the river near the battle-ground, where my dearest husband had discovered some Columbine plants. & behold it was scarlet for her roost. I never saw so many together. Pedate violets also gave a celestial aspect to all the nooks & sheltered places, & the ground was a beautiful mosaic of [illegible], darker blue violets, houstonias & everlasting. About the first of May the cherry trees began to bloom & now (19th) pear, apple & peach are all in full glory. I never before saw pear trees in blossom. Two in our large orchard are very superb. They look like fountains of flower-wreaths, throwing out their long branches in noble curves. & snowy white bloom. The apple looks like a <u>heap</u> of flowers rather, because its twigs & branches are so uneven & jagged

sense, & decidedly Alcotty in countenance – very much altered since I saw him last autumn. Mr L. I thought very handsome, of the picturesque, tropical beauty. Ellery came to tea in the afternoon, to escape a great talk at Mr Emerson's between a Mr Bennett Mr Lane &c. And in the evening we were delighted to recieve George Bradford, as pure a spirit as GOD ever made. The next morning he called again to take a letter for me to Mother. That evening 8th Monday Father arrived, his first visit to us since our marriage. He stayed till Saturday morning 13th We did not walk while he was here, because I did not like to leave him; but Saturday afternoon we went to a rocky field on the banks of the river near the battleground, where my dearest husband had discovered some columbine plants – & behold it was scarlet for harvest. I never saw so many together. Pedate violets also gave a celestial aspect to all the nooks & sheltered places, & the ground was a beautiful mosaic of lovelier, darker blue violets, housatonias & everlasting. About the first of May the cherry trees began to bloom & now (19th) pear, apple & peach are all in full glory. I never before saw pear trees in blossom. Two in our large orchard are very superb. They look like fountains of flower-wreaths, throwing out their long branches in noble curves – & snowy white blooms. The apple looks like a heap of flowers rather, because its twigs & branches are so uneven & jagged.

The air is filled with the fragrance from these
myriad chalices. For a day or two I observe
that the petals are falling constantly, a
summer snow storm, & the flakes do not melt
but cover the ground like little white moons.
The venerable lilacs round two sides of our old
abbey are beginning to unfold their buds—
very slowly. There has been no rain for nearly
a fortnight, & vegetation seems to be retarded
on that account. We have taken note
of the arrival of several birds. One morning
I heard a sweet chattering as of greetings & loving
interchange that struck my ear as new sounds
& looking from the window, behold the
trees & lilac bushes & fence adorned with
living turquoises, of celestial blue— in the
shape of blue birds. They had evidently just
arrived. It was in April. Another day notes
clear as diamond, rich as gold actually made
my heart throb with a noble emotion—
I looked out, but though I constantly heard
the lordly tone, the cause seemed hidden
like the god in Memnon's statue. Finally
however, a minute sunlet, a sunset abridged
darted through the trees, & I recognized the
splendid ~~aureole~~ oriole. He had arrived that day.
So the sweet little yellow birds alighted like
bits of sunshine all at once & uttered their
pleasant warble.

One morning this week I went to see
Mrs Emerson, & found her very feeble & pale.
They will have no company this summer so
that she can have rest. & I am truly thankful.
She intends putting herself under Homeopathic
treatment & now I expect she will get well.

The air is filled with the fragrance from these myriad chalices. For a day or two I observe that the petals are falling constantly, a summer snow storm, & the flakes do not melt but cover the ground like little white moons. The venerable lilacs round two sides of our old Abbey are beginning to unfold their buds – very slowly. There has been no rain for nearly a fortnight, & vegetation seems to be retarded on that account. We have taken note of the arrival of several birds. One morning I heard a sweet chattering as of greetings & loving interchange that struck my ear as new sounds & looking from the window, behold the trees & lilac bushes & fence adorned with living turquoises, of celestial blue – in the shape of blue birds. They had evidently just arrived. It was in April. Another day notes clear as a diamond, rich as gold actually made my heart throb with a noble emotion – I looked out, but though I constantly heard the lordly tone, the cause seemed hidden like the god in Mammon's statue. Finally however, a minute sunset, a sunset abridged, darted through the trees, & I recognized the splendid aureole ↑oriole↓. He had arrived that day. So the sweet little yellow birds alighted like bits of sunshine all at once & uttered their pleasant warble.

One morning this week I went to see Mrs Emerson & found her very feeble & pale. They will have no company this summer so that she can have rest. I am truly thankful. She intends putting herself under Homeopathic treatment & now I expect she will get well.

On Thursday afternoon my beloved went with
me to call on Ellen & Ellery Channing at
their funny little red house. Ellen received us
at the door. She is enchanted with her home
entirely & looked very happy, though weary, for
she is not quite arranged. My dear husband
went out to see the chief of the domain, who
was at work on his acres, & as I saw him
from the window, very much of a brownie in
his appearance. I was delighted with the view
from Ellen's chamber window. A broad, level,
tranquil plain skirted by low hills & woods.
Its effect was most reposeful & sweet.
Ellen thought it supereminent in loveliness.
In that direction they have the unobstructed
rising sun. From the other chamber they have
the setting sun & Mr Emerson's house.
Ellen said she had seen no columbines nor
Thalictroides Anemones! & as we purposed
to go home through the woods, I determined
to gather her some. My dearest love had
discovered a bank of the last mentioned, &
we came that way. First we saw hundreds
of pedate violets, & new sweet fern, which
we plucked for its sweetness. It was a
dim, half shining afternoon, without wind,
& delightful for sauntering. We could not
find the grand path which we aimed
at, but became entangled in an open
wood, & finally retraced our steps.
Then we found ourselves on quite an eminence
from which was a fine view. A friendly
hospitable broad stump invited us to sit
& together we accepted the invitation.
Thence we saw the village & Caesar's house
& lovely slopes of fresh new grass &

On Thursday afternoon my beloved went with me to call on Ellen & Ellery Channing at their funny little red house. Ellen recieved us at the door. She is enchanted with her home entirely & looked very happy, though weary, for she is not quite arranged. My dear husband went out to see the chief of the domain, who was at work on his acre, & as I saw him from the window, very much of a brownie in his appearance. I was delighted with the view from Ellen's chamber window. A broad, level, tranquil plain skirted by low hills & woods. Its effect was most reposeful & sweet – Ellen thought supereminent in loveliness. In that direction they have the unobstructed rising sun. From the other chamber they have the setting sun & Mr Emerson's house. Ellen said she had seen no columbines nor Thalectroides anemones! & as we purposed to go home through the woods, I determined to gather her some. My dearest love had discovered a bank of the last mentioned, & we came that way. First we saw hundreds of pedate violets, & new sweet fern, which we plucked for its sweetness. It was a dim, half shining afternoon, without wind, & delightful for sauntering. We could not find the grand path which we arrived at, but became entangled in an open wood, & finally retraced our steps. Then we found ourselves on quite an eminence from which was a fine view. A friendly hospitable broad stump invited us to sit & together we accepted the invitation. Thence we saw the village & Cesar's tower & lovely slopes of fresh new grass &

trees of tender foliage. I was particularly struck with the beauty of the young oaks. Their new leaves were of crimson & pale yellow, & beautiful blossoms - or aments of red hung beneath little canopies of separate bunches of leaves in this way. The new foliage of the birches also was very beautiful the leaves so exquisitely shaped, & highly polished & their slender peduncles giving them such an airy movement. They look like little pyramids on the wing, in ethereal dance. While we sat on the good old stump, a mocking bird entertained us by means of his single throat, with the notes of all the birds & sounds in Nature, even the frog's croak. He sat alone on a tree & amused himself apparently as well as us. Finally we descended the hill & went through Sleepy Hollow & visited the bank of Thalectroides. I never saw so many. I sat down in the midst & gathered till I thought gloomy Dis would gather me. My husband also had as many as his hand could clasp. When we gave up the harvesting, we met an apple tree with a broken arm, all in bloom, & we purloined the rosy blossoms, seeing that the apples could not ripen. Then we climbed the hill opposite our house, & came home. I put the Thalects. & all the Columbines I had into a tin basket & sent them to Ellen that night, greatly to her joy, as she said by Mary. I thought of my mother a great deal & wished they were going to her, & at last concluded I could not rest satisfied unless

trees of tender foliage. I was particularly struck with the beauty of the young oaks. Their new leaves were of crimson & pale yellow, & beautiful blossoms – or amounts of red hung beneath little canopies of separate branches of leaves in this way. The new foliage of the birches also was very beautiful – the leaves so exquisitely shaped, & highly polished & their slender pedanceles giving them such an airy movement. They look like ↑little↓ pyramids on the wing, in etherial dance. While we sat on the good old stump, a mocking bird entertained us by means of his single throat, with the notes of all the birds & sounds in Nature, even the frog's croak. He sat alone on a tree & amused himself apparently as well as us. Finally we descended the hill & went through Sleepy Hollow & visited the bank of Thalectroides. I never saw so many. I sat down in the midst & gathered till I thought gloomy Dis would gather me. My husband also had as many as his hand could clasp. When we gave up the harvesting, we met an apple tree with a broken arm, all in bloom, & we purloined the rosy blossoms, seeing that the apples could not ripen. Then we climbed the hill opposite our house, & came home. I put the Thalces. & all the columbines I had into a tin basket & sent them to Ellen that night, greatly to her joy, as she said by Mary. I thought of my mother a great deal & wished they were going to her, & at last concluded I could not rest satisfied unless

I sent her as splendid a collection. 45
So after dinner yesterday my lord & I went to the columbine rock & found still more than before & a few pedate violets. My love intended to go to the Thalectrides' bank & gather fresh ones but just as we arrived at the avenue, they announced that Ellery Channing had come to fish, & so there was an end of our plan. This morning, (Saturday 19th) I rose betimes, & with exceeding joy & satisfaction packed up columbines, wood-anemones & Thalectrides, & white & pedate violets, & Arethusas, which Mary Hosmer brought me, & Mary Bryan carried them to the stage.

This week I have planted my flower garden. It is the first time I ever put any seeds into the earth. Miss Catharine Barrett, Mrs Emerson & Louisa Hawthorne had supplied me. I have China asters, Gilly Flower, Amaranths gold & white, Lavateras, Columbines, Escholchia, Lychnis, Musk plant, Marble Peas, Foxgloves, white & purple Candytufts, dahlias, nasturtiums, morning glories, snapdragons, mourning brides, & many others. My dear husband has also about finished planting his garden this week. For more than a fortnight we have had asparagus on the table. He has planted potatoes, corn, squashes, peas, beans, tomatos, cucumbers, melons, turnips, carrots, rad#ishes, sweet herbs.

I find that the humming bird, that most exquisite of God's creations, frequents the cherry trees, & upon those near our chamber window I have often seen them this month. They are a type of fine fancy, & perhaps suggested Ariel to the

I sent her as splendid a collection. So after dinner yesterday my lord & I went to the columbine rocks & found still more than before, & a few pedate violets. My love intended to go to the Thalectroides' bank & gather fresh ones but just as we arrived at the avenue, Mary announced that Ellery Channing had come to fish, & so there was an end of our plan. This morning, (Saturday 19th) I rose betimes, & with exceeding joy & satisfaction packed up columbines, wood anemones & Thalectroides & white & pedate violets, & Arethusas, which Mary Hosmer brought me, & Mary Byran carried them to the stage.

This week I have planted my flower garden. It is the first time I ever put any seeds into the earth. Miss Catharine Barret, Mrs Emerson & Louisa Hawthorne had supplied me. I have China Astors, Gilly Flower, Amaranths gold & white, Lavateras, Columbines, Scholchis, Lycnis, Musk plant, Marble Perus, Foxgloves, white & purple candytufts, dahlias, nasturtiums, morning glories, snap dragons, mourning brides, & many others. My dear husband has also about finished planting his garden this week. For more than a fortnight we have had asparagus on the table. He has planted potatoes, corn, squashes, peas, beans, tomatos, cucumbers, melons, turnips, carrots, raddishes, sweet herbs.

I find that the humming bird, that most exquisite of GOD's creations, frequents the cherry trees, & upon those near our chamber window I have often seen them this month. They are a type of fine fancy, & perhaps suggested Ariel to the imagination of Shakspeare. In form, color, motion they are perfection of beauty. If the viler & ignoble reptiles & animals respond to what is low in man & prove him fallen from his high estate, then also the humming bird proves that he is divine & of angel beauty still.

It has been an inexpressible happiness to watch the coming of Summer & Spring step by step with such a Synonyme & Harmonie of Nature as my husband. I am rejoiced I never before saw its approach. I could never have appreciated it with half a soul as I once possessed. Now it seems as if indeed we were first born & saw the world fresh from God's hand as on the morning of Creation.

May 23d Tuesday. This morning we found upon awaking that there was falling a blessed rain. It has not rained before since Mayday when it poured in the morning & cleared up in the afternoon. On that day at ½ past 11. my sister Mary was married to Mr Horace Mann, & went directly to England on board after the ceremony. This marriage was a sudden conclusion & they had but a month to prepare for a six months tour in Europe. It was a most happy event in my life as well as the crowning joy of hers, for I never could be reconciled to her hard labor for others, & her sad countenance. Now she is entirely content & may GOD be praised & bless her forever. It is about ten o'clock & the rain has ceased I hope only for a few hours, for the earth cannot yet have quenched her thirst. The aspect of every green thing is superb now, & how the new seeds & young

imagination of Shakspeare. In form, color, motion they are perfection of beauty. If the viler & ignoble reptiles & animals respond to what is low in man & prove him fallen from his high estate, then also the humming bird proves that he is divine & of angel beauty still.

It has been an inexpressible happiness to watch the coming of summer & spring step by step with such a synonym & harmonic of Nature as my husband. I am rejoiced. I never before saw its approach. I could never have appreciated it with half a soul as I once possessed. Now it seems as if indeed we were first born & saw the world fresh from GOD's hand as on the morning of Creation.

May 23^{d} Tuesday. This morning we found upon awaking that there was falling a blessed rain. It has not rained before since May-day – when it poured in the morning & cleared up in the afternoon On that day at ½ past 11. my sister Mary was married to Mr Horace Mann, & went directly to England an hour after the ceremony. This marriage was a sudden conclusion & they had but a month to prepare for a six months tour in Europe. It was a most happy event in my life as well as the crowning joy of hers, for I never could be reconciled to her hard labor for others, & her sad countenance. Now she is entirely content, & may GOD be praised – & bless her forever. It is about ten oc'lk & the rain has ceased I hope only for a few hours, for the earth cannot yet have quenched her thirst. The aspect of every green thing is superb now, & how the new seeds & young plants rejoice.— Very early, while we were yet in bed, my dear husband announced a bird in the gallery. I arose to see what kind of bird & found a sparrow. He flew backwards & forwards, & I opened the window for him to go out if he liked. How he got in is a mystery.— On Sunday afternoon Ellery & Ellen Channing came to tea. We had a very pleasant visit. Ellery shines, & he seems perfectly to idolize my darling husband.

Monday morning I began the bust of the noblest head in Christendom or Heathendom, that of my own dear Lord.

June 2d. Friday. Last night, there came a frost, which has done great damage to my garden. The beans have suffered very much; although, luckily, not more than half that I planted had come up. The squashes, both summer and winter, appear to be almost killed. As to the other vegetables, there is little mischief done — the potatoes not being yet above ground, except two or three; and the peas and corn are of a hardier nature. It is sad that Nature will play such tricks with us poor mortals, inviting us with sunny smiles to confide in her; and then, when we are entirely within her power, striking us to the heart. Our summer, as my little wife sagely observes, commences at the latter end of June, and as I no less truly added, terminates somewhere about the first of August. There are certainly not more than six weeks of the whole year, when a frost may be deemed anything remarkable.

The above disappointment, however, is but a trifle to another, which, I fear, has befallen us within a day or two. Let my dearest wife record it, if she will; or perhaps it may be better not to shadow another page with such a recital. God can restore all. Let us trust that He will.

plants rejoice – ! Very early, while we were yet in bed, my dear husband announced a bird in the gallery. I uprose to see what kind of bird & found a sparrow. He flew backwards & forwards, & I opened the window for him to go out if he liked. How he got in is a mystery. On Sunday afternoon Ellery & Ellen Channing came to tea. We had a very pleasant visit. Ellery shines, & he seems perfectly to idolize my darling husband. Monday morning I began the bust of the noblest head in Christendom or Heathenesse, that of my own dear Lord.

June 2d/· Friday. Last night, there came a frost, which has done great damage to my garden. The beans have suffered very much; although, luckily, not more than half that I planted had come up. The squashes, both summer and winter, appear to be almost killed. As to the other vegetables, there is little mischief done – the potatos not being yet above ground, except two or three; and the peas and corn are of a hardier nature. It is sad that Nature will play such tricks with us poor mortals, inviting us with sunny smiles to confide in her, and then, when we are entirely within her power, striking us to the heart. Our summer, as my little wife sagely observes, commences at the latter end of June; and as I no less truly added, terminates somewhere about the first of August. There are certainly not more than six weeks of the whole year, when a frost may be deemed anything remarkable.

The above disappointment, however, is but a trifle to another, which, I fear, has befallen us within a day or two. Let my dearest wife record it, if she will; or perhaps it may be better not to shadow another page with such a recital. God can restore all. Let us trust that He will.

June 6th. Tuesday My beloved has gone to fish. It is a cloudy, warm day & last night came down sheets of water. A week ago to day in the afternoon we took a walk along Peter's path. It was a most lovely afternoon & the earth was blue with lupins & grandiflora blue violets, with here & there a rose flush from wood-pinks & a gold sheen from yellow stars. We brought home an armful of flowers. One groupe of violets gave out a delicious odor. It seemed a peculiar clique with its own fine rare fragrance. There were great varieties of them. Some palest azure, some deep purple with gold eyes - some ultra marine blue with dark eyes & stems nine inches long.

The next day & for several days I was not very well. I read Carlyle's Past & Future in the bed. The style is detestable but the purpose & thoughts are noble. It is like struggling through a tangled wood with excessive irritation about the feet, while constantly the heavens are over your head birds sing in the branches, pines murmur of the infinite & as my husband said, thunder rolls & lightning flashes at times. One may either be wholly occupied with the snarls & thickets beneath, or listen to better music, just as one is inclined. Carlyle's humanity makes any thing he writes tolerable to me. He is born to represent. No one can pretend ignorance of the evils in England after he has spoken.

I have read also "The Home" by Frederika Bremmer. It is charming. A divine mother, a noble father, loving sisters & a brother with a head like an angel & most true tender

June 6.th ↑Tuesday↓ My beloved has gone to fish. It is a cloudy, warm day & last night came down sheets of water. A week ago today in the afternoon, we took a walk along Peter's path. It was a most lovely afternoon & the earth was blue with lupins & grandiflora blue violets, with here & there a rose flush from wood-pinks & a gold sheen from yellow stars. We brought home an armful of flowers. One group of violets gave out a delicious odor. It seemed a peculiar clique with its own fine rare fragrance. There were great varieties of them. Some palest azure, some deep purple with gold eyes – some ultra marine blue with dark eyes – & stems nine inches long.

The next day & for several days I was not very well. I read Carlyle's Past & Future on the bed. The style is detestable but the purpose & thoughts are noble. It is like struggling through a tangled wood with excessive vexation about the feet, while constantly the heavens are over your head, birds sing in the branches, pines murmur of the infinite & as my husband said, thunder rolls & lightning flashes at times. One may either be wholly occupied with the snarls & thickets beneath, or listen to better music, just as one is inclined. Carlyle's humanity makes any thing he writes tolerable to me. He is born to represent. No one can pretend ignorance of the evils in England after he has spoken.

I have read also "The Home" by Frederika Bremmer. It is charming. A divine mother, a noble father, loving sisters – & a brother with a head like an angel & most true tender heart. The Assessor is a thunder cloud with a rainbow in it. Mrs Gunilla is busy rain & blend sunshine.

We have heard from Mary Mann just a month from her departure. She says she feels "perfect satisfaction." This is to hear rich music. Beethoven could not surpass that strain for my heart. When a person is married truly, they pass into perfect spheres & sail off into the infinite on their own account, complete in themselves, & subject & bound no more except to the great laws of the Universe. I was the first to pass off from the family in this way with a fine sound of cymbals, called spherical harmony, & now Mary has shott into her orbit, having found the other half of her globe. To her as to me nothing is wanting but that those left behind should also roll in full circles through the blue depths of joy. But we can never ~~never~~ feel independent of those who are not quite so happy as we. She & I can now nod our heads gravely at each other in saucy defiance. & say "I am as happy as you!" (secretly believing happier than—) I wish Elizabeth could take up the wondrous tale & echo "And I as you!"

I have been thinking of the flood of "People's" books lately falling like a new kind of deluge all printed in the vilest small type, on the vilest black paper. It seems a crusade against eyesight however much it be intended to benefit the wits. We shall probably become a very wise nation, but totally blind—& perhaps it will be no matter when we come to know as much as Milton did

heart. The assessor is a thunder cloud with a rainbow in it. Mrs Gunilla is busy rain & blessed sunshine.

We have heard from Mary Mann just a month from her departure. She says she feels "perfect satisfaction." This is to hear rich music. Beethoven could not surpass that strain for my heart. When a person is married truly, they pass into perfect spheres & sail off into the infinite on their own account, complete in themselves, & subject & bound no more except to the great laws of the Universe. I was the first to part off from the family in this way with a fine sound of cymbals, called spherical harmony, & now Mary has shot into her orbit, having found the other half of her globe. To her as to me nothing is wanting but that those left behind should also roll in full circles through the blue depths of joy. But we can never ~~XXXX~~ feel independent of those who are not quite so happy as we. She & I can now nod our heads grandly at each other in saucy defiance – & say I am as happy as you! (secretly believing happier than –) I wish Elizabeth could take up the wondrous tale & echo "and I as you!"

I have been thinking of the flood of "People's" books lately falling like a new kind of deluge – all printed in the vilest small type, on the vilest black paper. It seems a crusade against eyesight however much it be intended to benefit the wits. We shall probably become a very wise nation, but totally blind – & perhaps it will be no matter, when we come to know as much as Milton did before the 'drop serene' quenched his orbs. The United States will be a great Blind Institution, saving a few Dr Howeses, who saved their sight by being able to read in decent books, & they will take care of us. Considering that the really poor people cannot afford bright & sufficient candle light, I think it is a pity this should be so. I wish there could retrenchment somewhere else, & clear, fair pages could be presented to the hungerers & thirsters after knowledges, who have few pennies to spare.

June 23d. Friday. Summer has come at last, — the longest days, and the blazing sunshine and fervid heat. Yesterday glowed like molten brass; last night was the most uncomfortably and unsleepably sultry that we have experienced since our residence in Concord; and to-day is another scorcher. I have a sort of enjoyment in these seven-times heated furnaces of mid-summer, even though they make me droop like a thirsty plant. The sunshine can scarcely be too much or too intense for my taste; but I am no enemy to summer showers. Could I only have the freedom to be perfectly idle now — no duty to fulfil — no mental or physical labor to perform — I could be as happy as a squash, and much in the same mode. But the necessity of keeping my brain at work eats into my comfort as the squash-bugs do into the heart of the vines. I keep myself uneasy, and produce little, and almost nothing that is worth producing.

The garden looks well now; the potatoes flourish; the early corn waves in the wind, and the latter is immeasurably advanced; the squashes, both for summer and winter use, are more forward, I suspect, than those of any of my neighbors. I am forced, however, to carry on a continual warfare with the squash-bugs, who, were I to let them alone for a whole day together, would perhaps quite destroy the pros-

before the 'drop serene' quenched his orbs. The United States will be a great Blind Institution, saving a few Dr Howeses, who saved their sight by being able to read in decent books, & they will take care of us. Considering that the really poor people cannot afford bright & sufficient candle light, I think it is a pity this should be so. I wish there could retrenchment somewhere else, & clear, fair pages could be presented to the hungerers & thirsters after knowledge, who have few pennies to spare.

June 23d. Friday. Summer has come at last; – the longest days, and the blazing sunshine and fervid heat. Yesterday glowed like molten brass; last night was the most uncomfortably and unsleepably sultry that we have experienced since our residence in Concord; and to-day is another scorcher. I have a sort of enjoyment in these seven-times heated furnaces of mid-summer, even though they make me droop like a thirsty plant. The sunshine can scarcely be too much or too intense for my taste; but I am no enemy to summer showers. Could I only have the freedom to be perfectly idle now – no duty to fulfil – no mental or physical labor to perform – I could be as happy as a squash, and much in the same mode. But the necessity of keeping my brain at work eats into my comfort as the squash-bugs do into the heart of the vines. I keep myself uneasy, and produce little, and almost nothing that is worth producing.

The garden looks well now; the potatoes flourish; the early corn waves in the wind, and the later is measurably advanced; the squashes, both for summer and winter use, are more forward, I suspect, than those of any of my neighbors. I am forced, however, to carry on a continual warfare with the squash-bugs, who, were I to let them alone for a whole day together, would perhaps quite destroy the pros-

48

pects of the whole summer. It is impossible not to feel bitterly angry with these unconquerable vermin, who scruple not to do such infinite mischief to me, with only the profit of a meal or two to themselves. For their own sakes they ought at least to wait till the squashes are better grown. There is an absolute pleasure in taking vengeance on them. Why is it, I wonder, that Nature has provided such a host of enemies for every useful esculent, while the weeds are suffered to grow unmolested, and are provided with such tenacity of life, and such methods of propagation, that the gardener must maintain a continual struggle, or they will hopelessly overwhelm him! What hidden virtue is there in these things, that it is granted them to sow themselves with the wind, and to grapple hold of the earth with this immitigable stubbornness, and to flourish in spite of obstacles, and never to suffer blight beneath any sun or shade, but always to mock their enemies with the same wicked luxuriance! It is truly a mystery. There is a sort of sacredness about them. Perhaps if we could penetrate Nature's secrets, we should find that what we call weeds are more essential to the well-being of the world than the most precious fruit or grain. This may be doubted, however; for there is an unmistakeable analogy between these wicked weeds and the bad habits and sinful propensities which have overrun the moral world; and we may as well imagine that there is good in one as in the other.

Our peas are in such forwardness that I should not wonder if we had some of them on the table within a week. The beans have come up ill, and I planted a fresh supply only the day before yesterday. We have watermelons in good advancement; and muskmelons have come up within three or four days. I set out some tomatoes, last night, also some capers. It is my purpose to plant some more corn at the end of the month, or sooner. My little wife should take these to be-

pects of the whole summer. It is impossible not to feel bitterly angry with these unconscionable vermin, who scruple not to do such infinite mischief to me, with only the profit of a meal or two to themselves. For their own sakes, they ought at least to wait till the squashes are better grown. There is an absolute pleasure in taking vengeance on them. Why is it, I wonder, that Nature has provided such a host of enemies for every useful esculent, while the weeds are suffered to grow unmolested, and are provided with such tenacity of life, and such methods of propagation, that the gardener must maintain a continual struggle, or they will hopelessly overwhelm him! What hidden virtue is there in these things, that it is granted them to sow themselves with the wind, and to grapple hold of the earth with this immitigable stubbornness, and to flourish in spite of obstacles, and never to suffer blight beneath any sun or shade, but always to mock their enemies with the same wicked luxuriance! It is truly a mystery. There is a sort of sacredness about them. Perhaps, if we could penetrate Nature's secrets, we should find that what we call weeds are more essential to the well-being of the world than the most precious fruit or grains. This may be doubted, however; for there is an unmistakeable analogy between these wicked weeds and the bad habits and sinful propensities which have overrun the moral world; and we may as well imagine that there is good in one as in the other.

Our peas are in such forwardness, that I should not wonder if we had some of them on the table within a week. The beans have come up ill, and I planted a fresh supply only the day before yesterday. We have water-melons in good advancement; and musk melons have come up within three or four days. I set out some tomatos, last night; also, some capers. It is my purpose to plant some more corn at the end of the month, or sooner. My little wife should take shame to her-

self for not keeping a record of her flower-~~garden~~, and of
the succession of the wild flowers, as minutely, at least,
as I do of the kitchen vegetables and pot-herbs. Above
all, she ought not to omit the appearance of the first
roses, nor of the Arethusa, one of the delicatest, gracefullest, and in every manner sweetest of the whole race
of flowers. For a fortnight past, I have found it in the
swampy meadows, growing up to its chin in heaps of
wet moss; its hue is a delicate pink, of various depth
of shade, and somewhat in the form of a Grecian helmet. Little wife is surely much amiss not to have
described it — a feat beyond my powers. I leave her,
likewise, to describe the visit of two of her friends who
came yesterday, and left us this morning. They may fitly
enough be mentioned among flowers. I wonder, too,
that she has neglected to mention the birth into this
wicked world of a little white dove — ~~perhaps the har-~~
~~binger of another birth, which at some inscrutable period~~
~~may gladden our old abbey~~. Oh, she is very naughty!

I never observed, until the present season, how long
and late the twilight lingers, in these longest days. The
orange hue of the western horizon remains till ten o'clock,
at least, and how much later I am unable to say. The
night before last, I could distinguish letters by this lingering gleam, between nine and ten o'clock. The dawn,
I suppose, shows itself as early as two o'clock; so that
the absolute dominion of night has dwindled to almost
nothing. There seems to be, also, if not a diminished
necessity, yet at all events a much less possibility
of sleep, than at other periods of the year. I get
scarcely any sound repose, just now;— tossings and
turnings, and the turmoil of dreams, consume the
night. We should grow old and wear out twice as
fast if there were no winter;— it is summer, and not
winter, that steals away mortal life. Well; we get the
value of what is taken from us.

self for not keeping a record of her flower-garden, and of the procession of the wild-flowers, as minutely, at least, as I do of the kitchen vegetables and pot-herbs. Above all, she ought not to omit the appearance of the first roses; nor of the Arethusa, one of the delicatest, gracefullest, and in every manner sweetest of the whole race of flowers. For a fortnight past, I have found it in the swampy meadows, growing up to its chin in heaps of wet moss; its hue is a delicate pink, of various depth of shade, and somewhat in the form of a Grecian helmet. Little wife is surely much amiss not to have described it – a feat beyond my power. I leave her, likewise, to describe the visit of two of her friends, who came yesterday, and left us this morning. They may fitly enough be mentioned among flowers. I wonder, too, that she has neglected to mention the birth into this wicked world of a little white dove – ~~perhaps the harbinger of another birth, which, at some inscrutable period, may gladden our old abbey.~~ Oh, she is very naughty!

I never observed, until the present season, how long and late the twilight lingers, in these longest days. The orange hue of the western horizon remains till ten o clock, at least; and how much later I am unable to say. The night before last, I could distinguish letters by this lingering gleam, between nine and ten o clock. The dawn, I suppose, shows itself as early as two o clock; so that the absolute dominion of night has dwindled to almost nothing. There seems to be, also, if not a diminished necessity, yet at all events a much less possibility of sleep, than at other periods of the year. I get scarcely any sound repose, just now; – tossings and turnings, and the turmoil of dreams, consume the night. We should grow old and wear out twice as fast, if there were no winters; – it is summer, and not winter, that steals away mortal life. Well; we get the value of what is taken from us.

49

~~[illegible]~~. GOD gives us all that is of eternal worth — consummate Love — perfect health — even a lovely home — & in still addition — the power to receive friends & make them happy — Sweetest husband — has He put a very heavy yoke on us?

Wonderful! At this moment as I sat musing with my eyes fixed on the unsightly old poplar, & thought how ugly its dead limbs looked — a gorgeous oriole alighted on the very spot where my eyes rested. How was the old tree glorified! I accept it as an intimation from GOD.

On the 22^d of this month the first roses bloomed. The sweet briar bush on the southern side of our house first unfolded its flowers. It was the day that golden Anna Shaw, & her sister Sarah — the Rose of Sharon, came to see us — & it was a very fit time. We had a most charming visit from them, dearest, did we not? They arrived at nine o'clk on the loveliest day we had had, a true midsummer day. Our familiar Spirit overtook them as they were walking from the stage office & brought their carpet-bag, & conversed with them all the way in a very impartial manner, they said, turning first to one & then to the other. Thou, beloved, didst greet them at the door of thy study with the most celestial smile & gleam that they ever beheld, though it is my daily privilege. Then they went to their chamber — & when they came forth again they went into ~~our~~ golden apartment & were delighted with ~~its~~ the furniture in its place which they had seen under my hand in Boston. Then I took them down into the dining room to eat some gingerbread wh I had made for them, & drink some of our

7

[24 June, Saturday]

GOD gives us all that is of eternal worth – consummate Love – perfect health – even a lovely home – & in still addition – the power to recieve friends & make them happy. Sweetest husband – has He put a very heavy yoke on us?

Wonderful! At this moment as I sat musing with my eyes fixed on the unsightly old poplar, & thought how ugly its dead limbs looked – a gorgeous oriole alighted on the very spot where my eyes rested. How was the old tree glorified! I accept it as an intimation from GOD.

On the 22^d^ of this month the first roses bloomed. The sweet briar bush on the southern side of our house first unfolded its flowers. It was the day that golden Anna Shaw, & her sister Sarah – the Rose of Sharon, came to see us – & it was a very fit time. We had a most charming visit from them, dearest, did we not? They arrived at nine oc'lk on the loveliest day we had had, a true midsummer day. Our familiar spirit overtook them as they were walking from the stage office & brought their carpet-bag, & conversed with them all the way in a very impartial manner, they said, turning first to one & then to the other. Thou, beloved, didst greet them at the door of thy study with the most celestial smile & gleam that *they* ever beheld, though it is *my* daily privilege. Then they went to their chamber – & when they came forth again they went into our golden apartment & were delighted with it ~~XX~~ the furniture in its place which they had seen under my hand in Boston. Then I took them down into the dining room to eat some gingerbread w'h I had made for them, & drink some of our delicious water. Then we stayed in the parlor a while & they were charmed with the room. the curtains, the couch & all. Golden Anna threw herself on the flowered Carpet, a more splendid flower, than all. & the Rose of Sharon half reclined on the Ottoman. beautiful ornaments for my parlor! Then we came up into the gallery & talked. & Sarah wanted to hear Mary's letters from London & so I read aloud. Anna's attention wandered, however, for she said she felt on enchanted ground & kept falling into trances. In the midst my dearest husband came out of his study & thou didst look most lovely, beloved, & thou wentst to the village & to Mr Emerson's to find if he would return for our dinner. After thou hadst gone, Anna went into our chamber & took a nap on our little white couch by the window. While she was there Sarah & I had some marriage talk. & I finished Mary's letters. Before Anna awoke, thou didst return, bringing three velvet roses. Thou didst present one to Sarah with a smile that might have created light. I was truly sorry that Anna could not recieve hers from thy hand. But when she dawned from our chamber, with a rose flush from sleep in her cheeks, looking like Aurora with her gold hair streaming, Sarah gave the rose to her. & they both carried them home as relics. Thou didst disappear into thy study till Mr Emerson came; for lo! as I was looking down the avenue, who should appear at the gate but Plato himself. He came literally in "hot haste". He had just arrived from Boston & hurried hither at once. Anna & Sarah descended into the parlor to see him & I requested thee to come

delicious water. Then we stayed in the parlor a while & they were charmed with the room – the curtains, the couch & all. Golden Anna threw herself on the flowered carpet, a more splendid flower, than all – & the Rose of Sharon half reclined on the Ottoman – beautiful ornaments for my parlor! Then we came up into the gallery & talked – & Sarah wanted to hear Mary's letters from London & so I read aloud. Anna's attention wandered, however, for she said she felt on enchanted ground & kept falling into trances. In the midst my dearest husband came out of his study & thou didst look most lovely, beloved, & thou wentst to the village & to Mr Emerson's to find if he would return for our dinner. After thou hadst gone, Anna went into our chamber & took a nap on our little white couch by the window. While she was there Sarah & I had some marriage talk & I finished Mary's letters. Before Anna awoke, thou didst return, bringing three velvet roses. Thou didst present one to Sarah with a smile that might have created light – I was truly sorry that Anna could not recieve hers from thy hand. But when she dawned from our chamber, with a rose flush from sleep in her cheeks, looking like Aurora with her gold hair streaming, Sarah gave the rose to her & they both carried them home as relics. Thou didst disappear into thy study till Mr. Emerson came: for lo! as I was looking down the avenue, who should appear at the gate but Plato himself. He came literally in hot haste. He had just arrived from Boston & hurried hither at once. Anna & Sarah descended into the parlor to see him & I requested thee to come

50

too, dearest. Our dinner was very pleasant. Mary Bryan prepared it excellently — lamb, our own asparagus, maccaroni & potatoes — & for the second course a custard pudding, most refreshingly cool, & which Sarah pronounced very nice. Mr Emerson was very agreeable & talked a great deal. He remained after dinner a long time holding vivid discourse with Anna — Sarah was obliged to go & lie down before he went away. Thou, dearest husband, didst thy part & more, considering thy inclinations, & Anna asked afterwards whether thou wast not unusually sociable, for from what she had heard, she did not expect so much intercourse with thee. She said it was beautiful to meet thine eyes, because there was such a friendly glance in them. I should think it was about five when Mr E. took leave & thou didst accompany him to speak for a cariole to convey them to Stowe in the morning. How thou didst beam & shine as with the most hospitable countenance thou spokest with Anna about the vehicle & the hour, & how gracefully thou didst urge her to go at a later hour. Thou dost fulfil all my dreams of beautiful hostship as well as of every thing else desirable. When you both had left, Anna would carry herself the put chair out upon the lawn & sat there awhile, but when Sarah came down from her nap, she threw herself along the grass, looking like one of Dian's nymphs or Dian herself. There we talked much. She said she had expected to have a beautiful time but the reality far exceeded her hopes. As we sat there Anna ran up stairs & returned with some Democratic

too, dearest. Our dinner was very pleasant. Mary Bryan prepared it excellently – lamb, our own asparagus maccaroni & potatoe – & for the second course a custard pudding, most refreshingly cool, & which Sarah pronounced very nice. Mr Emerson was very agreable & talked a great deal. He remained after dinner a long time, holding vivid discourse with Anna – Sarah was obliged to go & lie down before he went away. Thou, dearest husband, didst thy part & more, considering thy inclinations, & Anna asked afterwards whether thou wast not unusually sociable, for from what she had heard, she did not expect so much inter course with thee. She said it was beautiful to meet thine eyes, because there was such a friendly glance in them. I should think it was about five when Mr E. took leave & thou didst accompany him to speak for a cariole to convey them to Stowe in the morning. How thou didst beam & shine as with the most hospitable countenance thou spokest with Anna about the vehicle & the hour, & how gracefully thou didst urge her to go at a later hour. Thou dost fulfil all my dreams of beautiful hostship as well as of every thing else desirable. When you both had left, Anna would carry herself the ↑great↓chair out upon the lawn & sat there awhile, but when Sarah came down from her nap, she threw herself along the grass, looking like one of Dian's nymphs or Dian herself. Thus we talked much. She said she had expected to have a beautiful time but the reality far exceeded her hopes. As we sat there Anna ran up stairs & returned with some Democratics –

but just as she returned, thou didst walk up the avenue & she dropped her books & sat down on the step. I besought her to resume her reclination on the grass & she did. I wanted thee to see how lovely she looked in that attitude. Thou wentst on a raid against squash bugs a little while & then it was tea-time. After tea & when the sun was low enough, we all walked to the terrace & Anna adorned the rock between the two young elms & then Sarah. The river was still & glassy & shaded & in its best condition. We visited the monument & went up the avenue to the road & then thou didst kindly escort them to Sleepy Hollow. Meanwhile I came home & arranged their chamber for the night with Mary Bryan's assistance & provided tubs of water for their bathing. Sarah retired soon after her return; for it was then nine o'clk though daylight. Anna resumed her position on the grass, with now a ~~blanket~~ shawl beneath her. There she lay, with a low cricket to rest her arms upon, all the evening & Sydnean showers of sweet discourse distilled upon us with the dew. She pointed us out several of the constellations ~~[illegible]~~ in the magnificent fields of space, uncommonly clear that night– Cassiopeia's chair, Sagittarius, Lyra, &c. Finally she also went to bed. It was a red hot night & thou & I did not sleep hardly– We had no air on our side of the house– but excepting for thy sake, I was very glad they had some to keep them comfortable. The morning dawned bright & at seven o'clk or half past, they departed in a light

but just as she returned, thou didst walk up the avenue & she dropped her books & sat down on the step. I besought her to resume her reclination on the grass & she did. I wanted thee to see how lovely she looked in that attitude. Thou wentest on a raid against squash bugs a little while & then it was tea time. After tea & when the sun was low enough, we all walked to the terrace & Anna adorned the rock between the two young elms & then Sarah. The river was still & glassy & shaded, & in its best condition. We visited the monument & went up the avenue to the road & then thou didst kindly escort them to Sleepy Hollow. Meanwhile I came home & arranged their chamber for the night with Mary Bryan's assistance & provided tubs of water for their bathing. Sarah retired soon after her return; for it was then nine o'clk though daylight. Anna resumed her position on the grass, with now a blanket shawl beneath her. There she lay, with a low cricket to rest her arms upon, all the evening & Lydnean showers of sweet discourse distilled upon us with the dew. She pointed us out several of the constellations ~~XXXX~~ in the magnificent fields of space, uncommonly clear that night – Cassiopeia's chair, Sagittarius, Lyra, &c. Finally she also went to bed. It was a red hot night & thou & I did not sleep hardly. We had no air on our side of the house – but excepting for thy sake, I was very glad they had some to keep them comfortable. The morning dawned bright & at seven o'clk or half past, they departed in a light

51

cariole, with a driver. It was a most successful visit. Every thing happened just right, & thou wast perfect as usual, doing every thing in the most elegant way.

To day bloomed the first damask roses (24th June). Dearest, how shall I better describe the arethusa than thou hast done? It is of a pink-purple with five curved petals of exquisite form. It was about the first of June that thou didst bring some home to me, beloved. This is a dark crimson flower of rich grave aspect. I do not know its name. The wild lupin, blue & white abounded for a long time in May & the first part of June. My garden does not entirely succeed. Not all the seeds I planted have come up & but one dahlia of the five which Father put in the ground when he was here the second week in May. I have weeded my garden pretty well. I have not taken a walk abroad with thee since the 29th of May. But on the 21st, the longest day of the year, thou tookst me out in the boat. We saw many green headed, orange throated frogs sprawled upon the water with their noses out, looking imperturbably grave. We saw an Iris too (Sister have just come) but could not pluck it with safety. I paddled a little to help thee when the tide & wind were strong against us.

July 6th. Wednesday. We had our first mess of green peas (a very small one) yesterday. Every day for the last week has been tremendously hot; and our garden flourishes like Eden itself — only Adam could hardly have been doomed to contend with such a tremendous banditti of weeds.

cariole, with a driver. It was a most successful visit. Every thing happened just right, & thou wast perfect as usual, doing every thing in the most elegant way.

Today bloomed the first damask roses (24$^{th.}$ June). Dearest, how shall I better describe the arethusa than thou hast done? It is of a pink-purple with five curved petals of exquisite form. It was about the first of June that thou didst bring some home to me, beloved. This & a dark crimson flower of rich grave aspect. I do not know its name. The wild lupin, blue & white abounded for a long time in May & the first part of June. My garden does not entirely succeed. Not all the seeds I planted have come up & but one dahlia of the five which Father put in the ground when he was here the second week in May. I have weeded my garden pretty well. I have not taken a walk abroad with thee since the 29th of May. But on the 21$^{st.}$, the longest day of the year, thou tookst me out in the boat. We saw many green headed, orange throated frogs sprawled upon the water with their noses out, looking imperturbably grave. We saw an Iris too (Irises have just come) but could not pluck it with safety. I paddled a little to help thee when the tide & wind were strong against us.

July 1st. Saturday. We had our first mess of green peas (a very small one) yesterday. Every day for the last week has been tremendously hot; and our garden flourishes like Eden itself – only Adam could hardly have been doomed to contend with such a tremendous banditti of weeds.

July 9th Saturday. This is the anniversary of our wedding day, my dearest love. It is the loveliest weather & the moon is about full. What a sweet return of that happy hour. But I think that we of all persons make small account of dates & anniversaries & all outward marks of life. I doubt if ever there were lovers who thought less of gifts & visible tokens of united spirit. It is because we truliest love & therefore live in the spirit & need no appurtenances to testify perfect accord. We have been in the free ranges of Eternity ever since we first recognized each other & Time is beneath our feet. How can we bestow any thing upon each other when we are an indivisible soul? What note should we take of set times & seasons, when there are no such measures in Eternity, but only succession of States. Our state now is one of far deeper felicity than last 9th of July. Then we had visions & dreamed of Paradise. Now Paradise is here & our fairest visions stand realized before us. We are happier than we then knew, or perhaps than we now know, for who can tell what is to come? Who can tell what lower deep is beneath the lowest depth? We cannot search out unfathomable hearts nor count the stars of love. [illegible]

July 9th Sunday. This is the anniversary of our wedding day, my dearest love. It is the loveliest weather & the moon is about full. What a sweet return of that happy hour. But I think that we of all persons make small account of dates & anniversaries & all outward marks of life. I doubt if ever there were lovers who thought less of gifts & visible tokens of united spirits. It is because we trulyest love & therefore live in the spirit & need no appurtenances to testify perfect accord. We have been in the free ranges of Eternity ever since we first recognized each other & Time is beneath our feet. How can we bestow any thing upon each other when we are an indivisible soul? What note should we take of set times & seasons, when there are no such measures in Eternity, but only successions of States. Our state now is one of far deeper felicity than last 9th. of July. Then we had visions & dreamed of Paradise. Now Paradise is here & our fairest visions stand realized before us. We are happier than we then knew, or perhaps than we now know, for who can tell what is to come? Who can tell what lower deep is beneath the lowest depth? We cannot search out unfathomable hearts nor count the shews of love. ~~My XXXXXXXXXXXXXX XXXXXXX with the XXXXXXXXXXXXX XXXXXXXXXXXXXXXXXXXXXXXX XXXXGODXXXXXXXXXXXXXXXXX XXXXXXXXXXXXXXXXXXXXXXX XXXXXXXXXXXXXX she has any one yet, XXXXXXXXXXXXXXXXX GOD'S infinite XXXXXXXXXXXX plan of His Providence! XXXXX this XXXXXXXXXXXXXXXXXX XXXXXXXXXXXXXXXXXXXXXXXXXX~~

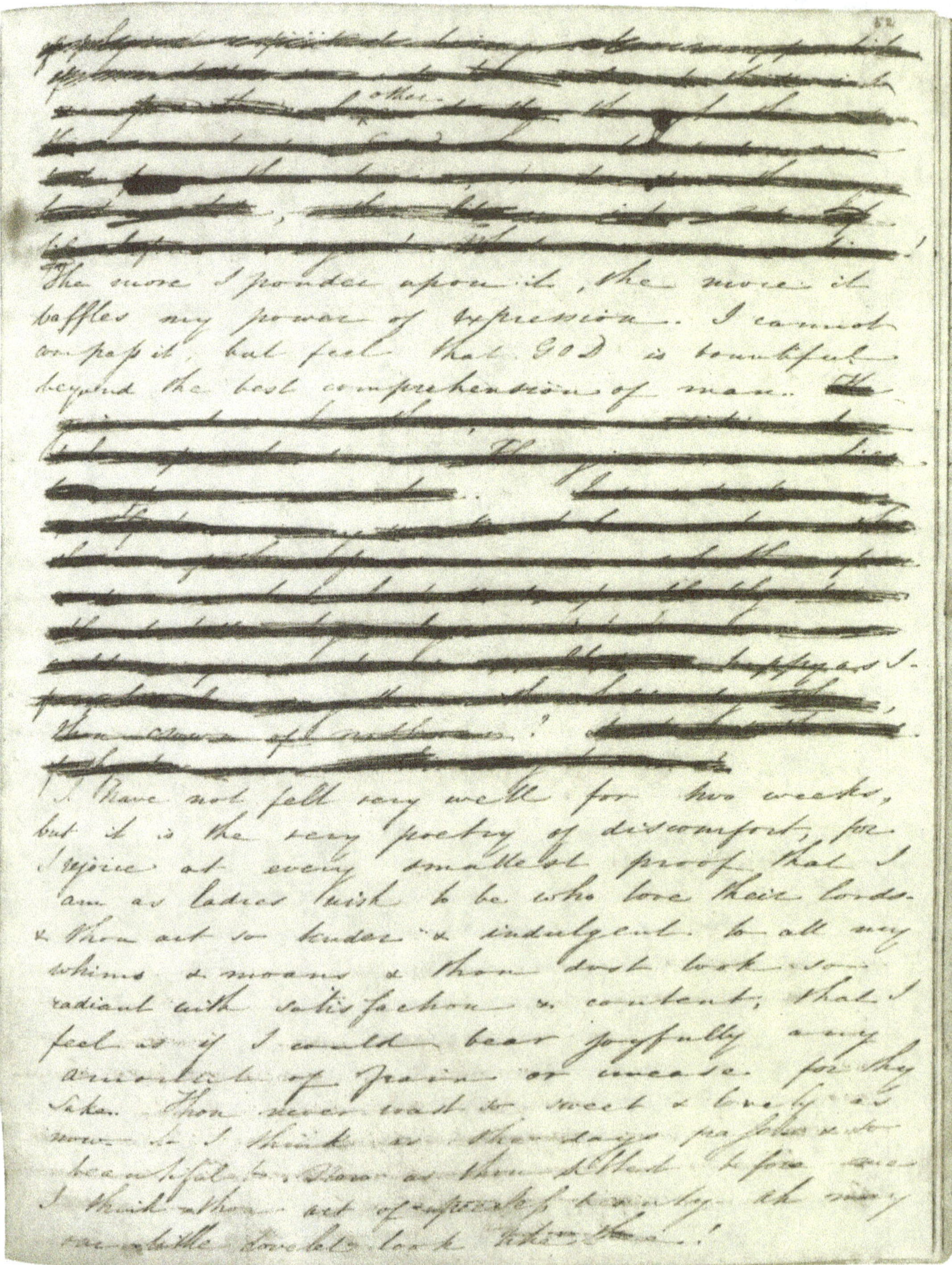

The more I ponder upon it, the more it baffles my power of expression. I cannot compass it, but feel that GOD is bountiful beyond the best comprehension of man.

I have not felt very well for two weeks, but it is the very poetry of discomfort, for I rejoice at every smallest proof that I am as ladies wish to be who love their lords—& Thou art so tender & indulgent to all my whims & moans & thou dost look so radiant with satisfaction & content, that I feel as if I could bear joyfully any amount of pain or unease for thy sake. Thou never wast so sweet & lovely as now—& I think as thou sayest perfect & so beautiful—Now as thou sittest before me I think thou art of exquisite beauty. Oh may our little lovelet look like thee—!

XXXX [other] XXXX GOD XXXX, & then XXXX life before XXXX! What XXXX! The more I ponder upon it, the more it baffles my power of expression. I cannot compass it, but feel that GOD is bountiful beyond the best comprehension of man. The XXXX I XXXX happy as I — XXXX with child by thee, thou crown of nobleness? XXXX

I have not felt very well for two weeks, but it is the very poetry of discomfort, for I rejoice at every smallest proof that I am as ladies wish to be who love their lords – & thou art so tender & indulgent to all my whims & moans & thou dost look so radiant with satisfaction & content, that I feel as if I could bear joyfully any amount of pain or unease for thy sake. Thou never wast so sweet & lovely as now. So I think as the days pass & so beautiful! Now as thou sittest before me I think thou art of peerless beauty – ah may our little dovelet look like thee!

July 9th. Sunday. Dearest love, I know not what to say, and yet cannot be satisfied without marking with a word or two this holiest anniversary of our life. But life now heaves and swells beneath us like a brim-full ocean; and the endeavor to comprise any portion of it in words, is like trying to dip up the ocean in a goblet. We never were so happy as now — never such wide capacity for happiness, yet overflowing with all that the day and every moment brings to us. Methinks this birth-day of our married life is like a cape, which we have now doubled, and find a more infinite ocean of love stretching out before us. God bless us and keep us; — for there is something more awful in happiness than in sorrow — the latter being earthly and finite, the former composed of the texture and substance of eternity, so that spirits still embodied may well tremble at it.

July 18th. Tuesday. This morning, I gathered our first summer squash. We should have had them some days earlier, but for the loss of two of the vines, either by a disease of the root or by those infernal bugs. We have had turnips and carrots, several times. Currants are now ripe, and we are in the full enjoyment of cherries, which turn out much more delectable than I anticipated. George Hillard and his wife paid us a visit on Saturday last; — he left us on Monday afternoon, and she still remains here.

July 28th. Friday. We had green corn for dinner yesterday, and shall have some more to-day — not quite full grown, but sufficiently so to be palatable. There has been no rain, except one moderate shower, for many weeks; and the earth appears to be wasting away in a slow fever. This weather, I think, affects the temper and spirits very unfavorably; — there is an irksomeness, a restlessness, a pervading dissatisfaction, together with an absolute incapacity to bend the mind to any serious effort. With me, as regards literary production, the summer has been idle and unprofitable; and I can only hope that my forces-

July 9th. Sunday. Dearest love, I know not what to say, and yet cannot be satisfied without marking with a word or two this holiest anniversary of our life. But life now heaves and swells beneath me like a brim-full ocean; and the endeavor to comprise any portion of it in words, is like trying to dip up the ocean in a goblet. We never were so happy as now – never such wide capacity for happiness, yet overflowing with all that the day and every moment brings to us. Methinks this birth-day of our married life is like a cape, which we have now doubled, and find a more infinite ocean of love stretching out before us. God bless us and keep us; for there is something more awful in happiness than in sorrow – the latter being earthly and finite, the former composed of the texture and substance of eternity, so that spirits still embodied may well tremble at it.

July 18th. Tuesday. This morning, I gathered our first summer-squash. We should have had them some days earlier, but for the loss of two of the vines, either by a disease of the root or by those infernal bugs. We have had turnips and carrots, several times. Currants are now ripe, and we are in the full enjoyment of cherries, which turn out much more delectable than I anticipated. George Hillard and his wife paid us a visit on Saturday last; – he left us on Monday afternoon, and she still remains here.

July 28th. Friday. We had green corn for dinner yesterday, and shall have some more to-day – not quite full grown, but sufficiently so to be palateable. There has been no rain, except one moderate shower, for many weeks; and the earth appears to be wasting away in a slow fever. This weather, I think, affects the temper and spirits very unfavorably; – there is an irksomeness, a restlessness, a pervading dissatisfaction, together with an absolute incapacity to bend the mind to any serious effort. With me, as regards literary production, the summer has been idle and unprofitable; and I can only hope that my forces

63

are recruiting themselves for the autumn and winter. For the future, I shall endeavor to be so diligent during nine months of the year, that I may allow myself a free and full vacation of the other three.

July 31st. Monday. We had our first cucumber yesterday. It showed symptoms of rain on Saturday; and the weather has since been as moist as the thirstiest soul could desire.

are recruiting themselves for the autumn and winter. For the future, I shall endeavor to be so diligent during nine months of the year, that I may allow myself a free and full vacation of the other three.

~~My little wife is troubled with XXXXXXXXXXXXX XXXXXXXXXXXXXXXXXXXXXXXXXXXXX XXXXXXXXXXXXXXXXXXXXXXXXXX~~ God bless her and the ~~XXXXX~~ life within her bosom.

<u>July 31st. Monday</u>. We had our first cucumber yesterday. It showed symptoms of rain on Saturday; and the weather has since been as moist as the thirstiest soul could desire.

room free in a high idleness. Every
beautiful morning I have felt a sense
of suffocation when thou hast shut thyself
into thy study to toil & spin intellectual
yarn for the benefit of the nations. Yet
beloved, I cannot quite regret that there
is some necessity for thee to write sometimes
because so much wealth of wisdom & delicate
apprehension of folly & wrong would be
lost to the world, were thou quite
silent. I should be content with thy

[31 July-28 August?]

roam free in high idleness. Every beautiful morning I have felt a sense of suffocation when thou hast shut thyself into this study to toil & spin intellectual yarn for the benefit of nations. Yet beloved, I cannot quite regret that there is some necessity for thee to write sometime because so much wealth of wisdom & delicate reprehension of folly & wrong would be lost to the world, wert thou quite silent. I should be content with thy

54

at least whenever one comes so dispiriting as those of the last week. I am soon going to walk again. Let us go & spend days in the woods & throw care away as we did last summer. September is soon enough to become a prisoner within doors. Here thou cometh. I cannot finish this book to night.

August 29th Tuesday noon. My darling husband, I have been thinking whether I should send thee another letter or write to thee here. And I conclude to do the last; for thou mightest not get another letter in Salem before leaving, & in Boston Post Office thou wilt not expect to find one. Sweetest love, I received thy sweet letter yesterday morning & there are no words to express my joy. Thou wast best & kindest to write so soon. Thou didst know that though I resigned thee pretty heroically, & smiled at the last, that my heart was divided & bereaved by thy absence, & that I needed some token from thee as much as thou didst need to give it. Over & over & over again I read the beloved words. ~~[illegible]~~ This makes me laugh at all kind of outward mishaps. They cannot invade me, for I am bulwarked & shielded by the consciousness of thy precious love. I am proud & triumphant because of it. To me there could be

at least whenever one comes so dispiriting as those of the last week. I am soon going to walk again. Let us go & spend days in the woods & throw care away as we did last Summer. September is soon enough to become a prisoner within doors. Here thou comest. I cannot finish this book tonight.

August 29th Tuesday noon. My darling husband, I have been thinking whether I would send thee another letter or write to thee here. And I concluded to do the last; for thou mightest not get another letter in Salem before leaving, & in Boston Post Office thou wilt not expect to find one. Sweetest love, I recieved thy dearest letter yesterday morning & there are no words to express my joy. Thou wast best & tenderest to write so soon. Thou didst know that though I resigned thee pretty heroically, & smiled at the last, that my heart was divided & bereaved by thy absence, & that I needed some token from thee as much as thou didst need to give it. Over & over & over again I read the beloved words. ~~How thou lovest now! I wonder I am not wholly transfigured by such deep & heavenly love. My soul is transfigured & has been ever since thou first toldest me I was dearer to thee than all else. I am happy beyond the reach of circumstance for this reason.~~ This makes me laugh at all kind of outward mishaps. They cannot invade me, for I am bulwarked & sheilded by the consciousness of thy precious love. I am proud & triumphant because of it. To me there could be

no shadow or darkness but from its withdrawal....
It was the forgetfulness of us all that kept
the letter behind; but principally my fault.
Father sent it by mail the same day, & mother
answered it. It gave her great satisfaction to see
thee, my husband. She speaks of my "magnificent
Knight" & though regretting the letter she says
"but I saw a beautiful Spring sparkle" I rejoice with George Hillard & the Sunflower. So thou
art going to see the dark eyed Fanny Longley
I am glad thou wilt stay till Saturday for my
sake. I trust thou wilt bring me many tales
of the sea when thou comest. Oh thou wilt feel
so well refreshed. My pulses bound to think
of it. I am very well now, dearest. Yesterday
I was better & to day better still. My head
seems resuming its ease at last. I believe
it was Court which so disturbed it, for it was
at the close of the trial that I first had the
pain. It was probably continued & aggravated
by all that followed, but the quiet & freedom
from all care & action since have restored me.
Especially I feel easy about thee. After reading
my letter yesterday to thee, I read & did nothing
till twelve & then slept a while. After
dinner Ellery Channing came to talk with me
about Mr Allston & discover whether I could
give him any help & light. I could not; but
he stayed a great time & was very agreeable
& presently Father came from hoeing & talked
to him about the lovely families of Knapp,
Crowninshield & White, & the murder of
the old Man was discussed. Father finally
left us & Ellery said he admired to hear old
gentlemen tell stories. He said Mrs Fuller
had been gone some days. In the evening

no shadow or darkness but from its withdrawal.

It was the forgetfulness of us all that kept the letter behind, but principally my fault. Father sent it by mail the same day, & mother answered it. It gave her great satisfaction to see thee, my husband. She speaks of my "magnificent Knight" & though regretting the letter she says "but I saw a beautiful living epistle" I rejoice with George Hillard & the Sunflower. So thou art going to see the dark eyed Fanny Longlady.

I am glad thou wilt stay till Saturday for thy sake. I trust thou wilt bring me many tales of the sea when thou comest. Oh thou will feel so well & refreshed. My pulses bound to think of it. I am very well now, dearest. Yesterday I was better & today better still. My head seems resuming its ease at last. I believe it was Court which so disturbed it, for it was at the close of the trial that I first had the pain. It was probably continued & aggravated by all that followed, but the quiet & freedom from all care & action since have restored me. Especially I feel easy about thee. After sending my letter yesterday to thee, I read & did nothing till twelve & then slept a while. After dinner Ellery Channing came to talk with me about Mr. Allston & discover whether I could give him any help & light. I could not; but he stayed a great time & was very agreable & presently Father came from hoeing & talked to him about the lovely families of Knapp, Crowninshield & White, & the murder of the old man was discussed. Father finally left us & Ellery said he admired to hear old gentlemen tell stories. He said Mrs Fuller had been gone some days. In the evening

55

I lighted the Solar lamp & we sat in the parlor, Father reading 'Change for Dickens' notes,' & I 'Les Memoires de Luther' till half past eight, when I went to sea in a tub & thence to bed. Do not I behave well! This morning soon after five I debouched & grieved for thy sake to find it cloudy. Father appeared shortly after & went to the garden to hoe till breakfast. After breakfast he pulled up the rest of the summer savory, & we spread it out on the floors of two attics. A fine, large squash & three ears of corn he gathered for dinner, but forgot the potatoes, & went far off to see Squire Barrett till dinner time. So we will have rice to-day instead. He would not gather beans, because he thought they were not needed. When he was gone I went out & pulled one more ear of corn & plucked some cucumbers, of which there is a fearful number dear love. We are actually overrun with cucumbers & summer squashes! I mended all thy bosomettes this morning & at eleven plunged into the tin tub. A shabby gentleman came just now for the boat. I never saw such a strange man. He was either crazy, drunk or a knave. His face prevented all confidence & his manner equally. I do not know as we shall ever see our Water Lily again. He was dressed in a worn black velvet frock coat. He made me shudder.

August 30th Wednesday noon. Best beloved. The hero of the velvet coat brought back the boat safely at about seven at night, so that whatever else bad he may do, he does not steal boats.

[illegible]

I lighted the Solar lamp & we sat in the parlor, Father reading Change for Dickens' notes, & I 'Les Memoires de Luther' till half past eight, when I went to sea in a tub & thence to bed. Do not I behave well? This morning soon after five I debouted, & grieved for thy sake to find it cloudy. Father appeared shortly after & went to the garden to hoe till breakfast. After breakfast he pulled up the rest of the Summer savory, & we spread it out on the floors of two attics. A fine, large squash & three ears of corn he gathered for dinner; but forgot the potatoes, & went far off to see Squire Barrett till dinner time. So we will have rice today instead. He would not gather beans, because he thought they were not needed. When he was gone I went out & pulled one more ear of corn & plucked some cucumbers, of which there is a fearful number, dear love. We are actually overrun with cucumbers & summer squashes! I mended all thy bosomettes this morning & at eleven plunged into the tin tub. A shabby gentleman came just now for the boat. I never saw such a strange man. He was either crazy, drunk or a knave. His face prevented all confidence & his manner equally. I do not know as we shall ever see our Water lily again. He was dressed in a worn black velvet frock coat He made me shudder.

August 30th. Wednesday noon. Best beloved – The hero of the velvet coat brought back the boat safely at about seven at night, so that whatever else bad he may do, he does not steal boats. ~~Sweetest, I love thee! What a heavenly lot it is to~~

be [illegible] through all heights & depths, unspeakably
~~[illegible]~~ What profanity it is to speak of real
love as if it could ever become like a tale
that is told. I feel the enchantment of thy love
more now than ever before. It can no more
be worn than the face of the sun which
for uncounted years has kindled the world
with light every morning. This will outlast
all suns & vivify us with life & warmth
through vanishing eternities. We are far
~~more comprehensively lovers than ever~~
What is called the fine illusion, the bloom
fragrance, the indefinable charm remain
as if GOD had set His seal upon them to
show that all the appliances of true love are as
permanent as His throne. Would it not be
mockery otherwise? What is this point of
mortal life as a measure for the enjoyment
& realization of a sentiment that seems in its
very nature to be made up of uncreated soul!
The word "forever" is much desecrated. We
know how to use it with sacred reverence, because
we stand on the heights of being, blended spirits
~~the dearest & [illegible] indeed that thou with~~
~~thy gorgeous & [illegible] nature art half~~
~~my soul! my own husband's forever~~

Father stayed at Squire Barrett's
to dine & after waiting for him till ½ past
I sat down alone, being as hungry as the wolf
that ate little red-riding hood. He did not
return till after six at night. At table I
missed thee, beloved, for thy chair was empty
But where do I not miss thee? Mrs Bab. spent
the day with Mary. As she cannot eat, she is not
a very expensive guest! I walked in the
avenue a long time in the afternoon -

~~be loved through all hieght & depths, infinitely, by thee!~~ What profanity it is to speak of real love as if it could ever become like a tale that is told. I feel the enchantment ~~of thy love~~ more now than ever before. It can no more be worn than the face of the sun which for uncounted years has kindled the world with light every morning. This will outlast all suns & vivify us with life & warmth through vanishing eternities. ~~We are far more comprehensively <u>lovers</u> than ever.~~ What is <u>called</u> the fine illusion, the bloom & fragrance, the indefinable charm remain as if GOD had set His seal upon them to show that all the appliances of true love are as permanent as His Throne. Would it not be mockery otherwise? What is this point of mortal life as a measure for the enjoyment & realization of a sentiment that seems in its very nature to be made up of uncreated soul!

The word "forever" is much desecrated. We know how to use it with sacred reverence, because we stand on the hieghts of being, blended spirits. ~~Oh dearest it is true indeed that thou with thy gorgeous & profound nature art half my soul! my own husband forever.—~~

Father stayed at Squire Barrett's to dine & after waiting for him till ½ past 2 I sat down alone, being as hungry as the wolf that ate little red-riding hood. He did not return till after six at night. At table I missed thee, beloved, for thy chair was empty. But where do I not miss thee? Mrs Bab. spent the day with Mary. As she cannot eat, she is not a very expensive guest! I walked in the avenue a long time in the afternoon.

After tea we sat in the parlor & I read Sots-
till Father put down the Change for
American notes & declared that it was too
dull a book to read, & then we talked
a while. By mistake I sat up later
than I intended; but was in bed before
ten. This morning I was lazier & rose not
till six. I breakfasted alone, for Father was
so interested in his weeds, that I could not
persuade him to come in before eight, &
I was famishing. He has bought him a
small, low crowned straw hat for sixpence,
& today with that & thy blue frock on, he
was a spectacle to behold. He says "it is very
hard to stop hoeing, for one weed lies close
by the next." After breakfast I arranged
my flowers & solar lamp, & then partly
mended thy russia gown. Ellery Channing
came to say Caroline Sturgis was at Mr
Emerson's & he wished to go out with
her in the boat this afternoon. So he
went to see whether it would do. He
sat down awhile & talked of Mr Thoreau's
father's lead pencils, as being as good as the
English & he wished they might be used
instead. He brought a letter to Elizabeth
about them. He said he "hated the English"
& had rather use American things.
Mary had not time to fill the great tub
& so at eleven I went to sea in a bowl
otherwise green oval tub. Father has now
gone to the village & I am about to
array myself, being in deshabille from
the bath. There are two most lovely
summer squashes, twins on one stalk, of
exquisite shape, which we conclude to save for

After tea we sat in the parlor & I read Tasso till Father put down the Change for American notes & declared that it was too dull a book to read, & then we talked a while. By mistake I sat up later than I intended; but was in bed before ten. This morning I was lazier & rose not till six. I breakfasted alone, for Father was so interested in his weeds, that I could not persuade him to come in before eight, & I was famishing. He has bought him a small, low crowned straw hat for six pence, & today with that & thy blue frock on, he was a spectacle to behold. He says "it is very hard to stop hoeing, for one weed lies close by the next." After breakfast I arranged my flowers & solar lamp, & then partly mended thy russia gown. Ellery Channing came to say Caroline Sturgis was at Mr Emerson's & he wished to go out with her in the boat this afternoon. So he went to see whether it would do. He sat down awhile & talked of Mr Thoreau's father's lead pencils, as being as good as the English & he wished they might be used instead. He brought a letter to Elizabeth about them. He said he "hated the English" & had rather use American things. Mary had not time to fill the great tub & so at eleven I went to sea in a bowl otherwise green oval tub. Father has now gone to the village & I am about to array myself, being in deshabille from the bath. There are two most lovely summer squashes, twins on one stalk, of exquisite shape, which we conclude to save for

seed. Good bye darling.
September 1st. Sweetest husband I sent thee a letter yesterday instead of writing here. Father went after dinner to Squire Barrett's & stayed to tea. Ellery & Caroline did not come to go in the boat. I sent Mary to the Post with my letter, though in that case I was left alone, because I wanted it to go that afternoon. As I sat in the Hall, in the profound solitude & silence, I heard the apples drop one by one in the orchard. It was a sound of the fulness of time. I thought of Bryant
"When the sound of falling nuts is heard."
But above all, I thought of thee. No one was here & I wanted thee with my whole soul. After tea I went to see Mrs Prescott & found only Miss Abby at home. We sat in the Hall in the evening without a light & "wholly destroyed" as Mary said, with "muskitties." Father had bathed in the river the night before & enjoyed it very much, but seemed to hesitate about going again. I found at last that he felt lonely to go by himself, & I thought as he was an old man & some accident might happen to him, he had better not. So I told him Mary & I would go & sit on the wall while he went into the river. We did so, & watched the half moon struggling with clouds both in the heavens & in the placid water while Father swam about. It was very hot. I was in bed at nine o'clk. At five I was awake & soon up, & first went into the orchard & gathered some fine yellow apples

seed. Goodbye darling.

September 1st. Sweetest husband I sent thee a letter yesterday instead of writing here. Father went after dinner to Squire Barrett's & stayed to tea. Ellery & Caroline did not come to go in the boat. I sent Mary to the Post with my letter, though in that case I was left alone, because I wanted it to go that afternoon. As I sat in the Hall, in the profound solitude & silence, I heard the apples drop one by one in the orchard. It was a sound of the fullness of time. I thought of Bryant

"When the sound of falling nuts is heard."

But above all, I thought of thee. No one was here & I wanted thee with my whole soul. After tea I went to see Mrs Prescott & found only Miss Abby at home. We sat in the Hall in the evening without a light & "wholly destroyed" as Mary said, with "muskitties." Father had bathed in the river the night before & enjoyed it very much, but seemed to hesitate about going again. I found at last that he felt lonely to go by himself, & I thought as he was an old man & some accident might happen to him, he had better not. So I told him Mary & I would go & sit on the wall while he went into the river. We did so, & watched the half moon struggling with clouds both in the heavens & in the placid water while Father swam about. It was very hot. I was in bed at nine o'clk. At five I was awake & soon up, & first went into the orchard & gathered some fine yellow apples

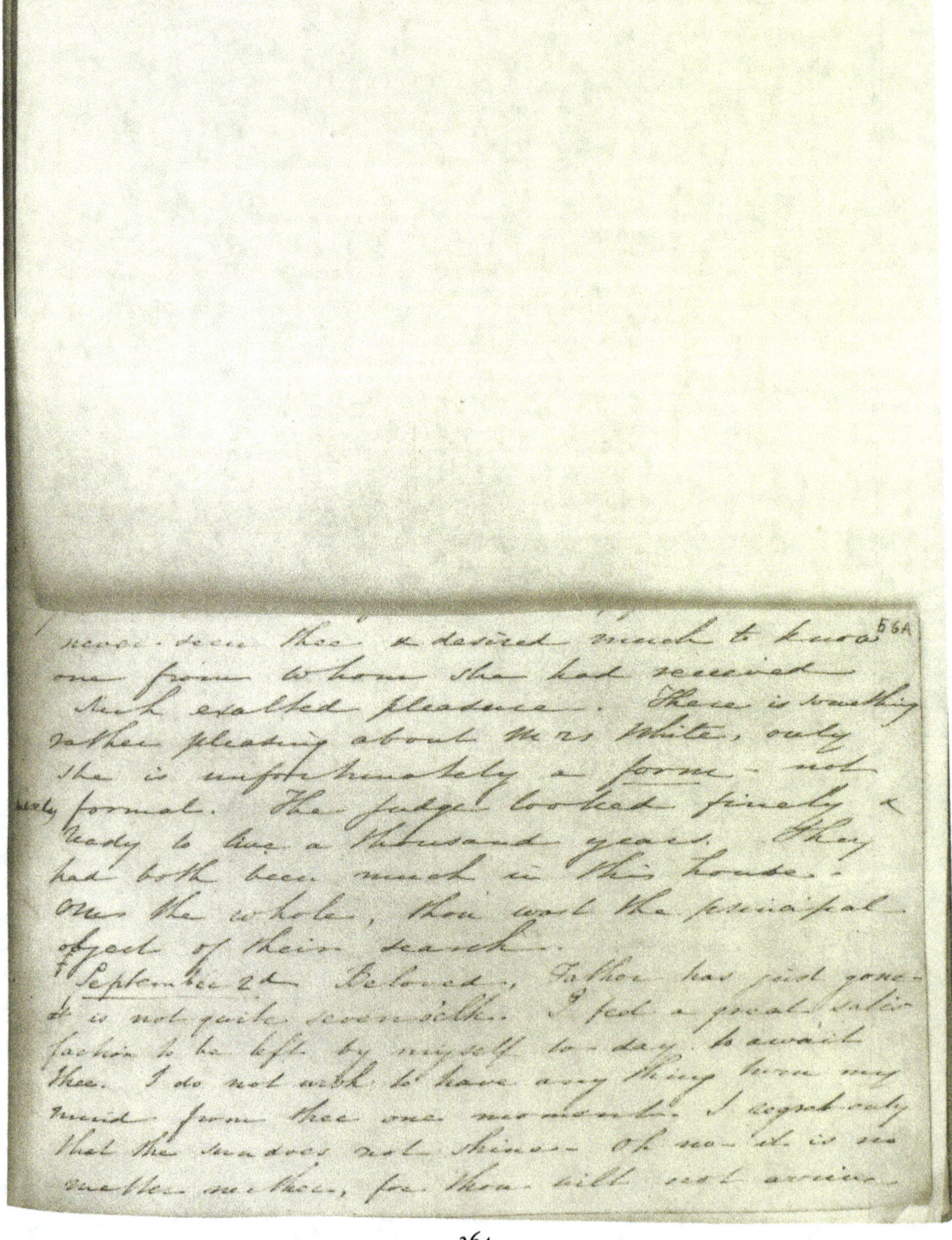

never seen thee & desired much to know 56A
one from whom she had received
such exalted pleasure. There is something
rather pleasing about Mrs White, only
she is unfortunately a forme— not
merely formal. The Judge looked finely &
ready to live a thousand years. They
had both been much in this house.—
Over the whole, thou wert the principal
object of their search.
September 2d Beloved, Father has just gone—
it is not quite noon still. I feel a great satisfaction to be left by myself to-day to await
thee. I do not wish to have any thing turn my
mind from thee one moment. I regret only
that the sun does not shine— Oh no it is no
matter neither, for thou wilt not arrive

never seen thee & desired much to know one from whom she had recieved such exalted pleasure. There is something rather pleasing about Mrs White, only she is unfortunately a form – not ↑merely↓ formal. The Judge looked finely & ready to live a thousand years. They had both been much in this house. On the whole, thou wast the principal object of their search.

September 2^{d} Beloved, Father has just gone. It is not quite seven o'clk. I feel a great satisfaction to be left by myself to-day to await thee. I do not wish to have any thing turn my mind from thee one moment. I regret only that the sun does not shine. Oh no – it is no matter neither, for thou wilt not arrive

Sept 13th. Wednesday. There was a frost the night before last, according to George Prescott; but no effects of it were visible in our garden. Last night, however, there was another, which has nipped the leaves of the winter squashes and cucumbers, but seems to have done no other damage. This is a beautiful morning, and promises to be one of those heavenly days that render autumn, after all, the most delightful season of the year. My little wife and I mean to make a voyage on the river, this afternoon.

1842 Sept 23d. Friday. I have gathered the two last of our summer squashes to-day; they have lasted ever since the 18th of July, and have numbered fifty-eight eatable ones, and of excellent quality. Last Wednesday (I think it was) I harvested our winter-squashes; sixty-three in number, and mostly of fine size. Our last series of green corn, planted about the first of July, came into eating two or three days ago. We have still beans; and our tomatoes, though backward, supply us with

September 13th. Wednesday. There was a frost the night before last, according to George Prescott; but no effects of it were visible in our garden. Last night, however, there was another, which has nipped the leaves of the winter-squashes and cucumbers, but seems to have done no other damage. This is a beautiful morning, and promises to be one of those heavenly days that render autumn, after all, the most delightful season of the year. My little wife and I mean to make a voyage on the river, this afternoon.

1843 September 23d Sunday. I have gathered the two last of our summer squashes to-day; they have lasted ever since the 18th. of July, and have numbered fifty-eight eatable ones, and of excellent quality. Last Wednesday (I think it was) I harvested our winter-squashes, sixty-three in number, and mostly of fine size. Our last series of green corn, planted about the first of July, came into eating two or three days ago. We have still beans; and our tomatos, though backward, supply us with a dish every day or two. My potato crop promises to be pretty good; and on the whole, my first independent experiment in agriculture is quite a successful one.

This is a glorious day, bright, very warm, yet with an unspeakable gentleness both in its warmth and brightness. On such days, it is impossible not to love Nature; for she evidently loves us. At other seasons, she does not give me this impression; or only at very rare intervals; but in these happy autumnal days, when she has perfected her harvests, and accomplished every necessary thing that she had to do, she overflows with a blessed superfluity of love. It is good to be alive now. Thank God for breath—yes, for mere breath!—when it is made up of such a heavenly breeze as this. It comes to the cheek with a real kiss; it would linger fondly around us, if it might; but since it must be gone, it caresses us with its whole kindly heart, and passes onward, to caress likewise the next thing that it meets. There is a pervading blessing diffused all over the world. I look out of the window, and think—"Oh perfect day! Oh beautiful world! Oh good God!" And such a day is the promise of a blissful Eternity; our Creator would never have made such weather, and have given us the deep heart to enjoy it above and beyond all thought, if He had not meant us to be immortal. It opens the gates of Heaven, and gives us glimpses far inward.

Bless me! This flight has carried me a great way; so now let me come back to our old Abbey. Our orchard is fast ripening; and the apples and great thumping pears strew the grass in such abundance that it becomes almost a trouble, though a pleasant one. This happy breeze, too, shakes them down, as if it flung fruit to us out of the sky; and often, when the air is perfectly still, I hear the quiet fall of a great apple. Well; we are rich in blessings, though poor in money; ~~and it seems as if little [illegible]~~ ~~anticipate the greatest blessing that is yet to come~~

a dish every day or two. My potato crop promises to be pretty good; and on the whole, my first independent experiment in agriculture is quite a successful one.

This is a glorious day, bright, very warm, yet with an unspeakable gentleness both in its warmth and brightness. On such days, it is impossible not to love Nature; for she evidently loves us. At other seasons, she does not give me this impression; or only at very rare intervals; but in these happy autumnal days, when she has perfected her harvests, and accomplished every necessary thing that she had to do, she overflows with a blessed superfluity of love. It is good to be alive now. Thank God for breath – yes, for mere breath! – when it is made up of such a heavenly breeze as this. It comes to the cheek with a real kiss; it would linger fondly around us, if it might; but since it must be gone, it caresses us with its whole kindly heart, and passes onward, to caress likewise the next thing that it meets. There is a pervading blessing diffused all over the world. I look out of the window, and think – "Oh perfect day! Oh beautiful world! Oh good God!" And such a day is the promise of a blissful Eternity; our Creator would never have made such weather, and have given us the deep hearts to enjoy it above and beyond all thought, if He had not meant us to be immortal. It opens the gates of Heaven, and gives us glimpses far inward.

Bless me! This flight has carried ↑me↓ a great way; so now let me come back to our old Abbey. Our orchard is fast ripening; and the apples and great thumping pears strew the grass in such abundance that it becomes almost a trouble, though a pleasant one. This happy breeze, too, shakes them down, as if it flung fruit to us out of the sky; and often, when the air is perfectly still, I hear the quiet fall of a great apple. Well; we are rich in blessings, though poor in money;~~ and I see my little wife rounding apace, and anticipate the greatest blessing that is yet to come.~~

1848 (I think 1843)

October 6th Friday. Yesterday afternoon (leaving wife with my sister Louisa, who has been with us two or three days) I took a solitary walk to Walden Pond. It was a cool, north-west windy day, with heavy clouds rolling and tumbling about the sky, but still a prevalence of genial autumn sunshine. The fields are still green, and the great masses of the woods have not yet assumed their many-colored garments; but here and there, are solitary oaks of a deep, substantial red, or maples of a more brilliant hue, or chestnuts, either yellow or of a tenderer green than in summer. Some trees seem to return to their hue of May or early June, before they put on the brightest autumnal tints. In some places, along the borders of low and moist land, a whole range of trees were clothed in the perfect gorgeousness of autumn, of all shades of brilliant color, looking like the palette on which Nature was arranging the tints wherewith to paint a picture. These hues appeared to be thrown together without design; and yet there was perfect harmony among them, and a softness and delicacy made up of a thousand different brightnesses. There is not, I think, so much contrast among these colors as might at first appear; the more you consider them, the more they seem to have one element among them all—which is the reason that the most brilliant display of them soothes the observer, instead of exciting him. And I know not whether it be more a moral effect, or a physical one operating merely on the eye; but it is a pensive gaiety, which causes a sigh often, but never a smile. We never fancy, for instance, that these gaily-clad trees should be changed into young damsels in holiday attire, and betake themselves to dancing on the plain. If they were to undergo such a transformation, they would surely arrange themselves in a funeral procession, and go sadly along with their purple, and scarlet, and golden garments trailing over the withering grass. When the sunshine falls upon them, they seem to smile; but it is as if they were heart-broken. But it is in vain for me to attempt to describe these autumnal brilliancies, or to convey the impression which they make

1844 (I think 1843)

October 6th. Friday. Yesterday afternoon (leaving wifie with my sister Louisa, who has been with us two or three days) I took a solitary walk to Walden Pond. It was a cool, north-west windy day, with heavy clouds rolling and tumbling about the sky, but still a prevalence of genial autumn sunshine. The fields are still green, and the great masses of the woods have not yet assumed their many-colored garments; but here and there, are solitary oaks of a deep, substantial red, or maples of a more brilliant hue, or chesnuts, either yellow or of a tenderer green than in summer. Some trees seem to return to their hue of May or early June, before they put on the brighter autumnal tints. In some places, along the borders of low and moist land, a whole range of trees were clothed in the perfect gorgeousness of autumn, of all shades of brilliant color, looking like the palette on which Nature was arranging the tints wherewith to paint a picture. These hues appeared to be thrown together without design; and yet there was perfect harmony among them, and a softness and delicacy made up of a thousand different brightnesses. There is not, I think, so much contrast among these colors as might at first appear; the more you consider them, the more they seem to have one element among them all – which is the reason that the most brilliant display of them soothes the observer, instead of exciting him. And I know not whether it be more a moral effect, or a physical one operating merely on the eye, but it is a pensive gaiety, which causes a sigh often, but never a smile. We never fancy, for instance, that these gaily-clad trees should be changed into young damsels in holiday attire, and betake themselves to dancing on the plain. If they were to undergo such a transformation, they would surely arrange themselves in a funeral procession, and go sadly along with their purple, and scarlet, and golden garments trailing over the withering grass. When the sunshine falls upon them, they seem to smile; but it is as if they were heart-broken. But it is in vain for me to attempt to describe these autumnal brilliancies, or to convey the impression which they make in me. I have tried a thousand times, and always without the slightest self-satisfaction. Luckily, there is no need of such a record; for Nature renews the scene year after year, and even when we shall have passed away from the world, we can spiritually create these scenes; so that we may dispense now and hereafter with all further efforts to put them into words. 58

Walden Pond was clear and beautiful, as usual. It tempted me to bathe; and though the water was thrillingly cold, it was like the thrill of a happy death. Never was there such transparent water as this. I threw sticks into it, and saw them float suspended on an almost invisible medium; it seemed as if the pure air were beneath them, as well as above. If I were to be baptized, it should be in this pond; but then one would not wish to pollute it by washing off his sins into it. None but angels should bathe there. It would be a fit bathing-place for my little wife; and sometime or other, I hope, our blessed baby shall be dipt into its bosom.

In a small and secluded dell, that opens upon the most beautiful cove of the whole lake, there is a little hamlet of huts or shanties, inhabited by the Irish people who are at work upon the rail-road. There are three or four of these habitations, the very rudest, I should imagine, that civilized men ever made for themselves, constructed of rough boards, with protruding ends. Against some of them the earth is heaped up to the roof, or nearly so; and when the grass has had time to sprout upon them, they will look like small natural hillocks, or a species of ant-hills, or something in which Nature has a larger share than man. These huts are placed beneath the trees (oaks, walnuts, and white pines) wherever the trunks give them space to stand; and by thus adapting themselves to natural interstices, instead of making new ones, they do not break or disturb the solitude and seclusion of the place. Voices are heard, and the shouts and laughter of children, who play about like the sunbeams that come down through the branches. Women

on me. I have tried a thousand times, and always without the slightest self-satisfaction. Luckily, there is no need of such a record; for Nature renews the scene, year after year; and even when we shall have passed away from the world, we can spiritually create these scenes; so that we may dispense now and hereafter with all further efforts to put them into words.

Walden Pond was clear and beautiful, as usual. It tempted me to bathe; and though the water was thrillingly cold, it was like the thrill of a happy death. Never was there such transparent water as this. I threw sticks into it, and saw them float suspended on ↑an↓ almost invisible medium; it seemed as if the pure air was beneath them, as well as above. If I were to be baptized, it should be in this pond; but then one would not wish to pollute it by washing off his sins into it. None but angels should bathe there. It would be a fit bathing-place for my little wife; and sometime or other, I hope, our blessed baby shall be dipt into its bosom.

In a small and secluded dell, that opens upon the most beautiful cove of the whole lake, there is a little hamlet of huts or shanties, inhabited by the Irish people who are at work upon the rail-road. There are three or four of these habitations, the very rudest, I should imagine, that civilized men ever made for themselves, constructed of rough boards, with protruding ends. Against some of them the earth is heaped up to the roof, or nearly so; and when the grass has had time to sprout upon them, they will look ↑like↓ small natural hillocks, or a species of ant-hill, or something in which Nature has a larger share than man. These huts are placed beneath the trees, (oaks, walnuts, and white pines) wherever the trunks give them space to stand; and by thus adapting themselves to natural interstices instead of making new ones, they do not break or disturb the solitude and seclusion of the place. Voices are heard, and the shouts and laughter of children, who play about like the sunbeams that come down through the branches. Women are washing beneath the trees, and long lines of whitened clothes are extended from tree to tree, fluttering and gambolling in the breeze. A pig, in a stye even more extemporary than the shanties, is grunting, and poking his snout through the clefts of his habitation. The household pots and kettles are seen at the doors, and a glance within shows the rough benches that serve for chairs, and the bed upon the floor. The visitor's nose takes note of the fragrance of a pipe. And yet, with all these homely items, the repose and sanctity of the old wood do not seem to be destroyed or profaned; she overshadows these poor people, and assimilates them, somehow or other, to the character of her natural inhabitants. Their presence did not shock me, any more than if I had merely discovered a squirrel's nest in a tree. To be sure, it is a torment to see the great, high, ugly embankment of the rail-road, which is here protruding itself into the lake, or along its margin, in close vicinity to this picturesque little hamlet. I have seldom seen anything more beautiful than the cove, on the border of which the huts are situated; and the more I looked, the lovelier it grew. The trees overshadowed it deeply; but on one side there was some brilliant shrubbery which seemed to light up the whole picture with the effect of a sweet and melancholy smile. I felt as if spirits were there — or as if these shrubs had a spiritual life — in short, the impression was undefinable; and after gazing and musing a good while, I retraced my steps through the Irish hamlet, and plodded on along a wood-path.

According to my invariable custom, I mistook my way, and emerging upon a road, I turned my back, instead of my face, towards Concord, and walked on very diligently, till a guide-board informed me of my mistake. I then turned about, and was shortly overtaken by an old yeoman in a chaise, who kindly offered me a ride, and shortly set me down in the village.

are washing beneath the trees, and long lines of whitened clothes are extended from tree to tree, fluttering and gambolling in the breeze. A pig, in a stye even more extemporary than the shanties, is grunting, and poking his snout through the clefts of his habitation. The household pots and kettles are seen at the doors, and a glance within shows the rough benches that serve for chairs, and the bed upon the floor. The visiter's nose takes note of the fragrance of a pipe. And yet, with all these homely items, the repose and sanctity of the old wood do not seem to ↑be↓ destroyed or prophaned; she overshadows these poor people, and assimilates them, somehow or other, to the character of her natural inhabitants. Their presence did not shock me, any more than if I had merely discovered a squirrel's nest in a tree. To be sure, it is a torment to see the great, high, ugly embankment of the rail-road, which is here protruding itself into the lake, or along its margin, in close vicinity to this picturesque little hamlet. I have seldom seen anything more beautiful than the cove, on the border of which the huts are situated; and the more I looked, the lovelier it grew. The trees overshadowed it deeply; but on one side there was some brilliant shrubbery which seemed to light up the whole picture with the effect of a sweet and melancholy smile. I felt as if spirits were there – or as if these shrubs had a spiritual life – in short, the impression was undefinable; and after gazing and musing a good while, I retraced my steps through the Irish hamlet, and plodded on along a wood-path.

According to my invariable custom, I mistook my way, and emerging upon a road, I turned my back, instead of my face, towards Concord, and walked on very diligently, till a guide-board informed me of my mistake. I then turned about, and was shortly overtaken by an old yeoman in a chaise, who kindly offered me a ride, and shortly set me down in the village.

53

November 17th This Indian summer is very beautiful. Yesterday & the day before it was so exceedingly warm here, that I was really uncomfortable in walking out at noon, but the dulcet air & stillness were lovely. Today it is cooler yet still mild. This morning we watched the opal dawn & the stars becoming pale before it, as also the old moon, which rose between five & six & in the form of a boat of pure silvery gold, floated up the sea of rosy air. ~~Our bed now stands so that we command a view of the eastern heaven a part of the evening. I am so very early a riser that the first faint light usually finds me out of bed, but this morning I lay & watched the coming of day with my lord.~~

My beloved husband's study looks charmingly now. As we abandon our drawing room this winter, I have dismantled it of pictures, & hung the Comos upon his walls, & the Loch Lomond all of which I painted expressly for him; & over the fire-place still hangs Raphael's Madonna del Pesce. I have also placed the parlor couch there between the western windows, covering it with pretty patch to keep its damask unsullied by stove dust: & the little mahogany centre-table, belonging to the parlor, stands beneath the hanging astral, covered with a crimson cloth. The antique table, once there, broke one day beneath my dear husband's arms & down tumbled desk with a mighty sound upon the floor, astounding me beneath. It is mended & will stand & I have put it in the gallery, in place of the antique one formerly there, & ~~when danger confirmed~~ I shall take it into my chamber. On one of the secretaries I have put the lovely half statue of Ceres & opposite, on the other, is Margaret's bronzed vase. In the afternoon

November 19.th This Indian summer is very beautiful Yesterday & the day before it was so exceedingly warm here, that I was really uncomfortable in walking out at noon, but the dulcet air & stillness were lovely. Today it is cooler yet still mild. This morning we watched the opal dawn & the stars becoming pale before it, as also the old moon, which rose between five & six & in the form of a boat of pure silvery gold, floated up the sea of rosy air. ~~Our bed now stands so that we can command a view of the eastern heaven & part of the avenue –~~ I am so very early ~~a riser that the first faint light usually finds me out of bed, but this morning I lay & watched the coming of day with my lord.~~

My beloved husband's study looks charmingly now. As we abandon our drawing room this winter, I have dismantled it of pictures, & hung the Comos upon the walls, & the Loch Lomond all of which I painted expressly for him, & over the fire-place still hangs Raphael's Madonna del Pesce. I have also placed the parlor couch there between the western windows, covering it with pretty patch to keep its damask unsullied by stove dust: & the little mahogany centre-table, belonging to the parlor, stands beneath the hanging astral, covered with a crimson cloth. The antique table, once there, broke one day beneath my dear husband's arms & down tumbled desk with a mighty sound upon the floor, astounding me beneath. It is mended & will stand & I have put it in the gallery, in place of the antiquer one, formerly there, & ~~when I am confined,~~ I shall take it into my chamber. On one of the secretaries I have put the lovely ↑half↓ statue of Ceres & opposite, on the other, is Margaret's browned vase. In the afternoon,

when the sun fills the room it is beautiful: still more so
perhaps, when the astral emulates the sun, & pours shine
upon all objects, & shows beneath the noblest head
in Christendom, in the ancient chair with its
sculptured back, & whenever I look up, two
stars beneath a brow of serene white, radiate
love & sympathy upon me. My dearest love is
reading Shakspere aloud to me this winter, & I can
truly say I never had an idea of it before. As
made apparent by his voice, it is a magnificent
gallery of pictures, illustrated by noble sentiments.
What is great is greater, & what is less noble
shows itself more plainly, for the mere act of his
reading it, criticises it acutely. Can there be a
happier life? The rich intellectual feasts, ~~and the~~
~~perpetual joy of the new hope in my bosom for~~
~~both of us~~, & the overbending, surrounding, penetrating
love which makes illustrious every moment,
& the quiet of Eternity & its permanence superadded
That downy bloom of Happiness which unfaithful
& ignoble poets have persisted in declaring
always vanishes at the touch & wear of life,
is delicate & fresh as ever, & must remain so
if we remain unprofane & identical. What!
would the benign & wise GoD design otherwise?
Oh no! it is man who violates & then says "It is
inevitable "The contrary is only a dream."
I never believed it, & my reality has proved
wholly ideal & will ever, for the sacredness,
the loftiness, the ethereal delicacy of such
a soul as my husband's, will keep Heaven
about us through the long blue vistas of
futurity. My thought does not yet compass
him. He rises upon me daily like a
new sun. It is so refreshing to find one person
without theories of any kind, without party or

when the sun fills the room, it is beautiful: still more so perhaps, when the astral enacts the sun, & pours shine upon all objects, & shows beneath the noblest head in Christendom, in the ancient chair with its sculptured back, & whenever I look up, two stars beneath a brow of serene white, radiate love & sympathy upon me. My dearest love is reading Shakspere aloud to me this winter, & I can truly say I never had an idea of it before. As made apparent by his voice, it is a magnificent gallery of pictures, illustrated by noble sentiments. What is great is greater, & what is less noble shows itself more plainly, for the mere act of his reading it, criticizes it acutely. Can there be a happier life? The rich intellectual feasts, ~~& the perpetual joy of this new hope in my bosom for both of us,~~ & the overbending, surrounding, penetrating love which makes illustrious every moment, & the quiet of Eternity & its permanence superadded that downy bloom of Happiness which unfaithful & ignoble poets have persisted in declaring always vanishes at the touch & wear of life, is delicate & fresh as ever, & must remain so, if we remain unprofane & identical. What? could the benign & wise GOD design otherwise? Oh no! it is man who violates & then says "It is inevitable "The contrary is only a dream." I never believed it, & my reality has proved wholly ideal & will ever; for the sacredness, the loftiness, the etherial delicacy of such a soul as my husband's, will keep Heaven about us through the long blue vistas of futurity. My thought does not yet compass him. He rises upon me daily like a new sun. It is so refreshing to find one person without theories of any kind, without party or

60

sectarian tendency, free from earthly clogs, & floating like a star on its own way, without rule except GOD's hand. This is one secret of his perennial charm & newness. He lives, transparent to Heaven & pure thought, & can thought be exhausted? He does not meddle with Truth & it lays upon him like the blessed sunshine, full & broad. No microscopes nor burning glasses, nor any of those impertinent littler dividers & dissectors nor large magnifiers disturb its serene wholeness & greatness. I hourly thank GOD that he is my husband — all nature in a man! He is as unfathomable as any other counsel of GOD; for it is only when men insist upon holding up their own minute reflectors to Truth that they shut it out & nail platforms over the depths of soul, & such people are tedious & soon tire. We cannot get farther than the platform & who can stand always on that? But to be drawn forever into lower deeps, seeing only space beyond space, this is the true enchantment, the endless communion, & this is his — this is my mystery.

Indian arrow heads found by my husband exactly marked from the originals

sectarian tendency, free from earthly clogs, & floating like a star on its own way, without rule except GOD'S hand. This is one secret of his perennial charm & newness. He lives, transparent to Heaven & pure Thought, & can thought be exhausted? He does not meddle with Truth & it lays upon him like the blessed sunshine, full & broad. No microscopes nor burning glasses, nor any of those impertinent littler dividers & dissectors nor large magnifiers disturb its serene wholeness & greatness. I hourly thank GOD that he is my husband – all nature in a man! He is as unfathomable as any other counsel of GOD; for it is only when men insist upon holding up their own minute reflectors to Truth that they shut it out & nail platforms over the depths of the soul, & such people are tedious & soon tire. We cannot get farther than the platform & who can stand always on that? But to ↑be↓ drawn forever into lower deeps, seeing only space beyond space, this is the true enchantment, the endless communion, & this is his – this is my mystery.

Indian arrow heads found by my husband exactly marked from the originals

Textual Notes

The Common Journal of
Nathaniel and Sophia Hawthorne

THESE NOTES, organized by entry number, author, date, and leaf numbers, clarify complex textual situations, detail Sophia Hawthorne's editorial alterations to the manuscript, and identify variants between the manuscript and the earliest printed versions of Nathaniel Hawthorne's journal entries edited for publication by Sophia Hawthorne in *The Atlantic Monthly* and *Passages from the American Note-Books.*

All editorial alterations to the manuscript leaves were, unless otherwise specifically noted, presumably made by Sophia Hawthorne in the process of preparing MA 580 for publication and, possibly, for transmission to her heirs. The following types of editorial alterations are reported and described in the textual notes:

a) Excisions of passages or leaves;
b) Words and/or passages over-inked in black, still largely unrecoverable;
c) Words and/or passages over-inked in blue, later recovered by librarians at the Morgan via a process of ink lightening;
d) Words and/or passages lightly canceled in pencil;
e) Words and/or passages overwritten in ink or pencil;
f) Words and/or passages underlined in pencil;
g) Interlineations made in ink or pencil; and
h) Asterisks, crosses, and slash marks made in pencil and possibly belonging to a private system of notation devised by SH in her editing of the manuscript. At times, these marks seem to correlate with passages omitted from publication; at other times, the significance of the marks is unclear.

In reporting publication histories, references on the left are to manuscript readings and references on the right are to readings in the printed texts. Since the printed text of *Passages* follows the printed text in *The Atlantic* in all but punctuation and accidentals, only one reading of the printed texts—that of *The Atlantic*—is given here. The following abbreviations have been used for published works:

AM *The Atlantic Monthly Magazine*
Passages *Passages from the American Note-Books*, 2 vols., edited by Sophia Hawthorne. Boston: Ticknor and Fields, 1868

1. Sophia Hawthorne, [9 July–5 August] 1842 (2)

Editorial Alterations to the MS

2 wife] The first extant entry in the common journal begins in medias res: one or two leaves are missing between the front flyleaf and the first extant leaf of the notebook.

2. Nathaniel Hawthorne, 5 August 1842 (2v–3v)

Editorial Alterations to the MS

3.8 Paradise] followed by two-thirds of a line over-inked in black

Publication History

NH's 5 August 1842 entry was first printed, with omissions and alterations, in *AM* vii (July 1866): 40–41; it was reprinted without further substantive textual alterations in *Passages*, vol. 2, pp. 60–63:

2v.1 *SH added* Concord *to the entry's heading, perhaps alerting readers to the change of scene occasioned by the Hawthornes' marriage*
2v.1 Friday] silently omitted
2v.1–5 and I...banished me] silently omitted
2v.5 has banished me] *altered to* I am therefore banished
2v.6–7 but she...if the] *altered to* but perhaps the
2v.8 should] *altered to* will
2v.9 at all] silently omitted
2v.14–15 in the...long embrace] silently omitted
2v.17 spirits] *altered to* souls
2v.19 The] *altered to* This
2v.24 our] *altered to* the
2v.30–31 at the...angelic personage] silently omitted
2v.32 so far favored...to be] silently omitted
2v.32–33 (with a...Ellery Channing)] silently omitted
2v.33 Thorow] *standardized* Thoreau
2v.35–36 Elizabeth Hoar] *abbreviated to* E---- H----
3.8 ~~XXXXXXXXXX~~] inked over passage silently omitted
3.12 a portion] *altered to* portions
3.14–15 my wife...to record] *altered to* Would that I were permitted to record
3.15 ethereal] *altered to* celestial
3.19 intruded] *altered to* entered
3.22 Paradise] *altered to* Eden
3.31 Intolerable!] *followed by* (though our stout handmaiden really fetches our water)

3.31–33 I shall...look out] silently omitted
3v.4 do] *altered to* does
3v.9 towards the house] *altered to* hitherward

3. Nathaniel Hawthorne, 6 August 1842 (3v–4v)

Editorial Changes to the MS

4.17 ~~and wear...my bosom~~] over-inked in blue; later recovered

Publication History

NH's 6 August 1842 entry was first printed, with omissions and alterations, in *AM* vii (July 1866): 41–42; it was reprinted without further substantive textual alterations in *Passages*, vol. 2, pp. 63–66:

3v.12 August 6th Saturday] *transposed* Saturday, August 6
3v.14–15 fill our...beneficent downpouring] *altered to* supply us well with their beneficent outpouring
3v.29 others] *followed by* and
4.4 this] *altered to* the
4.7–8 which, likewise, ...lily draws] *altered to* which the yellow lily likewise draws
4.8–9 perfume] *altered to* odor
4.13 a few] *altered to* Some
4.15 spotless and fragrant] *transposed* fragrant and spotless
4.16–19 I possess...yellow companion] omission indicated with ellipses
4.26–30 my wife...they can] omission indicated with ellipses
4v.8 as] *followed by* it
4v.9 There are...to be] *altered to* It is said there are
4v.10 captures] *followed by* hitherto
4v.16 hand,] *followed by* it
4v.21 along its quiet bosom] *altered to* over its bosom
4v.24 margin] *altered to* brink
4v.29 the purpose of] silently omitted
4v.31 is alive] *altered to* be alive
4v.33 our river] *altered to* the Concord
4v.34 north-west] *altered to* northwestern

4. Nathaniel Hawthorne, 7 August 1842 (5–5v)

Editorial Alterations to the MS

5v.1a with] below a cross mark in pencil

Publication History

NH's 7 August 1842 entry was first printed, with omissions and alterations, in *AM* vii (July 1866): 42–43; it was reprinted without further substantive textual alterations in *Passages*, vol. 2, pp. 66–68:

5.1 August 7th Sunday] *transposed* Sunday, August 7
5.34 soul,] *followed by* though
5v.9 broad] *altered to* wide
5v.10 crowned] *altered (mistranscribed?)* covered
5v.11 Concord] silently omitted
5v.18 Had my...with me] *altered to* Had I not then been alone
5v.20 her] *altered to* another
5v.27–29 May the...afar off!] omission indicated with ellipses
5v.30–31 so long...the world;] *transposed* homeless in the world so long!
5v.31–33 for no...threshold] omission indicated with ellipses

5. Nathaniel Hawthorne, 8 August 1842 (6–7v)

Editorial Alterations to the MS

6.5 ga~~m~~ble] *corrected to* gable, *possibly by SH*

Publication History

NH's 8 August 1842 entry was first printed, with omissions and alterations, in *AM* vii (July 1866): 43–45; it was reprinted without further substantive textual alterations in *Passages*, vol. 2, pp. 68–72:

6.1 August 8th Monday] *transposed* Monday, August 8
6.5 the house] *altered to* it
6.9–10 The rooms,...never been] *altered to* The rooms seemed never to have been
6.18 musty] *altered to* ancient
6.18–19 where the...a century,] silently omitted
6.31 front] silently omitted
6.33 ever] *altered to* usually
6.36–6v.1 for the...of this] *altered to* by the aid of the
6v.4 -side] silently omitted
6v.5 have] *followed by* at present
6v.5 bed-] silently omitted
6v.5–6 chamber] *followed by* and the
6v.5–7 which I...adorned it] silently omitted
6v.7 room is...as a] *altered to* one a
6v.8 and] *altered to* which
6v.10 those] *altered to* these
6v.11 long] silently omitted
6v.18–23 but it...the bureau] *altered to* but there is a happier disposal of things now. There is a little vase of flowers on one of the book-cases, and a larger bronze vase of graceful ferns that surmounts the bureau.
6v.33 abutment] *altered to* abutments
7.1 house] *altered to* home
7.3 though none...as ourselves] silently omitted

7.12 my wife] silently omitted
7.13 parlor] *followed by* we
7.15 when she told me)] silently omitted
7.15–16 she heard a] *altered to* there was a
7.28 venerable] *altered to* reverend
7.33 panelling] *altered to* wainscoting
7.36 card-vases] *altered to* card-tables
7v.1 card-vases] *altered to* flower-vases

6. Nathaniel Hawthorne, 9 August 1842 (7v–8v)

Publication History

NH's 9 August 1842 entry was first printed, with omissions and alterations, in *AM* vii (July 1866): 45–46; it was reprinted without further substantive textual alterations in *Passages*, vol. 2, pp. 72–74:
7v.7 Tuesday] silently omitted
7v.17 burthens] *standardized* burdens
7v.19 cooking] *followed by* (But we have yet to have practiced experience of the fruit.)
7v.22 shadow] *altered to* shadows
7v.26 the sale] *altered to* their sale
7v.31 the living] *altered to* us
8.19 There is...number of] *altered to* There are a good many
8.29 our] *altered to* the
8.32 abundant] *altered to* prosperous
8v.1–2 If my...be obtained] omission indicated with ellipses
8v.3 into] *altered to* in
8v.4–5 his flesh] *altered to* him

7. Sophia Hawthorne, 10 August 1842 (8v–9)

Editorial Alterations to the MS

8v.36] One or two leaves have been excised between 8/8v and 9/9v, creating a significant textual gap in SH's description of her wedding day.

8. Nathaniel Hawthorne, 10 August 1842 (9–10v)

Publication History

NH's 10 August 1842 entry was first printed, with omissions and alterations, in *AM* vii (July 1866): 46–47; it was reprinted without further substantive textual alterations in *Passages*, vol. 2, pp. 74–78:
9.31 Wednesday] silently omitted
9v.2 mess of] silently omitted
9v.3 esculants] *altered to* esculant

9v.5 their] *altered to* its
9v.6 a new] silently omitted
9v.11 on] *followed by* a
9v.11–12 inspection] *altered to* observation
9v.12 delicate] *altered to* tender
9v.13 depths of] silently omitted
9v.24–25 of considerable depth] *altered to* deeper
9v.27 beautifully] *altered to* lovely
9v.27 china-ware] *altered to* china
9v.33 belly] *altered to* rotundity
9v.33 autumnal] *altered to* autumn
10.2 the latter] *altered to* them
10.4 and thus] *altered to* and have thus
10.7 considerable] *altered to* great
10.21 contributed] *altered to* given them
10.22 therefore] *altered to* so
10.25 the] *altered to* a
10.29 Heaven] *followed by* that
10.33 hen] *altered to* hens
10.33 pig] *altered to* pigs
10v.1 there is...pleasanter than] *altered to* it is very pleasant
10v.5 account] *altered to* idea
10v.6 certainly, it] *transposed* it certainly
10v.15 neither my...nor I] *altered to* we neither of us
10v17 Sarah] *followed by* the cook
10v.17–18 Tomatoes] *followed by* too
10v.18 bye] *standardized* by
10v.20–21 season at] *altered to* garden to

9. Nathaniel Hawthorne, 13 August 1842 (10v–12)

Editorial Alterations to the MS

11v.1a made brighter] below a cross mark in pencil
12.1a spend a lifetime] below a cross mark in pencil

Publication History

NH's 13 August 1842 entry was first printed, with omissions and alterations, in *AM* viii (August 1866): 189–190; it was reprinted without further substantive textual alterations in *Passages*, vol. 2, pp. 78–80:

10v.22 *SH added the place*, Concord *and the year*, 1842, *to the heading in AM*
10v.22 August 13th Saturday] *transposed* Saturday, August 13, 1842
10v.28 his] silently omitted
11.2 life] *altered to* living
11.15 for my wife] silently omitted
11.20 pantaloons] *altered to* trousers

11.24 of tainted fame, or] silently omitted
11.28 the pond lilies] *altered to* these
11v.8 return] *followed by* home
11v.8–25 to my wife,...disposed of,] omission indicated with ellipses
11v.25 of,] *followed by* Then
11v.26 (or, possibly, sleep!)] silently omitted
11v.29 a] *altered to* our
11v.29–32 with my...record it] omission indicated with ellipses
11v.32 Then] *altered to* So
11v.35 and] *altered to* but

10. Nathaniel Hawthorne, 15 August 1842 (12–13v)

Editorial Alterations to the MS

12.18–22 ~~and afterwards,...the world~~] over-inked in blue; later recovered
12.24 ~~as my lily~~] over-inked in blue; later recovered
13v.5 ~~my sweetest wife entertaining~~] over-inked in blue; later recovered

Publication History

NH's 15 August 1842 entry was first printed, with omissions and alterations, in *AM* viii (August 1866): 190–191; it was reprinted without further substantive textual alterations in *Passages*, vol. 2, pp. 80–83:

12.6 August 15th Monday] *transposed* Monday, August 15th
12.10–11 wife and a] silently omitted
12.16 my wife and I] *altered to* we
12.18–24 and afterwards,...lily. However,] omission indicated with ellipses
12.26 morning,] *followed by* and
12.26.28 which would...and bright] omission indicated with ellipses
12.29–30 as my...or slap-jacks,] silently omitted
12.30 of] silently omitted
12.30 we] *altered to* I
12.31 of] silently omitted
12.31 pouts] *altered to* pout
12.35–36 He, from...into church,] silently omitted
12.36 then] *altered to* he
12v.2 a visit] a *silently omitted*
12v.2 Mr. Edmund Hosmer] *abbreviated* Mr. -------
12v.4 but] *altered to* and
12v.5–6 somewhat uncouth...at, but] silently omitted
12v.7 seemed to have] *altered to* had
12v.12 and smell] silently omitted
12v.15–31 Methought however,...a hundred;] omission indicated with ellipses
12v.33–13.1 It would...sense, all] silently omitted
13.1–2 hard and substantial] silently omitted
13.3 earth] *altered to* ground

13.3–5 Mr. Emerson...his grasp] silently omitted
13.6 Mr. Hosmer] *abbreviated* Mr.
13.11 hills,] *followed by* –it is
13.16 slimy] silently omitted
13.21–22 not only...that bath] *altered to* my spirit, as well as corporeal person, were refreshed by that bath
13.24 those] *altered to* these
13.25–30 at which...and hostess] omission indicated with ellipses
13.35 needless] silently omitted
13.36–13v.1–2 that my...after-supper ramble] *altered to* as to make it rather wet for our afternoon ramble
13v.3 burthen] *altered to* burden
13v.3 clematis] *altered to* clematis-vine
13v.5 my sweetest wife entertaining] silently omitted
13v.6 Mr. and Mrs. Storer and Elizabeth Hoar] *abbreviated* Mr. and Mrs. ------ *and* E----- H------.
13v.7 sate up...ten o'clock] *altered to* sat up late
13v.8 o'clock] silently omitted
13v.8–11 and, at...her hospitality] silently omitted
13v.12–15 and pleased...it herself] silently omitted

11. Nathaniel Hawthorne, 16 August 1842 (13v–14v)

Publication History

This entry was not selected for publication in *The Atlantic Monthly* or in *Passages from the American Note-Books*. In *Passages*, an ellipsis indicates a gap between entries for August 15, 1842 and August 22, 1842.

12. Sophia Hawthorne, 20 August 1842 (14v–14a)

Editorial Alterations to the MS

14v.36] One entire leaf following 14v has been excised, and two-thirds of the next extant leaf, 14a, has been excised. Although it is likely that the missing text was part of SH's 20 August entry, it is possible that another entry was lost as well (see note for NH's 22 August 1842 entry).

13. Nathaniel Hawthorne, [22 August] 1842 (14av)

Editorial Alterations to the MS

14av] The top two-thirds of this leaf have been partly excised. Though generally scrupulous about preserving NH's entries, here SH's excision produced gaps not only in her 20 August entry, but in NH's entry for 22 August as well, the heading and opening lines of which have been lost in the cut. The entry can be dated precisely on the basis of internal evidence.
15v.2 take] followed by a slash mark in pencil

Publication History

NH's 22 August 1842 entry was first printed, with omissions and alterations, in *AM* viii (August 1866): 191–192; it was reprinted without further substantive textual alterations in *Passages*, vol. 2, pp. 83–86:

14av.2–3 behind her] silently omitted
14av.9 to be...death by] *altered to* where one is tormented by
15.1 midst of...of bushes] *altered to* midst of bushes
15.3 a multitudinous gripe] *altered to* their multitudinous grip
15.5 further] *altered to* farther
15.6 scrape] *altered to* moil
15.11 lonely] *mistranscribed (?)* lovely
15.12 nobody] *altered to* no one
15.14–15 sabbath in...the trees] *altered to* Sabbath on their summits
15.26 in] *altered to* on
15.29 their] *altered to* his
15.30 they] *altered to* Crows
15.36 crickets] *altered to* cricket
15v.5 vallies] *altered to* valleys
15v.17 all the most glorious] *altered to* –the most glorious
15v.22 what is caused] *altered to* that caused
15v.24 in the same breath] *altered to* at the same time
15v.35 remote] *altered to* away
15v.36 lying] *altered to* reclining
16.4 getting] *altered to* being
16.12 intruder] *altered to* person
16.15–17 who, in...the woods—] silently omitted
16.21 Mr. Emerson and Margaret] *transposed* Margaret and Mr. Emerson
16.21 house] *altered to* home
16.22–31 where my...desolate husband] omission indicated with ellipses

14. Sophia Hawthorne, 24 August 1842 (16v–17v)

15. Nathaniel Hawthorne, 24 August 1842 (17v–18v)

Editorial Alterations to the MS

17v.27 ~~'s arms~~] over-inked in blue; later recovered
18.26 whetted] ted *added later in ink, possibly by SH*

Publication History

NH's 24 August 1842 entry was first printed, with omissions and alterations, in *AM* viii (August 1866): 192–193; it was reprinted without further substantive textual alterations in *Passages*, vol. 2, pp. 87–89:

17v.27 August 24th Wednesday] *transposed* Wednesday, August 24th
17v.27 my Sophie's arms] *altered to* home
17v.35 promises to do so] *altered to* probably will

18.15 fish] *altered to* of fishes
18.17 along] *altered to* across
18.25 pasture] *altered to* the pastures
18.26 mower] *altered to* man
18.26 whet] *altered to* whetted
18.34 flat] silently omitted
18v.2 fish] *altered to* fishes
18v.8 you feel] *altered to* one feels
18v.9–10 my little...she said] *altered to* its character was admirably expressed last night by some one who said

16. Nathaniel Hawthorne, 27 August 1842 (18v–19v)

Publication History

NH's 27 August 1842 entry was first printed, with omissions and alterations, in *AM* viii (August 1866): 193–194; it was reprinted without further substantive textual alterations in *Passages*, vol. 2, pp. 89–90:

18v.20 August 27th Saturday.] *transposed* Saturday, August 27th.
18v.21 kitchen] silently omitted
18v.22 burthened] *altered to* burdened
18v.24–25 In a...be ripe] silently omitted
18v.26 burthen] *altered to* burden
18v.27 eaten] *followed by* at
18v.31 when] *followed by* behold
18v.31 down come...our ears] *altered to* a dozen come thumping about our ears
18v.32 an] *altered to* the
18v.32 in] *altered to* of
18v.34–35 two or three] *altered to* few
18v.63–19.1 and all his household] silently omitted
19.3 those] *altered to* these
19.8 George Bradford] *abbreviated* G----- B------
19.9 Community] *followed by* at Brook Farm
19.9 us] *altered to* me
19.29–34 I have...should decline] silently omitted
19v.4 at a] *altered to* in the
19v.8 of] *followed by* the

17. Nathaniel Hawthorne, 28 August 1842 (19v–20v)

Publication History

NH's 28 August 1842 entry was first printed, with omissions and alterations, in *AM* viii (August 1866): 194–195; it was reprinted without further substantive textual alterations in *Passages*, vol. 2, pp. 91–93:

19v.10 Concord] *followed by* (not two months ago)

19v.13 that] *altered to* which
19v.17 their] *altered to* the
19v.25 and] silently omitted
19v.26 bubbling] *altered to* babbling
20.1 were] *followed by* as
20.2–3 half sullen, half cheerful] *transposed* half cheerful, half sullen
20.9 ordinary] *altered to* some
20.11 my little wife seems] *altered to* others seem
20.12 her own...and mind] *altered to* their own hearts and minds
20.12 pervade her] *altered to* pervade them
20.13 she conquers] *altered to* they conquer
20.13 drives it] *altered to* drive it
20.13 her sphere] *altered to* their sphere
20.14 creates] *altered to* create
20.16 she contrives] *altered to* such persons contrive
20.16–17 for she...heart, and] silently omitted
20.17 shines] *altered to* shining
20.19–20 my wife read us] *altered to* we read
20.20–22 most beautifully...an utterance] silently omitted
20.24 for our dinner] silently omitted
20.27 cow-hide] silently omitted

18. Nathaniel Hawthorne, 30 August 1842 (20v–22)

Editorial Alterations to the MS

21.1a main current] below an asterisk in pencil
21.24 in the world] followed by an asterisk in pencil
21.34 in the world] followed by an asterisk in pencil

Publication History

NH's 30 August 1842 entry was first printed, with omissions and alterations, in *AM* (August 1866): 195–197; it was reprinted without further substantive textual alterations in *Passages*, vol. 2, pp. 93–96:
20v.15 August 30th Tuesday] *transposed* Tuesday, August 30th
20v.15 My wife promised] *altered to* I was promised
20v.16 yesterday] *altered to* Monday
20v.18 that ever was made] *altered to* ever made
20v.19 bye] *standardized* by
20v.20–22 and what ...wet roses!] silently omitted
20v.36 downward] *altered to* downwards
21.11 these] *altered to* those
21.16–19 But let...so truly] omission indicated with ellipses
21.20 Mr. Frost] *abbreviated* Mr. -----
21.21 the colleague... Dr. Ripley] silently omitted

21.21–28 I find...old one] silently omitted
21.28 Mr. Frost] *abbreviated* Mr. -----
21.33–35 when they...our conversation] silently omitted
21v.2 enough] silently omitted
21v.14–16 That dear...manuscript volume] silently omitted
21v.16 It] *altered to* Her manuscript
21v.26 about] *altered to* around
21v.27 that] *followed by* some
21v.28 around] *altered to* about
21v.31 that] *altered to* who
21v.32 yet] *altered to* and
22.2 when they...they need] *altered to* professing to need
22.8 ever] *altered (mistranscribed?) to* even

19. Nathaniel Hawthorne, 1 September 1842 (22–23)

Publication History

NH's 1 September 1842 entry was first printed, with omissions and alterations, in *AM* ix (September 1866): 288–289; it was reprinted without further substantive textual alterations in *Passages*, vol. 2, pp. 96–98:

22.10 *SH added the place,* Concord, *and the date,* 1842, *to the heading in AM and Passages*
22.10 September 1st Thursday] *transposed* Thursday, Sept. 1
22.10 Thorow] *standardized* Thoreau
22.11–28 He is...in him] omission indicated with ellipses
22.28 Mr. Thorow] *altered to* He
22v.5 a] silently omitted
22v.6 men] *altered to* man
22v.9 especially] *followed by* for
22v.9–11 although more...with them] silently omitted
22v.11 He] *altered to* and he
22v.12 one] *altered to* a
22v.16 minute] *altered to* innate
22v.19 then there...the article] *transposed* Then there are in the article passages
22v.20–21 partly affected...his intellect] silently omitted
22v.23 him] *altered to* them
22v.24 and] *followed by* of
22v.24–27 however imperfect...the whole] silently omitted
22v.30 ripened] *altered to* grown
22v.30 Thorow] *standardized* Thoreau
22v.33 the river] silently omitted
22v.33 Thorow] *standardized* Thoreau
22v.33 further] *altered to* farther
23.6 caps] *altered to* hats

23.6 water] *altered to* tide
23.6 Thorow] *standardized* Thoreau
23.10 since] *altered to* ago
23.12–13 being in...of money] silently omitted
23.13 the poor fellow] *altered to* he
23.14 he is] *altered to* he was
23.15 give him his price] *altered to* take it
23.15–16 (only seven dollars)] silently omitted
23.17 its] *altered to* the
23.18 at as...a rate] silently omitted

20. Nathaniel Hawthorne, 2 September 1842 (23–24)

Editorial Alterations to the MS

23v.22 he knows not what)] preceded by a cross mark in pencil
23v.27 verses as too sacred] preceded by a cross mark in pencil
23v.30 for them.] followed by a cross mark in pencil

Publication History

NH's 2 September 1842 entry was first printed, with omissions and alterations, in *AM* ix (September 1866): 289–290; it was reprinted without further substantive textual alterations in *Passages*, vol. 2, pp. 98–100:
23.19 Friday] silently omitted from the heading
23.19–21 while my...our orchard,] silently omitted
23.24 Thorow] *standardized* Thoreau
23.25 were] *followed by* lately
23.25 a week...two since] silently omitted
23.27–28 My little...husband's proficiency] omission indicated with ellipses
23.31 Thorow] *standardized* Thoreau
23.34 but] *followed by* it is
23v.5 bye] *standardized* by
23v.6–8 especially after...or inanimate] omission indicated with ellipses
23v.9 of] *followed by* the
23v.14 Thorow] *standardized* Thoreau
23v.14 has] *followed by* made
23v.16 a voyage...eighty miles] silently omitted
23v.16 vessel] *altered to* craft
23v.17 Ellery Channing] omission of name indicated with -------- ---------
23v.18 the Boston Miscellany] *altered to* a Boston periodical
23v.20 He is...young men] *altered to* He is an odd and clever young man
23v.20 young men] *followed by* with
23v.20-23 whom Mr. Emerson...There is] silently omitted
23v.26 and, ridiculously...for them] silently omitted
24.1 gives] *altered to* give

21. Nathaniel Hawthorne, 4 September 1842 (24)

Publication History

NH's 4 September 1842 entry was first printed, with omissions and alterations, in *AM* ix (September 1866): 290; it was reprinted without further substantive textual alterations in *Passages*, vol. 2, pp. 100–101:

24.10 long years ago] silently omitted
24.11 Oh] *altered to* O
24.17–22 My wife . . . I believe] silently omitted

22. Sophia Hawthorne, 8 September 1842 (24–25)

Editorial Alterations to the MS

24v.36] Three or four leaves following 24/24v have been excised.

23. Nathaniel Hawthorne, 18 September 1842 (25–26v)

Publication History

NH's 18 September 1842 entry was first printed, with omissions and alterations, in *AM* ix (September 1866): 290–291; it was reprinted without further substantive textual alterations in *Passages*, vol. 2, pp.101–104:

25.25 Sunday] omitted from the headings in *AM* and *Passages*
25.30–31 (my dearest...her mother)] silently omitted
25v.17 intrusion] *altered to* presence
25v.23 Thorow] *standardized* Thoreau
25v.24–25 seem ready...down, and] silently omitted
25v.26 headlong in] *transposed in* headlong
25v.28 here] *altered to* there
25v.28 stand] *altered to* stood
25v.29 their] silently omitted
25v.31 birches] *altered (mistranscribed?)* bushes
25v.31 elder-trees] *altered to* alder-trees
25v.32 over the water] silently omitted
25v.36–26.1 more complete] *altered to* deeper
26.1 mine did] *altered to* my boat
26.14 At all events] *altered to* At any rate
26.17 scene] *altered to* picture
26.17 arrayed] *altered to* dressed
26.25 settled] *altered to* settling
26.29 and yet] *altered to* with yet
26.30 down the stream] *altered to* along
26.31–32 what it is in] *altered to* that of
26.35 wherever] *altered to* whenever
26v.6 at] *altered to* of
26v.8–9 and partly...cleaning them] silently omitted

24. Nathaniel Hawthorne, 10 October 1842 (26v–27)

Publication History

NH's 10 October 1842 entry was first printed, with omissions and alterations, in *AM* ix (September 1866): 291–292; it was reprinted without further substantive textual alterations in *Passages*, vol. 2, pp.104–106:

26v.20 I] *followed by* have
26v.21 slept] *altered to* spent
26v.21 my belovedest wife] *altered to* home
26v.21 spent the] *altered to* were that
26v.23 further] *altered to* farther
26v.31 bring them...little wife] *altered to* pluck them
26v.32 our] *altered to* an
26v.35 David Roberts] *abbreviated* D----- R------
26v.36 My wife...describe him] silently omitted
27.1 which I...description of] *transposed* of which I would give a description
27.14–15 a considerable] *altered to* some
27.23 indeed] *followed by* in price
27.25 bushels] *followed by* of potatoes

25. Nathaniel Hawthorne, 8 November 1842 (27v–28)

Publication History

NH's 8 November 1842 entry was first printed, with omissions and alterations, in *AM* ix (September 1866): 292–293; it was reprinted without further substantive textual alterations in *Passages*, vol. 2, pp. 106–107:

27v.1 Tuesday] omitted from the headings in *AM* and *Passages*
27v.2–3 unless my...in hand] silently omitted
27v.21 My wife and I] *altered to* We
27v.32 trees] *altered to* boughs
27v.33 through] *altered to* over
27v.36 I found] silently omitted
28.1 which] silently omitted

26. Nathaniel Hawthorne, 24 November 1842 (28)

Editorial Alterations to the MS

28.20 overflown] *overwritten* overflowed

Publication History

NH's 24 November 1842 entry was first printed, with omissions and alterations, in *AM* ix (September 1866): 293; it was reprinted without further substantive textual alterations in *Passages*, vol. 2, pp. 106–107:

28.10 Nov[r] 24th Thursday] *transposed* Thursday, November 24
28.11 my wife and I] *altered to* we
28.18 one] *altered to* one's self

28.20 overflown] *altered to* overflowed
28.23 my wife and I] *altered to* we
28.30 into] *altered to* in

27. Sophia Hawthorne, 11 December–[?] 1842 (28v–30a)

Commentary

At some point subsequent to the excisions made by SH, but prior to the numbering and foliation of the notebook done at the Morgan, two loose leaves now numbered 29/29v and 30/30v but containing entries belonging to 1843 were mislaid following 28/28v, creating an error in the chronological sequence of the notebook's text. This edition of the common notebook follows Patrica Valenti's transcription of SH's portions of MA 580 by restoring the manuscript leaves to where they apparently belong chronologically. Here, 30a/30av follows 28/28v; 29/29v and 30/30v follow 37/37v.

30a.3] The transcription of the second half of the line is conjectural.

30a.4] The word or words following 'to' are illegible; Patricia Valenti offers the following conjectural reading: "stoop & [ ]."

Editorial Alterations to the MS

28v.36 unmanageable] Two or three leaves following 28/28v have been excised.

30a/30av] Three-quarters of 30a/30av has been cut away. The nature of SH's excisions makes it impossible to determine whether the text on 30a belongs to the 11 December entry or to another entry, as well as precisely how many entries were lost between 11 December and NH's next extant entry nearly four months later on 31 March.

30a.1–4 ~~every day…& XXX~~] over-inked in black

28. Nathaniel Hawthorne, 31 March 1843 (30av–32)

Editorial Alterations to the MS

30av] The opening leaf of NH's entry has been almost wholly excised (see the preceding entry by SH). Although SH seems to have been generally scrupulous in preserving NH's entries, it is impossible to know for sure what—and whose—text has been lost in the cut.

31.1a broad] below a cross mark in pencil

31.22–24 ~~One grief…preceding pages~~] over-inked in blue; later recovered

31.25–29 ~~We do…earlier period~~] over-inked in blue; later recovered

Publication History

NH's 31 March 1843 entry was first printed, with omissions and alterations, in *AM* ix (September 1866): 293–294; it was not reprinted in *Passages*:

30av.1 March 31st 1843. Friday.] *transposed* Friday, March 31, 1843
31.5 home] *altered to* mansion
31. 18–33 My dear…of marriage] omission indicated with ellipses

31v.3 prospects] *altered to* prospect
31v.11–13 and the...empty pockets] silently omitted
31v.17–28 My wife...boundless heart!] omission indicated with ellipses
31v.30 in so good condition] *altered to* in a better condition
31v.33–35 and a...substantial viands] silently omitted
31v.36 home] *altered to* home again
32.1–3 Salem—at...bachelor habits] *altered to* I alone went to Salem, where I resumed all my bachelor habits
21.12 Molly Bryant] *altered to* our servant

29. Nathaniel Hawthorne, 7 April 1843 (32–32v)

Editorial Alterations to the MS

32.14 belovedest] ve *interlined with a caret in a different ink*
32v.1 Mr. Emerson's brother] preceded by an asterisk in pencil
32v.9 removal; —] followed by an asterisk in pencil

Publication History

NH's 7 April 1843 entry was first printed, with omissions and alterations, in *AM* ix (September 1866): 294–295; it was reprinted without further substantive textual alterations in *Passages*, vol. 2, pp. 110–111:

32.14 April 7th Friday] *transposed* Friday, April 7
32.14–17 My belovedest...six months] *altered to* My wife has gone to Boston to see her sister M----, who is to be married in two or three weeks, and then immediately to Europe for six months.
32.17–20 A wagon...sight. Then] omission indicated with ellipses
32.22 inquietness] *altered to* unquietness
32.30–32 for the...rough road] omission indicated with ellipses
32v.6 physically] silently omitted
32v.6–8 morally and...these respects] silently omitted
32v.9 removal] *followed by* but
32v.9–10 also, world] silently omitted
32v.10 On] *altered to* on
32v.15–21 He says...Mr. Thoreau] omission indicated with ellipses
32v.26 my departure] silently omitted
32v.26–27 I should...as well] silently omitted

30. Nathaniel Hawthorne, 8 April 1843 (32v–33v)

Editorial Alterations to the MS

33.2 ~~Where was...then~~] lightly canceled in pencil
33.34 if] canceled in a different ink, possibly by SH
33v.1 seemed] below an asterisk in pencil
33v.15 Mr.] followed by an asterisk in pencil
33v.22 developements] "e" canceled, possibly by SH

Publication History

NH's 8 April 1843 entry was first printed, with omissions and alterations, in *AM* ix (September 1866): 295; it was reprinted without further substantive textual alterations in *Passages*, vol. 2, pp. 111–113:

32v.28 April 8th Saturday] *transposed* Saturday, April 8
32v.29 supper-time] *altered to* tea-time
32v.35–33.1 How much...little wife!] silently omitted
33.1 nine,] *followed by* and
33.2 Where was...wife then?] silently omitted
33.4–5 have been...my wife] *altered to* have not been intended for me
33.8–9 Before seven...I arose] silently omitted
33.16 Gaffer Flint] *altered to* Mr. Flint
33.17 Gaffer] *altered to* he
33.18 of Gaffer] silently omitted
33.19 also;] *followed by* he
33.21 Gaffer] *altered to* Mr. Flint
33.22–24 with no...loving smile] *altered to* without the usual heart-spring
33.25 Molly] *followed by* the cook
33.34 experiencing] *altered to* to have had
33.35–33v.1 My little...the kind] silently omitted
33v.1 seemed fullest] *altered to* spoke
33v.3–5 He apotheosized...worth considering] silently omitted
33v.6 supper-bell] *altered to* tea-bell
33v.6 spoke] *altered to* discoursed
33v.8 Sam Ward] *altered to* Sam G. Ward
33v.9 He seems...for them] omission indicated with ellipses
33v.9 he] *altered to* He
33v.10–12 and thinks...or nothing] silently omitted
33v.14–19 but Mr. Emerson...and fireside] omission indicated with ellipses
33v.23 Charles Newcomb] *abbreviated* C. N-------
33v.24 now] silently omitted
33v.28 discussed] *altered to* considered
33v.30 threatening to...very soon] silently omitted
33v.33 on the whole] silently omitted
33v.34 supper] *altered to* tea
33v.36 I would...my wife!] omission indicated with ellipses

31. Nathaniel Hawthorne, 9 April 1843 (34–35v)

Editorial Alterations to the MS

34v.28–30 ~~to my...not now~~] over-inked in blue; later recovered
34v.35–36 ~~to my dearest spouse~~] lightly canceled in pencil

Publication History

NH's 9 April 1843 entry was first printed, with omissions and alterations, in

AM x (October 1866): 450–452; it was reprinted without further substantive textual alterations in *Passages*, vol. 2, pp. 117–120:

34.1 April 9th Sunday] *transposed* Sunday, April 9; *SH also added the year,* 1843, *to the header*
34.1 Dear little Wife] omission indicated with ellipses
34.3–6 but the...cheerful either;] omission indicated with ellipses
34.6 my] *altered to* My
34.7–8 while thou art present] *altered to* when I am not alone
34.15–16 for thy...my difficulties] *altered to* for help in my difficulties
34.20 to] *altered to* at
34.21 thy] *altered to* a
34.22 that] silently omitted
34.23 Dearest wife,] silently omitted
34.24 thou canst not imagine] silently omitted
34.25–29 even though...deny it] silently omitted
34.30 letter] *altered to* note (enclosed)
34.33 thy dearest epistle] *altered to* my epistle
34.35 of looking...fairy penmanship] *altered to* for the sake of the penmanship
34v.1 went to bed] *altered to* retired
34v.10 thy husband's] *altered to* my
34v.11–12 during thy absence] silently omitted
34v.12 we] *altered to* I
34v.13–15 together, and...for thee] omission indicated with ellipses
34v.20 tail] *altered to* skirts
34v.21 on] *altered to* it
34v.22 finished] *followed by* reading
34v.23 and] *followed by* it
34v.27–32 But I...Husband. P.S.] omission indicated with ellipses
34v.35 5] *written* five
35.23 wake] *altered to* course
35.32 up] silently omitted
35v.9 legs] *altered to* feet

32. Nathaniel Hawthorne, 10 April 1843 (35v–36v)

Editorial Alterations to the MS

35v.30–31 ~~What is...in solitude?~~] lightly canceled in pencil
36v.6–7 ~~Come home...of speech.~~] lightly canceled in pencil

Publication History

NH's 10 April 1843 entry was first printed, with omissions and alterations, in *AM* x (October 1866): 452; it was reprinted without further substantive textual alterations in *Passages*, vol. 2, pp. 121–122:

35v.23 April 10th Monday] *transposed* Monday, April 10
35v.24–25 and my...with both;] omission indicated with ellipses

35v.25–26 lighted the lamp, and] silently omitted
35v.27 dearest] silently omitted
35v.27 could] *altered to* would
35v.28 Molly had...filled it] *altered to* it was duly filled
35v.28–36.2 Nevertheless, lacking...my side] omission indicated with ellipses
36.2 The] *altered to* This
36.11–13 Since my...the dinner-bell] silently omitted
36.18–20 Dearest love...man; yet] silently omitted
36.20 thy] *altered to* some
36.20–21 small as...might be,] silently omitted
36.24 thy company] *altered to* the company of another
36.31 the single...thy husband] *altered to* my single person
36v.2–4 Surely, thou...not ashamed?] omission indicated with ellipses
36v.6–7 Come home...of speech.] omission indicated with ellipses

33. Nathaniel Hawthorne, 11 April 1843 (36v–37)

Editorial Alterations to the MS

36v.12–17 ~~My greatest...couch; for~~] over-inked in blue; later recovered. Parts of "seek," "vasitude," and "couch" have been touched up in black ink for legibility.
37.22 Eve] followed by an excision of the remainder of the leaf

Publication History

NH's 11 April 1843 entry was first printed, with omissions and alterations, in *AM* x (October 1866): 452–453; it was reprinted without further substantive textual alterations in *Passages*, vol. 2, pp.122–123:
36v.9 1843] omitted from the headings
36v.10 lighted the lamp, and] silently omitted
36v.12–20 Bath and...that good?] silently omitted
36v.21 had] *altered to* has
36v.24 There was...Office; so] silently omitted
36v.26 if home...art not] *altered to* if home it may now be called
36v.28–32 It is...his ease] silently omitted
36v.34–35 wanted] *altered to* wished
37.15–16 Channing's] *altered* to Channing
37.19 the] *altered to* this
37.20–22 ten minutes...its Eve] silently omitted

34. Sophia Hawthorne, [11? – 22? April] 1843 (37v, 29, 29v, 30)

Editorial Alterations to the MS

37v.21 not] followed by an excision of the remainder of the leaf
29–30v] excised; later mislaid following 28v
29v.24 ~~sweet~~] over-inked in blue; later recovered

29v.27 ~~bosom~~] over-inked in blue; later recovered
29v.33 ~~blooming in his arms~~] over-inked in blue; later recovered
29v.36 ~~wholly, unreservedly his~~] over-inked in blue; later recovered
30.2–8 ~~XXXX...forever also?~~] over-inked in black

35. Sophia Hawthorne, 23 April 1843 (30, 30v, 38)

Editorial Alterations to the MS

30–30v] excised; later mislaid following 29/29v

36. Nathaniel Hawthorne, 25 April 1843 (38–39v)

Editorial Alterations to the MS

38.22–25 spot] followed by three lines over-inked in black
38.31 irritable] followed by three-fourths of a line over-inked in black; a period was inserted after "irritable," replacing NH's semi-colon

Publication History

NH's 25 April 1843 entry was first printed, with omissions and alterations, in *AM* x (October 1866): 453–454; it was reprinted without further substantive textual alterations in *Passages*, vol. 2, pp.123–126:
38.10 Tuesday] omitted from the headings
38.22–31 ~~XXXXX~~...irritable. ~~XXXXX~~] omission indicated with ellipses
38.32 Oh] *altered to* O
38.35 burthen] *standardized* burden
38v.5 of the] *altered to* in the
38v.12 latter] *altered to* later
38v.14 Some tracts] *altered to* Sometimes
38v.23 that] silently omitted
38v.29 A moment ago] *altered to* Just now
39.4 a pair of bars] *altered to* two rails
39.5 a considerable] *altered to* for some
39.19 considerable] *altered to* great
39.20 wait] *altered to (mistranscibed?)* went
39.21 now made themselves scarce] *altered to* disappeared
39.26 a] *altered to* the
39.32 I leave...to describe] *altered* I will not describe
39.32–33 I leave...her own kindred] omission indicated with ellipses
39.36 in] *altered to* on
39v.2 occasion] *altered to* subject
39v.6 one of them the crow-blackbird] silently omitted

37. Nathaniel Hawthorne, 26 April 1843 (39v–40v)

Editorial Alterations to the MS

40v.13 summer] "pring" *written over* "ummer," *possibly by SH*

Publication History

NH's 26 April 1843 entry was first printed, with omissions and alterations, in *AM* x (October 1866): 454–455; it was reprinted without further substantive textual alterations in *Passages*, vol. 2, pp.126–129:

39v.10 Wednesday] omitted from the headings
39v.19 But] silently omitted
40.9 the house] *altered to* this house
40.11–18 Methinks my...of May!] omission indicated with ellipses
40.20–22 My dearest...house; and] omission indicated with ellipses
40.22 the yard] *altered to* The yard
40.23 still greater] *altered to* great
40.25 my wife has] *altered to* are
40.26 intending to] *altered to* and we intend to
40.26–28 I wander...them away] omission indicated with ellipses
40.33 her] *altered to* its
40.34 her] *altered to* its
40.35 really] silently omitted

38. Nathaniel Hawthorne, 27 April 1843 (40v–41)

Editorial Alterations to the MS

41.35 I hate all labor] underlined later in pencil, possibly by SH

Publication History

NH's 27 April 1843 entry was first printed, with omissions and alterations, in *AM* x (October 1866): 455–456; it was reprinted without further substantive textual alterations in *Passages*, vol. 2, pp.129–131:

40v.14 April 27th Thursday] *transposed* Thursday, April 27
40v.15–16 observations] *altered to* observation
40v.27 as] *altered to* to be
40v.30 tracts] *altered to* places
40v.31 at a] *altered to* in the
40v.35 a fish] *altered to* fish
41.2 After we...to bed] silently omitted
41.3 we] *altered to* I
41.9 himself] *altered to* he was
41.31–36 I bought...the head] silently omitted

39. Sophia Hawthorne, 9 May 1843 (41v–45v)

Commentary

42v.34 Saturday] SH noted the date incorrectly; the 7th was Sunday
45.9 Saturday 19th] SH noted the date incorrectly; Saturday was the 20th

Editorial Alterations to the MS

42–45v] excised; later laid in

40. Sophia Hawthorne, 23 May 1843 (45v–46)

41. Nathaniel Hawthorne, 2 June 1843 (46)

Publication History

NH's 2 June 1843 entry was first printed, with omissions and alterations, in *AM* x (October 1866): 456; it was reprinted without further substantive textual alterations in *Passages*, vol. 2, pp.131:

46.14 June 2d Friday] *transposed* Friday, June 2
46.17 had] *altered to* have
46.22 play such tricks] *altered to* so sport
46.25–26 as my...sagely observes,] silently omitted
46.27 as I...truly added] silently omitted
46.31–36 The above...He will] silently omitted

42. Sophia Hawthorne, 6 June 1843 (46v–47v)

43. Nathaniel Hawthorne, 23 June 1843 (47v–48v)

Editorial Alterations to the MS

48v.17–19 ~~perhaps the...old abbey~~] over-inked in blue; later recovered

Publication History

NH's 23 June1843 entry was first printed, with omissions and alterations, in *AM* x (October 1866): 456–457; it was reprinted without further substantive textual alterations in *Passages*, vol. 2, pp. 131–134:

47v.13 June 23d Friday] *transposed* Friday, June 23
47v.14 and the] *altered to* with
47v.17–18 is another scorcher] *altered to* it scorches again
47v.21 too much...too intense] *altered to* too burning
47v.24 could] *altered to* should
47v.31–32 and the...measurably advanced] silently omitted
47v.36 whole day together] *altered to* day
48.1–2 bitterly] silently omitted
48.2 vermin] *altered to* insects
48.3 infinite] *altered to* excessive
48.6–7 There is...on them] silently omitted
48.14–15 hold of] silently omitted
48.19 mystery] *followed by* and also a symbol
48.23 grains] *altered to* grain
48.32 musk melons] *followed by* also
48.33 have come up] silently omitted
48.36–48v.1 My little... flower garden] *altered to* There ought to be a record of the flower-garden
48v.2 minutely] *altered to* minute

48v.3 I do] silently omitted
48v.4 she ought...to omit] *altered to* the noting of
48v.5 roses] *followed by* should not be omitted
48v.9 depth] *altered to* depths
48v.11–12 Little wife...described it] *altered to* To describe it is
48v.12–14 I leave...among flowers] *altered to* Also the visit of two friends, who may fitly enough be mentioned among flowers, ought to have been described.
48v.15 among flowers] *followed by* Mrs. F. S---- and Miss A. S----
48v.15–16 I wonder,...to mention] *altered to* Also I have neglected to mention
48v.16–17 into this wicked world] silently omitted
48v.17–19 perhaps the...very naughty] silently omitted
48v.28–29 if not...less possibility] *altered to* a diminished necessity, or, at all events, a much less possibility
48v.31 tossings and...no winters; —] silently omitted

44. Sophia Hawthorne, [24 June] 1843 (49–51)

Commentary

The entry can be dated on the basis of internal evidence.

Editorial Alterations to the MS

48v.36 us] One MS leaf following 48/48v, containing the opening lines of SH's entry, has been excised; two leaves (49/49v, 50/50v) have been cut out and laid in.
49.1–2 ~~XXXXX~~] one and a quarter lines heavily over-inked in black; although largely illegible, Patricia Valenti was able to discern two words, "bed...of."
49.36 our] followed by a cross mark in pencil

45. Nathaniel Hawthorne, 1 July 1843 (51)

Publication History

NH's 1 July 1843 entry was first printed, with omissions and alterations, in *AM* x (October 1866): 457; it was reprinted without further substantive textual alterations in *Passages*, vol. 2, p.134:
51.31 July 1st Saturday] *transposed* Saturday, July 1
51.31 mess] *altered to* dish
51.35–36 tremendous] *altered to* ferocious

46. Sophia Hawthorne, 9 July 1843 (51v–52)

Editorial Alterations to the MS

51v–52] These MS leaves were at some point glued together, presumably by SH, who may have glued them together to preserve the privacy of the entry on her wedding anniversary without wholly destroying it.

51v.27–52.7 ~~My XXX....What XXX!~~] over-inked in black; only scattered words remain legible: "My...with the...GOD...she has any one yet,... GOD's infinite...plan of His Providence!...this... other... GOD..., & then...life before...! What...!"

52.11–22 ~~The XXX...nobleness XXX~~] over-inked in black; only scattered words remain legible: "The...I...happy as I...with child by thee, thou crown of nobleness?"

47. Nathaniel Hawthorne, 9 July 1843 (52v)

Publication History

NH's 9 July 1843 entry was first printed, with omissions and alterations, in *AM* x (October 1866): 457–458; it was reprinted without further substantive textual alterations in *Passages*, vol. 2, pp. 134–135:

52v.1 July 9th Sunday] *transposed* Sunday, July 9
52v.1 Dearest love] silently omitted
52v.3 holiest] silently omitted
52v.3 of our life] silently omited
52v.4 heaves and swells] *transposed* swells and heaves
52v.7–12 We never...before us] omission indicated with ellipses
52v.15 texture and substance] *transposed* substance and texture

48. Nathaniel Hawthorne, 18 July 1843 (52v)

Publication History

NH's 18 July 1843 entry was first printed, with omissions and alterations, in *AM* x (October 1866): 458; it was reprinted without further substantive textual alterations in *Passages*, vol. 2, p.135:

52v.17 Tuesday] omitted from the headers
52v.18 summer-squash] *altered to* summer-squashes
52v.20 root] *altered to* roots
52v.24 his wife] *altered to* Mrs. Hillard
52v.24–25 he left...Monday afternoon] *transposed* On Monday afternoon he left us
52v.25 she] *altered to* Mrs. Hillard

49. Nathaniel Hawthorne, 28 July 1843 (52v–53)

Editorial Alterations to the MS

53.5–8 ~~My little...her bosom~~] over-inked in black; only scattered words remain legible: "My {little}wife is troubled with .... God bless her and the... life within her bosom."

Publication History

NH's 28 July 1843 entry was first printed, with omissions and alterations, in *AM* x (October 1866): 458; it was reprinted without further substantive textual alterations in *Passages*, vol. 2, p.135:

52v.26 July 28th Friday] *transposed* Friday, July 28
52v.31 temper and] silently omitted
52v.35–36 idle and] silently omitted
52v.36 can] silently omitted
53.2 during] silently omitted
53.3 free and full] *transposed* full and free
53.5–8 My little...her bosom] silently omitted

50. Nathaniel Hawthorne, 31 July 1843 (53)

Editorial Alterations to the MS

53.11 desire.] The remainder of the leaf has been excised; how many of NH's lines were lost in the process is unclear.

Publication History

NH's 31 July 1843 entry was first printed, with omissions and alterations, in *AM* x (October 1866): 458; it was reprinted without further substantive textual alterations in *Passages*, vol. 2, p. 136:
53.9 July 31st Monday] *transposed* Monday, July 31
53.10 It showed] *altered to* There were

51. Sophia Hawthorne, [31 July–28 August?] 1843 (53v–54)

Editorial Alterations to the MS

53v.1 roam] opening of entry excised (see note for previous entry)
53v.11 thy] remainder of leaf excised

52. Sophia Hawthorne, 29 August 1843 (54–55)

Editorial Alterations to the MS

54.25–31 ~~How thou...this reason~~] over-inked in blue; later recovered

53. Sophia Hawthorne, 30 August 1843 (55–56v)

Editorial Alterations to the MS

55.36–55v.2 ~~Sweetest, I...by thee!~~] over-inked in blue; later recovered
55v.4 of thy love] over-inked in blue; later recovered
55v.10–11 ~~We are...than ever~~] over-inked in blue; later recovered
55v.24–26 ~~Oh dearest...husband forever.—~~] over-inked in blue; later recovered

54. Sophia Hawthorne, 1 September 1843 (56v–56a)

Editorial Alterations to the MS

56a–56av] The top half of the MS leaf 56/56a has been excised; the excision created a gap in the middle of SH's 1 September entry.

55. Sophia Hawthorne, 2 September 1843 (56a–56av)

Editorial Alterations to the MS

56a–56av] The top half of the MS leaf 56/56a has been excised; the excision created a gap at the end of SH's 2 September 1843 entry.

56. Nathaniel Hawthorne, 13 September 1843 (56av)

Publication History

NH's 13 September 1843 entry was first printed, with omissions and alterations, in *AM* x (October 1866): 458; it was reprinted without further substantive textual alterations in *Passages*, vol. 2, p. 136:

56av.1 September 13th Wednesday.] *transposed* Wednesday, September 13
56av.8 My little...and I] *altered to* We

57. Nathaniel Hawthorne, 23 September 1843 (56av–57)

Editorial Alterations to the MS

57.35–36 ~~and I...to come~~] over-inked in blue; later recovered

Publication History

NH's 23 September 1843 entry was first printed, with omissions and alterations, in *AM* x (October 1866): 458–459; it was reprinted without further substantive textual alterations in *Passages*, vol. 2, pp. 136–137:

56av.10 September 23d Sunday.] *transposed* Sunday, September 23
56av.12 eatable] *altered to* edible
56av.12 and of] and silently omitted
56av.13 (I think it was)] *altered to* I think
56av.16 came into eating] *altered to* was good for eating
56av.16 have still] *transposed* still have
57.1–2 to be pretty good] *altered to* well
57.3 in] *altered to* of
57.10 her] *altered to* the
57.19 all over] *transposed* over all
57.23 have given] have *silently omitted*
57.24 hearts] *altered to* heart
57.31 pleasant one] *followed by* to gather them
57.35–36 and I...to come] omission indicated with ellipses

58. Nathaniel Hawthorne, 6 October 1843 (57v–58v)

Editorial Alterations to the MS

57v.1a *The date* 1844 *was added above the opening line; later, this notation was revised* (I think 1843).
58.29 like] interlined
58v.10 be] interlined

Publication History

NH's 6 October 1843 entry was first printed, with omissions and alterations, in *AM* x (October 1866): 459–460; it was reprinted without further substantive textual alterations in *Passages*, vol. 2, pp.137–141:

57v.1 October 6th Friday] *transposed* Friday, October 6
57v.1–2 (leaving...days)] silently omitted
57v.3 north-west] silently omitted
57v.27 but] *altered to* and
57v.28 should] *altered to* might
57v.31 a] silently omitted
58.2 Luckily] *altered to* Fortunately
58.3 scene] *altered to* picture
58.6 now and hereafter] silently omitted
58.6 further] silently omitted
58.13 was] *altered to* were
58.14–15 If I ...this pond] *altered to* It is fit for baptisms
58.15 then] silently omitted
58.15–16 to pollute...into it] *altered to* it to be polluted by having sins washed into it
58.17 there] *altered to* in it
58.17–18 It would...I hope] silently omitted
58.18–19 our blessed...its bosom] *altered to* but blessed babies might be dipped into its bosom
58.26 with] *followed by* the
58.30 ant-hill] *altered to* ant-hills
58.30 or] silently omitted
58v.1 beneath the trees] *altered to* in open spaces
58v.11 she] *altered to* It
58v.12 her] *altered to* its
58v.16 protruding] *altered to* thrusting
58v.26 undefinable] *altered to* indefinable
58v.30 a] *altered to* the
58v.34 ride] *altered to* drive

59. Sophia Hawthorne, 19 November 1843 (59–60)

Editorial Alterations to the MS

59–59v] excised; later laid in
59.9–14 ~~Our bed...my lord~~] over-inked in blue; later recovered
59.32 ~~when I am confined~~] over-inked in blue; later recovered
59v.15–17 ~~& the...of us~~] over-inked in blue; later recovered

Appendices

The Common Journal of
Nathaniel and Sophia Hawthorne

Appendix 1

A Calendar of the Sophia and Nathaniel Hawthorne Journal Entries, 1842–43

1842

1. SH, [9 July-5 August]
2. NH, 5 August
3. NH, 6 August
4. NH, 7 August
5. NH, 8 August
6. NH, 9 August
7. SH, 10 August
8. NH, 10 August
9. NH, 13 August
10. NH, 15 August
11. NH, 16 August
12. SH, 20 August
13. NH, 22 August
14. SH, 24 August
15. NH, 24 August
16. NH, 27 August
17. NH, 28 August
18. NH, 30 August
19. NH, 1 September
20. NH, 2 September
21. NH, 4 September
22. SH, 8 September
23. NH, 18 September
24. NH, 10 October
25. NH, 8 November
26. NH, 24 November
27. SH, [11 December]

1843

28. NH, 31 March
29. NH, 7 April
30. NH, 8 April
31. NH, 9 April
32. NH, 10 April
33. NH, 11 April
34. SH, [11? – 22? April]
35. SH, 23 April
36. NH, 25 April
37. NH, 26 April
38. NH, 27 April
39. SH, 9 May
40. SH, 23 May
41. NH, 2 June
42. SH, 6 June
43. NH, 23 June
44. SH, 24 June
45. NH, 1 July
46. SH, 9 July
47. NH, 9 July
48. NH, 18 July
49. NH, 28 July
50. NH, 31 July
51. SH, [31 July-28 August?]
52. SH, 29 August
53. SH, 30 August
54. SH, 1 September
55. SH, 2 September
56. NH, 13 September
57. NH, 23 September
58. NH, 6 October
59. SH, 19 November

Appendix 2
Entries with Wholly or Partly Excised Leaves

1. SH, [9 July-5 August] 1842
7. SH, 10 August 1842
12. SH, 20 August 1842
13. NH, [22 August] 1842
22. SH, 8 September 1842
27. SH, [11 December] 1842
28. NH, 31 March 1843
33. NH, 11 April 1843
34. SH, [11? – 22? April] 1843
35. SH, 23 April 1843
39. SH, 9 May 1843
44. SH, [24 June] 1843
50. NH, 31 July 1843
51. SH, [31 July-28 August?] 1843
54. SH, 1 September 1843
55. SH, 2 September 1843
59. SH, 19 November 1843

Appendix 3
Entries with Obliterated Passages

2. NH, 5 August 1842
3. NH, 6 August 1842
10. NH, 15 August 1842
15. NH, 24 August 1842
27. SH, [11 December] 1842
28. NH, 31 March 1843
31. NH, 9 April 1843
33. NH, 11 April 1843
34. SH [11?-22? April] 1843
36. NH, 25 April 1843
43. NH, 23 June 1843
44. SH, [24 June] 1843
46. SH, 9 July 1843
49. NH, 28 July 1843
52. SH, [31 July-28 August] 1843
53. SH, 30 August 1843
57. NH, 23 September 1843

Appendix 4
Entries with Sophia Hawthorne's Editorial Marks, Emendations, and Drawings

4. NH, 7 August 1842
5. NH, 8 August 1842
9. NH, 13 August 1842
13. NH, [22 August] 1842
15. NH, 24 August 1842
18. NH, 30 August 1842
20. NH, 2 September 1842
26. NH, 24 November 1842
28. NH, 31 March 1843
29. NH, 7 April 1843
30. NH, 8 April 1843
31. NH, 9 April 1843
32. NH, 10 April 1843
37. NH, 26 April 1843
38. NH, 27 April 1843
39. SH, 9 May 1843
44. SH, [24 June 1843]
58. NH, 6 October 1843
59. SH, 19 November 1843

Appendix 5

Examples of Published Entries in *The Atlantic Monthly* (1866) and *Passages from the American Note-Books* (1868)

1866.] *Passages from Hawthorne's Note-Books.* 191

but these bright waters washed it all away.

We returned home in due season for dinner. . . . . To my misfortune, however, a box of Mediterranean wine proved to have undergone the acetous fermentation; so that the splendor of the festival suffered some diminution. Nevertheless, we ate our dinner with a good appetite, and afterwards went universally to take our several siestas. Meantime there came a shower, which so besprinkled the grass and shrubbery as to make it rather wet for our after-tea ramble. The chief result of the walk was the bringing home of an immense burden of the trailing clematis-vine, now just in blossom, and with which all our flower-stands and vases are this morning decorated. On our return we found Mr. and Mrs. S——, and E. H——, who shortly took their leave, and we sat up late, telling ghost-stories. This morning, at seven, our friends left us. We were both pleased with the visit, and so I think were our guests.

Monday, August 22d.—I took a walk through the woods yesterday afternoon, to Mr. Emerson's, with a book which Margaret Fuller had left, after a call on Saturday eve. I missed the nearest way, and wandered into a very secluded portion of the forest; for forest it might justly be called, so dense and sombre was the shade of oaks and pines. Once I wandered into a tract so overgrown with bushes and underbrush that I could scarcely force a passage through. Nothing is more annoying than a walk of this kind, where one is tormented by an innumerable host of petty impediments. It incenses and depresses me at the same time. Always when I flounder into the midst of bushes, which cross and intertwine themselves about my legs, and brush my face, and seize hold of my clothes, with their multitudinous grip,—always, in such a difficulty, I feel as if it were almost as well to lie down and die in rage and despair as to go one step farther. It is laughable, after I have got out of the moil, to think how miserably it affected me for the moment; but I had better learn patience betimes, for there are many such bushy tracts in this vicinity, on the margins of meadows, and my walks will often lead me into them. Escaping from the bushes, I soon came to an open space among the woods,—a very lovely spot, with the tall old trees standing around as quietly as if no one had intruded there throughout the whole summer. A company of crows were holding their Sabbath on their summits. Apparently they felt themselves injured or insulted by my presence; for, with one consent, they began to Caw! caw! caw! and, launching themselves sullenly on the air, took flight to some securer solitude. Mine, probably, was the first human shape that they had seen all day long,—at least, if they had been stationary in that spot; but perhaps they had winged their way over miles and miles of country, had breakfasted on the summit of Greylock, and dined at the base of Wachusett, and were merely come to sup and sleep among the quiet woods of Concord. But it was my impression at the time, that they had sat still and silent on the tops of the trees all through the Sabbath day, and I felt like one who should unawares disturb an assembly of worshippers. A crow, however, has no real pretensions to religion, in spite of his gravity of mien and black attire. Crows are certainly thieves, and probably infidels. Nevertheless, their voices yesterday were in admirable accordance with the influences of the quiet, sunny, warm, yet autumnal afternoon. They were so far above my head that their loud clamor added to the quiet of the scene, instead of disturbing it. There was no other sound, except the song of the cricket, which is but an audible stillness; for, though it be very loud and heard afar, yet the mind does not take note of it as a sound, so entirely does it mingle and lose its individuality among the other characteristics of coming autumn. Alas for the summer! The grass is still verdant on the hills and in the valleys;

192 *Passages from Hawthorne's Note-Books.* [August,

the foliage of the trees is as dense as ever, and as green; the flowers are abundant along the margin of the river, and in the hedge-rows, and deep among the woods; the days, too, are as fervid as they were a month ago; and yet in every breath of wind and in every beam of sunshine there is an autumnal influence. I know not how to describe it. Methinks there is a sort of coolness amid all the heat, and a mildness in the brightest of the sunshine. A breeze cannot stir, without thrilling me with the breath of autumn, and I behold its pensive glory in the far, golden gleams among the long shadows of the trees. The flowers, even the brightest of them,—the golden-rod and the gorgeous cardinals,—the most glorious flowers of the year,—have this gentle sadness amid their pomp. Pensive autumn is expressed in the glow of every one of them. I have felt this influence earlier in some years than in others. Sometimes autumn may be perceived even in the early days of July. There is no other feeling like that caused by this faint, doubtful, yet real perception, or rather prophecy, of the year's decay, so deliciously sweet and sad at the same time.

After leaving the book at Mr. Emerson's I returned through the woods, and, entering Sleepy Hollow, I perceived a lady reclining near the path which bends along its verge. It was Margaret herself. She had been there the whole afternoon, meditating or reading; for she had a book in her hand, with some strange title, which I did not understand, and have forgotten. She said that nobody had broken her solitude, and was just giving utterance to a theory that no inhabitant of Concord ever visited Sleepy Hollow, when we saw a group of people entering the sacred precincts. Most of them followed a path which led them away from us; but an old man passed near us, and smiled to see Margaret reclining on the ground, and me sitting by her side. He made some remark about the beauty of the afternoon, and withdrew himself into the shadow of the wood. Then we talked about autumn, and about the pleasures of being lost in the woods, and about the crows, whose voices Margaret had heard; and about the experiences of early childhood, whose influence remains upon the character after the recollection of them has passed away; and about the sight of mountains from a distance, and the view from their summits; and about other matters of high and low philosophy. In the midst of our talk, we heard footsteps above us, on the high bank; and while the person was still hidden among the trees, he called to Margaret, of whom he had gotten a glimpse. Then he emerged from the green shade, and, behold! it was Mr. Emerson. He appeared to have had a pleasant time; for he said that there were Muses in the woods to-day, and whispers to be heard in the breezes. It being now nearly six o'clock, we separated,—Margaret and Mr. Emerson towards his home, and I towards mine. . . . .

Last evening there was the most beautiful moonlight that ever hallowed this earthly world; and when I went to bathe in the river, which was as calm as death, it seemed like plunging down into the sky. But I had rather be on earth than even in the seventh heaven, just now.

Wednesday, August 24th.—I left home at five o'clock this morning to catch some fish for breakfast. I shook our summer apple-tree, and ate the golden apple which fell from it. Methinks these early apples, which come as a golden promise before the treasures of autumnal fruit, are almost more delicious than anything that comes afterwards. We have but one such tree in our orchard; but it supplies us with a daily abundance, and probably will do so for at least a week to come. Meantime other trees begin to cast their ripening windfalls upon the grass; and when I taste them, and perceive their mellowed flavor and blackening seeds, I feel somewhat overwhelmed with the impending bounties of Provi-

Sample entry (22 August 1842) published in *The Atlantic Monthly* (1866)

Appendix 5
Examples of Published Entries in *The Atlantic* and *Passages* (continued)

stance, a sturdy fact, a reality, something to be felt and touched, whose ideas seem to be dug out of his mind as he digs potatoes, beets, carrots, and turnips out of the ground.

After leaving Mr. ——, we proceeded through wood paths to Walden Pond, picking blackberries of enormous size along the way. The pond itself was beautiful and refreshing to my soul, after such long and exclusive familiarity with our tawny and sluggish river. It lies embosomed among wooded hills, — it is not very extensive, but large enough for waves to dance upon its surface, and to look like a piece of blue firmament, earth-encircled. The shore has a narrow, pebbly strand, which it was worth a day's journey to look at, for the sake of the contrast between it and the weedy, oozy margin of the river. Farther within its depths, you perceive a bottom of pure white sand, sparkling through the transparent water, which, methought, was the very purest liquid in the world. After Mr. Emerson left us, Hillard and I bathed in the pond, and it does really seem as if my spirit, as well as corporeal person, were refreshed by that bath. A good deal of mud and river slime had accumulated on my soul; but these bright waters washed them all away.

We returned home in due season for dinner. . . . . To my misfortune, however, a box of Mediterranean wine proved to have undergone the acetous fermentation; so that the splendor of the festival suffered some diminution. Nevertheless, we ate our dinner with a good appetite, and afterwards went universally to take our several siestas. Meantime there came a shower, which so besprinkled the grass and shrubbery as to

make it rather wet for our after-tea ramble. The chief result of the walk was the bringing home of an immense burden of the trailing clematis-vine, now just in blossom, and with which all our flower-stands and vases are this morning decorated. On our return we found Mr. and Mrs. S——, and E. H——, who shortly took their leave, and we sat up late, telling ghost-stories. This morning, at seven, our friends left us. We were both pleased with the visit, and so, I think, were our guests.

. . . . .

Monday, August 22d. — I took a walk through the woods yesterday afternoon, to Mr. Emerson's, with a book which Margaret Fuller had left, after a call on Saturday eve. I missed the nearest way, and wandered into a very secluded portion of the forest; for forest it might justly be called, so dense and sombre was the shade of oaks and pines. Once I wandered into a tract so overgrown with bushes and underbrush that I could scarcely force a passage through. Nothing is more annoying than a walk of this kind, where one is tormented by an innumerable host of petty impediments. It incenses and depresses me at the same time. Always when I flounder into the midst of bushes, which cross and intertwine themselves about my legs, and brush my face, and seize hold of my clothes, with their multitudinous grip, — always, in such a difficulty, I feel as if it were almost as well to lie down and die in rage and despair as to go one step farther. It is laughable, after I have got out of the moil, to think how miserably it affected me for the moment; but I had better learn patience betimes, for there are many such bushy tracts

Sample entry (22 August 1842) published in *Passages from the American Note-Books* (1868)

in this vicinity, on the margins of meadows, and my walks will often lead me into them. Escaping from the bushes, I soon came to an open space among the woods, — a very lovely spot, with the tall old trees standing around as quietly as if no one had intruded there throughout the whole summer. A company of crows were holding their Sabbath on their summits. Apparently they felt themselves injured or insulted by my presence; for, with one consent, they began to Caw! caw! caw! and, launching themselves sullenly on the air, took flight to some securer solitude. Mine, probably, was the first human shape that they had seen all day long, — at least, if they had been stationary in that spot; but perhaps they had winged their way over miles and miles of country, had breakfasted on the summit of Greylock, and dined at the base of Wachusett, and were merely come to sup and sleep among the quiet woods of Concord. But it was my impression at the time, that they had sat still and silent on the tops of the trees all through the Sabbath day, and I felt like one who should unawares disturb an assembly of worshippers. A crow, however, has no real pretensions to religion, in spite of his gravity of mien and black attire. Crows are certainly thieves, and probably infidels. Nevertheless, their voices yesterday were in admirable accordance with the influences of the quiet, sunny, warm, yet autumnal afternoon. They were so far above my head that their loud clamor added to the quiet of the scene, instead of disturbing it. There was no other sound, except the song of the cricket, which is but an audible stillness; for, though it be very loud and heard afar, yet the mind does not take note of it as a

sound, so entirely does it mingle and lose its individuality among the other characteristics of coming autumn. Alas for the summer! The grass is still verdant on the hills and in the valleys; the foliage of the trees is as dense as ever, and as green; the flowers are abundant along the margin of the river, and in the hedge-rows, and deep among the woods; the days, too, are as fervid as they were a month ago; and yet in every breath of wind and in every beam of sunshine there is an autumnal influence. I know not how to describe it. Methinks there is a sort of coolness amid all the heat, and a mildness in the brightest of the sunshine. A breeze cannot stir, without thrilling me with the breath of autumn, and I behold its pensive glory in the far, golden gleams among the long shadows of the trees. The flowers, even the brightest of them, — the golden-rod and the gorgeous cardinals, — the most glorious flowers of the year, — have this gentle sadness amid their pomp. Pensive autumn is expressed in the glow of every one of them. I have felt this influence earlier in some years than in others. Sometimes autumn may be perceived even in the early days of July. There is no other feeling like that caused by this faint, doubtful, yet real perception, or rather prophecy, of the year's decay, so deliciously sweet and sad at the same time.

After leaving the book at Mr. Emerson's I returned through the woods, and, entering Sleepy Hollow, I perceived a lady reclining near the path which bends along its verge. It was Margaret herself. She had been there the whole afternoon, meditating or reading; for she had a book in her hand, with some strange title, which I did not understand, and have forgotten. She

Appendix 5
Examples of Published Entries in *The Atlantic* and *Passages* (continued)

said that nobody had broken her solitude, and was just giving utterance to a theory that no inhabitant of Concord ever visited Sleepy Hollow, when we saw a group of people entering the sacred precincts. Most of them followed a path which led them away from us; but an old man passed near us, and smiled to see Margaret reclining on the ground, and me sitting by her side. He made some remark about the beauty of the afternoon, and withdrew himself into the shadow of the wood. Then we talked about autumn, and about the pleasures of being lost in the woods, and about the crows, whose voices Margaret had heard; and about the experiences of early childhood, whose influence remains upon the character after the recollection of them has passed away; and about the sight of mountains from a distance, and the view from their summits; and about other matters of high and low philosophy. In the midst of our talk, we heard footsteps above us, on the high bank; and while the person was still hidden among the trees, he called to Margaret, of whom he had gotten a glimpse. Then he emerged from the green shade, and, behold! it was Mr. Emerson. He appeared to have had a pleasant time; for he said that there were Muses in the woods to-day, and whispers to be heard in the breezes. It being now nearly six o'clock, we separated, — Margaret and Mr. Emerson towards his home, and I towards mine. . . . .

Last evening there was the most beautiful moonlight that ever hallowed this earthly world; and when I went to bathe in the river, which was as calm as death, it seemed like plunging down into the sky. But I had rather be on earth than even in the seventh heaven, just now.

Wednesday, August 24th. — I left home at five o'clock this morning to catch some fish for breakfast. I shook our summer apple-tree, and ate the golden apple which fell from it. Methinks these early apples, which come as a golden promise before the treasures of autumnal fruit, are almost more delicious than anything that comes afterwards. We have but one such tree in our orchard; but it supplies us with a daily abundance, and probably will do so for at least a week to come. Meantime other trees begin to cast their ripening windfalls upon the grass; and when I taste them, and perceive their mellowed flavor and blackening seeds, I feel somewhat overwhelmed with the impending bounties of Providence. I suppose Adam, in Paradise, did not like to see his fruits decaying on the ground, after he had watched them through the sunny days of the world's first summer. However, insects, at the worst, will hold a festival upon them, so that they will not be thrown away, in the great scheme of Nature. Moreover, I have one advantage over the primeval Adam, inasmuch as there is a chance of disposing of my superfluous fruits among people who inhabit no Paradise of their own.

Passing a little way down along the river-side, I threw in my line, and soon drew out one of the smallest possible of fishes. It seemed to be a pretty good morning for the angler, — an autumnal coolness in the air, a clear sky, but with a fog across the lowlands and on the surface of the river, which a gentle breeze sometimes condensed into wreaths. At first I could barely discern the opposite shore of the river; but, as the sun arose, the vapors gradually dispersed, till only a warm, smoky

Sample entry (22 August 1842) published in *Passages from the American Note-Books* (1868)

Appendix 6

Excerpts from the Sophia Hawthorne / James T. and Annie Fields Correspondence, 1864–1868

To Annie Fields
n.d., [1864], upon Nathaniel Hawthorne's death

I wish to speak to you Annie.

A person of a more uniform majesty never wore mortal form.

In the most retired privacy it was the same as in the presence of men.

The sacred veil of his eyelids he scarcely lifted to himself – Such an unviolated sanctuary as was his nature, I his utmost wife – never conceived, nor knew.

So absolute a modesty was not before joined to so lofty a self respect.

But what must have been that self respect that he never in the smallest particular dishonored!

A conscience more void of offence never bore witness to GOD within.

It was the innocence of a baby and the grand comprehension of a sage –

To me – himself – even to me who was himself in unity – he was to the last the holy of holies behind the cherubim.

So unerring a judgment that a word from him would settle with me a chaos of doubts and questions that seemed perplexing to ordinary apprehension –

So equal a justice that I often wondered if he were human in this – for this seemed to partake of omniscience both of love and insight.

An impartiality of regard that solved all men and subjects in one alembick [sic].

Truth and right alone he deigned to regard – Far below him was every other consideration –

A tenderness so infinite – so embracing – that GOD's alone could surpass it – It folded the loathsome leper in as soft a caress as the child of his home affections –

Was not that divine!

Was it not Christianity in one action – What a bequest to his children – what a new revelation of Christ to the world was that!

And for him – when the sight and touch of unseemliness and uncleanness caused to shudder as an Eolian [sic] string shudders in the tempest.

Annie! to the last action in this house he was as lofty, as majestic, as imperial and as gentle – as in the strength of his prime as on the day he rose upon my eye and soul a King among men by divine right!

When he awoke that early dawn and found himself unawares standing among the "Shining Ones" – do you think they did not suppose he had been always with them – one of themselves – oh blessed be GOD for so soft a translation – as an infant wakes on its mother's breast so he woke on the bosom of GOD and can never be weary any more – nor see nor touch an unclean thing.

A demand for beauty and perfection that was inexorable yet though a flaw or a crack gave him so fine agony, no one no one was ever so tolerant as he!

To Annie Fields
n.d., [1864]

Dearest Annie,

I have your note this morning. Julian goes tomorrow, and so I write one word by him, but cannot properly answer it now. Dear Annie – I can neither write a book, nor would I, if able, so entirely set in opposition to my husband's express wish and opinion as to do so. We have not the power nor the right to suppose a total change of idea from change of plane – My instinct is the same as his was. I feel no call – I am conscious of no faculty for it. If I felt the call and had the faculty, it would be totally impossible for me to accomplish such a task for a very long time. I have as much as I can do now to keep quiet and preserve a mood of cheer for the children. I could not separate myself from them to do anything. My duty is to them and for them I live.

Ah dear Annie, believe me! The veil he drew around him no one should lift. He often referred to Tennyson's Poem with prophetic foreboding – that was his own sentiment. It is not as if he had not written – "His best he gave" – (he had no "worst" to "keep" –) He gave all he wished to give. Who shall wrench any more from him? With a common share of apprehension, the divine quality of his nature and his motive for action can be found in his pages. Details are not for him. The effect of his character, though so hidden from actual sight – will be felt as long as his books last. It was the only way he chose to present himself to the world. His friends only saw the more evidence from intimacy, of what his works promised. But by the guidance of them alone, multitudes of erring and suffering mortals came to him and told and wrote to him their lives to get his sympathy and his aid – so sure were they that he was indeed "the friend of sinners."

This is the way I view it now. Good night – No more at this moment.

Give my love to Mr Fields. I wish I could gratify you both by doing whatever you desire – I am so near the absconded one, that I am sure I shall not fail to know his counsel – . . . .

Ever lovingly yours
Sophia Hawthorne

To Annie Fields
2 August 1864

Beloved Annie –

. . . My darling Annie, I know well that you would not wish to do anything with the papers against my wish. But I shall in time copy out all that is possible – and I think there may be a good deal for the Atlantic – I shall copy all on separate sheets so as to have any part that is fitting available for the printers. And then we three will decide what to do. . . .

To James T. Fields
14 September 1864

My dear Mr Fields,

. . . I tremble at the prospect of plunging into the world again. It seems as if I were "without my cloak" as Shakespeare sings in his Sonnets. But I now seem summoned for the sake of others, and I must remember that such a call is imperative and put myself aside entirely –

Otherwise I ought to give up my name – Sophia Hawthorne.

At the same time I love my cousins very much and like to be with them.

But I only like to be with him better. . . .

Ever very sincerely yours,
Sophia Hawthorne

To James T. Fields
5 December 1864

Dear Mr Fields–

. . . You are altogether right about the fragment. I doubt very much whether it will do to print it, and great care will be requisite in deciding. The rain prevented our visit. My bag was all packed, and I had put in one or two early journals and my Flaxman's Dante for you, and I was eager to go. But I had worlds of business at home and so perhaps I had no right to go. . . .

. . . . but I have better things to do than long stitching and business. I wish to copy, copy, copy – Perhaps nothing will do to print – but I must copy all the same –

And I also wish to draw.

But now I ought to go to sleep – Good night dear Mr Fields –

Ever most truly yours
Sophia Hawthorne

To Annie Fields
30 March 1865

Dearest Annie –

. . . It is a tremendous effort to bring a human face out of the past. It seems as if I had made it. What a mystery it is, and how was it that I did it? This I can never understand, because the lines of each of all the myriad human faces belong alone to each face, and no variation of a hairline can be allowed. But here he is! . . .

. . . I hope I shall now be able to take hold of the English journals. I forgot the quill pens, but I think I can make our man of stationery send for them. . . .

Good night, my Poem –

Ever yours
Sophia Hawthorne

To James T. Fields
18 April 1865

My dear Heartsease,

You are perfectly right (AS USUAL) about the manuscript.

If I find anything more perfectly finished, I will copy it and submit it to you. But my first idea was that the journals were very rapid sketches – mere outlines – cartoons of the great pictures he meant to paint fully out.

What a history to be sure we are enacting! Nothing was ever so stupendous, so grand, so appalling – so glorious –

The consolations and compensations are all eternal – the horrors are transient. . . .

Always cordially yours
Sophia Hawthorne

To James T. Fields
2 October 1865

My dear Mr Fields,

It all at once struck me that probably a great part of the descriptive passages in the paper I sent you yesterday – was condensed in the Introduction to the Mosses. Upon reading that Introduction I find it is so – and so you will not be able to print them. I will read today, and find something else – I am immensely sorry that you should have to wait – but I will be as quick as I can – I will endeavor to get something ready for you when you come tomorrow to the wedding –

Very sincerely yours
Sophia Hawthorne

To James T. Fields
4 October 1865

My dear Mr Fields,

Upon considering the subject, I have quite a new idea, opposed to the one I suggested to you. It is that it is not of the least consequence (in my opinion) that some highly finished and condensed papers have already been printed from these journal sketches. For here we have all the richness of detail and blooming out, as it were and gleaming touches. Is not it something like the pen and ink and pencil sketches of the pictures of the old masters, in the contemplation of which we come so very near the creative soul of the artist?

There is more in this journal of the first year and part of the second of his married life; but I do not know as I can succeed in leaving myself out sufficiently to make a perfect whole of the rest. But I will do my best without regard to what is already published in the Introduction to the Mosses, and leave it to your option to take it or not. . . .

. . . I have found a whole volume of clear, fair manuscript which seems to be a portion of the English Romance – whether the first draft or the copy for print, I have not yet found out, for I have not had time to read it since I found it. . . .

. . . There is divine music in these sheets, is there not? Oh what a harp was that – no – what a harp is that!

I will go on with the Stratford visit – quite a different thing from these soft, mellifluous strains. . . .

I have written since breakfast and now it is eight, evening.

Your greatest enemy
S.H.

To James T. Fields
8 October 1865

I am undecided how to address you so I will give you a choice –

"You beautiful person,"!

"Angel of Benefits"!

"Gabriel, with lilies of promise"!

"Prospero, with the wand that summons (good) spirits from the vasty [sic] deep –

"Heart'sease"–! and so on, but I have no more time for beginnings. . . .

I wish now to ask you whether, if I copy and send you passages from the journal written previously to those you now have – whether they should not precede those you now have in publication?

I have found a journal of 1841 – before our marriage – partly at Brook Farm. Is it of consequence that this should precede the 1842 passages?

Would it not be well to add to your heading that the reader will find here the first records of what has since been published in the Introduction – it being supposed that all who care for him will like to come as near as possible to the full details? If all were eliminated that has been used in print, it would quite spoil the music of the original score.

I think that what I send now <u>must</u> come first – do not you?

Do you think these passages reveal too much?

Perhaps Dr. Ripley had better be only <u>Dr. R.</u> as his grandchildren are living.

There are thirteen <u>more</u> of Mr H's pages before the date of August 22d – which date commences what you already have. If herewith is not enough for the first paper for the Atlantic, there must be two <u>very long</u> papers –

Will you send me word whether this be long enough for one, or whether I must immediately send you more?

My hand is just now beyond penning for this day. . . .

Oct. 8. Evening,

I have just found the musing in Sleepy Hollow – with the date July 1844. So this will follow at the end of the MSS now in your hands.

I have also found that the journal at Brook Farm is very rich in passages – one about Brighton Fair – the other about SWINE – ! (perfectly "gorgeous –" as the children say) – and a picnic and also a sketch of a seamstress at Brook Farm – and Autumn glories again. I am going to try to send you the Brook Farm passages for the very first bit of autobiography. Just think of Apollo in a blue stuff frock! painted by himself – Is it not superb?

I do not know whether it will do to put Colonel George Prescott by name into the Old Manse Journal as the bringer of milk and flowers. But I thought perhaps it would be pleasant. You must judge. Later. I have made out to copy twelve pages of Brook Farm, and I will send them for you to read, and go on with the rest, so as to make a whole paper.

I believe you said you wished for sixteen of my pages for a paper. . . .

I shall finish this MSS with the seamstress. I will send it the moment it is copied if you like it well enough to take it.

Good night. It is past eleven.
Sophia Hawthorne

To James T. Fields
13 October [1865?]

Dear Mr Fields –

Instead of printing the passage I sent you this morning

about the girl who plants flowers over her lover's grave, this fuller passage on page 18 might be substituted – that is, if you retain either of them.

I suddenly have come to the end of 1836 and now comes in the Maine journal 1837. On the tenth page of this, I suppose all the part, beginning "Nevertheless" will have to be omitted, because the Gardiners are still extant, and will not like to have their father's affairs published. But it is a pity, is it not?

You will think my leaves fall upon you as thick and fast as autumn leaves now fall upon the ground. . . .

. . . and now I live all day long with my husband, pouring [sic] over his records.

What a day has this been – so glorious and golden.

But I think I have written enough – from nine this morning till nine this evening – a walk intervening to the Post only.

Good night –

Your affectionate friend –
S.H.

To James T. Fields
14 October 1865

My dear Mr Fields,

I just have your note of Friday – You are a perfect beauty. I am glad you estimate thus the short sentences. To me they are peculiarly interesting, but I did not know how much was due to my relation to him –

This morning I sent you the commencement of the Maine record. Yes – 1835 is the first date remaining, and the sheets I sent you are copied from the very beginning of all I have found, so that now we are all in order.

Just the Salem journal which you already have – then the first part of the Maine visits which I sent today –

On Monday you will have the rest of the visit to Mr Bridge.

If he journalized before 1835, he destroyed the books.

Alas for it.

Was there ever such delicate, minute, loving drawing of Nature and Man? To copy such studies is a great joy. My hours sing.

How he broods like a divine spirit over the face of the earth and the last, best creation! We get here at the heart of his vast charity. . . . I think he reveals himself exquisitely in these papers as no other person could portray him.

The world will not demand any more than this.

He considers nothing beneath his notice which concerns the humblest human being, and I think enacts human brotherliness as I never knew any one else to do. . . .

Perhaps you will think best to leave out the poor old sailor who lost his foot. Mr Hawthorne could not leave him out, because he was there. Is not the close of the Maine journal perfect music, with a happy gleam of hope. How soon must you have more copy?

Yours cordially
S Hawthorne

To James T. Fields
20 October 1865

My dear Mr Fields,

. . . Yesterday I copied another twenty pages. . . .

I am driven by a sort of iron necessity to keep copying – For I see that no other person could copy these journals, and as I am mortal, I wish to improve the time. Last Tuesday I thought I might be powerless for weeks – There is by and by something more very interesting about Browne's Hill. I shall like to take all these walks myself – at the same times of the year that he did, and I hope I shall, with his records in my hand. I shall feel easier when all is copied up to the European life.

Do you think walks were ever really transformed into language thoroughly before? As I copy, I seem to feel all the refreshment of a sauntering among the lovelinesses and glories of the earth and see, through his eyes what I might not see with my own. One virtue is that he does not obtrude himself – but is an eye and an ear for nature – except that his lovingness comes in always. His use of the word "little" reveals his tenderness for all things. I am glad you can read the MSS in your green bower at home, for they require a certain leisure and quiet. . . .

Do you prefer these huge sheets for the convenience of the typesetters – or is it of no consequence about the sizes of pages? . . .

Very sincerely yours,
Sophia Hawthorne

To James T. Fields
November [1865]

My dear Mr Fields –

No 1. – Annie told me that Miss {Larcom} said that there was a place or point in Salem called The Juniper to which people might walk. In the MSS I find it is plainly the Juniper without an S and with a capital J. And I find the J. of "Juniper-trees" is a capital in the MSS – and not a small letter as I copied it. But though I have altered it in the proof, perhaps it had better remain a small letter, just as we would write 'maples' or 'oaks' with a small letter.

No 2. – I find that the paragraph beginning "Sunday evening" is plainly a new entry, on a new day, and not a continuation of June 15 – So that all the difficulty about the year vanishes. And the wonderful Mr Nichols, your pearl of Proofreaders is all right in his nice criticism, without its being necessary to change the date. It is plainly 1835 in the MSS and the next year is 1836 in the notebook – and therefore a whole year would be here left out if this were not 1835. Very often there is an observation recorded without any date, just as this little incident of the setting sun is entered. Perhaps the true date might be put before "Sunday evening." It plainly comes between the 15th and 18th which day soever be Sunday.

No 3 – The word in the MSS is very plainly stone-wall and not stone-walls. But that may be as you judge best.

No 4. – I think Mr Nichols' suggestion about the date July 18th is without doubt correct. Though it is perfectly plain that it is July in the MSS – I think it was a slip of the pen – and should be June. I am immensely delighted with the delicacy of care with which Mr Nichols observes that the scenery is of June and not July. Pray weave him some sort of a crown.

No 5. – This book, dear Mr Fields is not truly a Diary, because by no means is there a daily record. It is, as Mr. N – says a note-book. So should not the title be "Passages from Hawthorne's Notebooks." There are such long intervals often – sometimes months interval – that it is in no wise a diary. And it is especially desirable that all the brackets should be "expunged" – and the lines put between the sentences as I have put them, and as they are put in the MSS by Mr Hawthorne himself – Thus

For otherwise I think the breaths of all the readers would be taken away, and they would be all dead men – for brackets cause one to suspend breath, as it were, in reading, and if this suspension continue too long, mortal life ceases.

No 6. – On page second of the proof Mr N. is again right. The word is "maples" and not "mosses," I see by referring to the M.S.S., but you would forgive me if you saw how much it looks like 'mosses.' Oh wonderful Mr Nichols!

No 6. – It is Rev. Nathl Rogers I find, though it looks very much like Ropes. But upon careful examination I see it is rs at the end –

No 7 – Yes – I omitted to put quotation-marks where they are put in the MSS in the sentence beginning "St Augustin." I should have placed them before "Then a dead body arose – and after thereby–" which ends the quotation.

No 8. – The expression "dreadful earnest" is the one Mr Hawthorne uses with great force – far more force it has than "dreadfully earnest." He uses the word earnest as a noun – and the epithet dreadful as meaning full of dread – not in the hacknied [sic] way. In this I disagree with Mr Nichols – It must remain I think "dreadful earnest –" unless we undertake to improve Mr Hawthorne's English, which I think cannot well be done, for he used words very thoughtfully and conscientiously.

No 9. – I have put the quotation marks to Mrs Sigourney's saying.

No 10. – Yes it is 'where' and not 'when' on page 7.

No 11. – I cannot make out any name but {'Florsman'} from the MSS. But if there were no such New England divine, perhaps the name had better be omitted and let the sentence be "an extempore prayer by a New England divine."

No 12. – I do not know what to do about the name "Walker"– It seems to be "Walker" in the MSS. Is it an English or American person? . . .

No 13. Why is the s. in 'Revelations' crossed out? St John's book of Revelations is referred to, I suppose.

No 14. My dear Mr Fields – that pathetic and interesting sentence "In this dismal chamber Fame was won" – should not be put as a part of a paragraph. It is in the MSS – quite by itself, and a page or two removed from the sentence about choosing wives. Pray have that altered – I hesitated about copying that line, which was heart-smiting to me – and to have it printed in this way, makes me think it had perhaps better be stricken out. But I thought it would be affecting to his friends and so copied it.

Page 8 of proof

No 15. Yes it is "sundry" in the MSS.

Page 9. No 16. Yes it is "there" in the sentence about the funeral garland.

And now let me say that there is not to be this great trouble for you in all the manuscripts. I am sure I grow more careful soon – I was excessively agitated in copying this first little book. I do not seem to have had undimmed eyes – But I will take the utmost care in future, so as even to satisfy Mr Nichols.

Oh how sorry I am that you have to read this long note.

And now I have finished with the proof, I am going to

succumb utterly – so tired – at least for this night.

Good night–

Ever yours cordially,
Sophia Hawthorne

P.S. I know you are more tired than I – alas! It is half past eleven.

❧

To James T. Fields
11 January 1866

My dear friend,

Your note dated New York went to my heart. How much I thank you for telling me these things – for I was not sure that others would care for these notes, which to me are so precious. I could not judge.

It is pleasant to think how many riches will come to these faithful lovers in future papers of which now only you and Annie and I know. . . .

My dear Heartsease I am
ever cordially yours
Sophia Hawthorne

❧

To James T. Fields
18 February 1866

My dear Mr Fields,

I have now finished the Old Manse records – all that I could copy. It has been difficult to leave myself out, but I think I have been pretty skilful. Whenever there has been left any reference, it was to save some lovely turn of expression or thought – but perhaps it had better be still more severely expurgated.

Ever since your New York note, I have been induced to copy more of his actual life and feeling than before for those loving friends. I rather dread the publicity of the wide spread Atlantic, because a periodical seems more public than a book: but as it is, I confide it to your judgment.

I have more to copy before the English Journals commence of which last I sent you a portion by Adams' express. . . .

Your very true friend
Sophia Hawthorne

❧

To Annie Fields
16 May 1866

Beloved Annie,

. . . P.S. This is what I see in the last Christian Register, a paper I have not seen since before my marriage.

"Hawthorne's notebook, doing so little justice to the genius of the writer, is again opened for people to gape over and wonder how such a man could write such commonplace things, and still more, how such a man's friends can wish to see them paraded before the world. His own delicate nature would have shrunk from it –"

Gail Hamilton had just been reassuring me about these notes by saying that the only trouble was that they could ever end, for she wished for more & more and more – and all such things she said. And Mr Fields has been reassured, has he not? It makes me shudder to think I may have done what Mr Hawthorne would not have approved –

What does Mr Fields think –

❧

To Annie Fields
4 July 1866

This is his birthday – 4th July '66

Dearest Annie–

. . . I shall be very sorry to have the MSS printed without my severest supervision. Especially as I may find it imperative to omit some things copied. I am subject to some awful doubts – So I hope I shall have all the other proof sheets without fail. . . .

Your loving friend
Sophia

❧

To James T. Fields
24 July 1866

My dear Mr Fields –

You will see I have made wild havoc with the proof. But I have grown wiser and look at the MSS from a less inward point of view, and so can adapt it better to the public. It is indeed very important indeed that I see every proof. I think I lost my head when I was copying the Old Manse Journal, and perhaps others – I seemed to forget that the delicious music must not be piped to all ears – As it is, perhaps I leave too much on the page.

But what word-painting of Nature is this! – even to the leaf that falls – curling as it dies, into a boat fit for fairies, floating with melancholy prettiness – and so on & so on – All the heavenly spring time of my married life comes back in these cadences – so rich and delicate – And what I cannot copy at all is of course sweeter than the rest. The stars in their courses do not cover such treasures in Space – as do the dots I substitute for words sometimes. . . .

Ever most sincerely yours
Sophia Hawthorne

❧

To James T. Fields
14 October 1866

My dear Mr Fields,

That plan of yours about the gradual publishing of the

volumes is the greatest proof yet of your strategic genius, – O Commander in Chief, General of the Army of men of letters! I had been much perplexed with the idea of overwhelming the public with so many volumes at once. I saw the wary Public clapping its hand on its pocket in alarm and holding its head in fear of apoplexy. You have untied the Gordian knot, O greater than Alexander, who cut it. "May you live a thousand years, and may your shadow never be less!" I could not be content without expressing to you my sense of your true might again.

Mr Hillard is retreating from his position about the "Twenty days." He says Julian's willingness, takes away more than half his objection. He has the MSS again for consideration.

Do you think I shall have means to do all for the children's culture that they should have done? Did not you say to me that you would be "very near me" in my widowhood, on that first day you came? This is why I ask you questions that concern me so nearly.

I crave a little freedom from anxiety before I lay down mortal life – but I do not know as I deserve it – indeed I know I do not deserve it – yet I crave it. Trouble is very subtle, and refines itself as we get over the gross obstacles. So watchful is our heavenly Father that we do not fall asleep on the near slopes of the Delectable Mountains. . . .

Ever sincerely yours
S. Hawthorne

To James T. Fields
28 March 1867

My dear Mr Fields,

After we left the Old Manse, Mr Hawthorne kept no journal for a very long time. The Study of the children in their daily life, of which I sent you a short portion, was all that he wrote in the way of notes till 1850. In that interval he collected the Mosses and wrote the Introduction to them – The Scarlet Letter – The House of the Seven Gables – The Wonder Book, Blithedale Romance and Tanglewood Tales. If he did write a journal, he burnt it – but I think he did not, for I should have known it.

My dear friend, I am on the brink of bankruptcy. . . . I wrote to Mr Hillard, and he says two banks in which was some of my money have been involved in some swindling transactions to the loss of $600,000 – and must lessen their dividends. So he cannot send me as much as was my due in April.

I am in debt to the tradesmen here, which I do not like – and I actually need cash in hand. Mr Hillard says you will pay me more money in July – but what will be the use of money in July if we all freeze and starve in April, May and June? So I wish to know whether you will be good enough to speak to Mr Hillard about it – and whether you can conveniently let me have some now – If not, perhaps I can borrow some, though I have a horror of that. Still it is no matter about my horror. I will do whatever ought to be done. But I wish to pay some bills in the first week of April to the butcher, grocer, and coalman – before I buy anything more –

I have note yet paid Dr Lewis a penny for Rose's teaching and board yet – and on the first of June her terms are over and she leaves –

In short – I am in a desperate strait – and think my cousin Mr George Peabody must hurry up and save me. Julian has been wearing turned and patched clothes and cobbled boots till I am quite mortified for him – . . . .

I write from noon to eve – and have nearly finished another volume.

I have not come to any separate part that would do for the Atlantic, or I could earn some money that way – But the twelve hundred dollars less that I have this year will make a vast difference in the turning of the wheels of life –

Mr Hillard proposes that we should all be drowned.

May your shadow never be less –

Ever sincerely yours
S.H.

To James T Fields
31 May [1867?]

Dear Mr Fields –

Today I have copied these additional extracts – about Brook Farm. Is it not like Apollo tending the herds of Admetus?

I therefore open my package and thrust these in –

Now will follow a visit to Salem – and then a return to Brook Farm in another portion.

Yrs
SH

To James T. Fields
31 May 1867

My dear Mr Fields –

I send you these sheets to know how they seem to you – These end 1840 – Do you think the extracts interesting to his public friends? I cannot judge. Oh such letters as I have been reading over! If we lived in a world of angels instead of prosaic men – what a glory would they be to publish. But it is impossible – impossible – I even feel like veiling myself when I read them –

Why am I not already transfigured into a Shining One by such a love, so expressed? The world never contained such letters before –

Yours ever
S H.

I shall go on.
Mr Fields –

Shall you have any money due to me in July? How much? I fear to be arrested for debt.

P.S. My dearest Fields – I find in the Atlantics which I have – the missing notes – which may make up the gap – but I supposed you wished all the leaves to lie together – must I dismember my Atlantics?

I have come across a long, minute account of the drowning and finding of the girl in Concord River, from which Zenobia's death is taken. In the Blithedale Romance it is very succinct. Shall I copy this wonderful photograph of the terrible night Mr Hawthorne spent with Mr Channing seeking and finding the body. . . .

To James T. Fields
7 July 1867

My dear Mr Fields –

. . . I write now for two or three reasons. One is to ask you whether you purpose now to begin the printing of the American Journal, now that it is all copied and ready –

Whether this month any monies will be due me for Copy Right – or whether you have already prepaid all of it for the past six months – . . . .

No one has hired my house. I remain, half packed up in the halls, waiting.

The sensations of Mahomet's tomb, suspended, can never come up to mine. Especially as Mahomet's tomb never was suspended.

I no more know what I am about to do than a rail-car going somewhere without halt, deaf, dumb and blind in its own particular.

But I possess my soul in patience and use the passing hour as well as I can.

With many blessings
Ever yours S.H.

PS. Forgive this shocking blotting paper

To James T. Fields
8 October 1867

My dear Mr Fields –

I have been looking over the journals; and in the package you gave me from the safe so long ago, and which I opened only this week for the first time, I find there is a great gap, from the middle of the Old Manse journal to May 1850.

Will you look and find these missing pages – so that I can go on with my revisal. I have already copied a great deal that I had left out before, and see that your counsel was (as usual) the best. Perhaps you will not think it well to print all I have now copied – as some sentences are mere memoranda; but yet, as the plan is to publish all that he has left which can be published, I suppose it is better to leave nothing out. The memoranda show what he is reading and thinking about – though not always his original thought.

O how exquisite is the Old Manse journal! It puts me back into Paradise whenever I read it.

I am at last rested and well, and now I shall work very hard.

No money has come in yet. But it was only a few days ago that I made the grand assault upon Mrs H. and the answer has not come. A fierce pack of hounds, in the shape of tradesmen are unleashed and ready for a spring upon me. If you do not hear of me again, you may fancy what has become of me. . . .

When my debts are paid, I shall be wholly at rest. . . .

. . . But I shall be almost too busy copying to paint.

I suppose your huge transactions, of which you told me, will contrive to prevent your printing the journals yet. The printing of them will be my Golconda mine – . . . .

SH.

To James T. Fields
3 November 1867

My dear Mr Fields –

I ought not to write but I must a little. I have a great objection that any of the extracts from the letters go into the Atlantic. Will not some other portion do as well? I hate not to do anything you ask me; but there is a certain intimateness of revelation in even these extracts from the letters, which I cannot bear to have go into a public journal. It seems to me as if they would be more sheltered in the volumes – Can you forgive me?

The American MSS are now ready, with the exception of the missing 'twenty days.' Had you rather I should apply to Mr Tolman myself? As I might recall to him how I asked him to put the package into the safe. Was he a careless and forgetful man? I grieve much over my debt to you for both our sakes – I was so unaware that I was running in debt to you, that I positively denied Mr Hillard's statement. It seems as if my very soul were mortgaged. Mr Hillard will be obliged to take of our scanty principal to pay my debts – and so the beginning of our ruin is at hand, unless the publishment of the journals saves us. But we may all find that too late a resource. What avails bread when there is no mouth to eat? It is not homeopathic but magnetic cure that I am having tried for my hand. It would be impossible for me to copy till my hand be better for I feel it all the way up to my arm socket now, and I fear it would become useless.

In haste

Most truly yours
SH.

To James T. Fields
30 January 1868

My dear Mr Fields –

I have been ingloriously laid low for nearly a week, and received your last note in that horizontal position which the pride of humanity is obliged to assume under difficulties. While thus, the Atlantic came, and I accidentally saw among the multitudes of the advertisements of your great House – one called "Good Stories," and among those mentioned was "The Christmas Banquet, by Nathaniel Hawthorne" – So then I understood the mistake – Una saw it in Newport – in something which had printed the word "Bouquet." "Hence all these tears." Typographical errors are as heinous as some others.

Today I am getting up and I am anxious to reply to your request for the "Twenty Days –" After the most careful consideration and consultation, I have finally decided that it must not be printed at all not in an Appendix nor in the Text. I am convinced that Mr Hawthorne would never have wished such an intimate domestic history to be made public, and I am astonished at myself that I ever thought of doing it. The unexpected addition of the Extracts from the letters will more than make up in bulk for the omission of the Twenty Days. I am especially distressed that that copy is lost somewhere in your House, because I should be very sorry to have any one (any profane person) read it – and unless it is burnt up, it must be in existence somewhere in Boston. I could severely chastise myself for ever putting it into any hands but yours.

Now I do hope you are not too much disappointed. Upon looking today at the original, I more than ever wonder how I could have ever dreamed of printing it. You know I gave it to Mr Longfellow, Mr Hillard – and Prof. Ticknor – and then doubted very much and wished to read it over before deciding. Today I have been doing so – So now this vexed question is settled forever and the loss of the MSS is probably quite providential as in my hurry, I might have committed the blunder of putting it in the book.

Above all things I would be loyal to what Mr Hawthorne would approve. I had rather starve than do what he might think an impropriety.

Do you hate me?

It makes me tremble to write, for I am very weak still. . . .

Yours sincerely
S. Hawthorne

To James T. Fields
20 May 1868

My dear Mr Fields –

I received the sharp-lined note written by your amanuensis, enclosing the account. But your clerk does not satisfy me at all, because he lumps my debts to you in a sum, and I have no more idea what I owe you that money for than before. . . .

I wish to be very clear and exact, and to understand what I am about. Do encourage – and help me, since I am trying to be good. Have I then swallowed up all the rest of the 10,000 dollars in your hands for the last year, as well as the copyright income?

I am afraid your heart misgives you about the American Notes. Do you prefer not to publish it? Is that the reason you delay so long – or is it because you have a thousand books to publish first.

I do not believe anyone can want money more than I do. I hope you will tell me at once if you had rather not undertake it. . . .

Most truly yours
S. Hawthorne

To James T. Fields
28 July 1868

My dear Mr Fields–

Your note has just come. . . . I have had no proofs for a good while, and have been wondering why not – as I am very anxious to get through with them. Shall you immediately begin with the English journal, when the American notes are finished? Will it be necessary to have all the volumes of the English journal copied, before you can begin to put any of it to press?

Yesterday, at a millener's shop

here, I was shown a letter in a newspaper purporting to be from Mr Hawthorne to a Mr B – speaking of the war. I was very sorry to see it, and if Mr {Bennock} was the person, I am amazed that an Englishman could so far put aside his customary delicacy as to allow a private letter to him to be published like that. I must write to him, and beg him to publish no more; for I know it would be very distasteful to Mr Hawthorne to be presented to the public in such an undress – It is really disloyal to him, and I feel obliged to do all I can to prevent the recurrence of such a thing – I was going to speak to you about it before your note came just now.

It seems to me that to allow a bad photograph or a private letter to be spread about of a person no longer able to defend himself is equally disloyal – I am much distressed – Yet I am sure I can persuade Mr {Bennock} to print no more – . . . .

I know Mr Hawthorne would be pained to have any opinion of his of the war or politics, which he confided to an intimate friend, made common talk – for he was <u>very</u> careful about such things – It seems like telling secrets. . . .

I have been looking over some of Mr Ticknor's letters to find what Smith and Elder gave for "Our Old Home" – but I have not yet discovered. Do you remember? for I have a curiosity to know. . . .

Yrs very truly
S.H.

To James T. Fields
n.d., [1868], on the receipt on *Passages*

My dear Mr Fields,

Fancy my emotion when I removed the wrappings and saw the Sacred, beloved name – And then opening the box found the beautiful books with the Hawthorne vine and the very elegant cloth outside, and the lovely paper within! I cannot thank you. I should like to weep for joy. When one reflects what a book is – a worthy book – how far above any other treasure that we can hold in our hands, it becomes plain what a lofty and benign position you hold as the dispenser of books. There is a grave and perfect elegance in these volumes. It seems as if he would like to see them.

But perhaps he has now looked into the "little book" which the 'mighty angel' held in his hand, who wore a rainbow upon his head, and a cloud for a mantle, and whose face was a sun, and who cried with a voice like seven thunders that there should be Time no longer – And if so, he would take no more interest in his earthly works, even in the fairest form.

Bibliography

The Common Journal of Nathaniel and Sophia Hawthorne

Badaracco, Claire M. "The Night-blooming Cereus: A Letter from the 'Cuba Journal' 1833-35 of Sophia Hawthorne Peabody, With a Check List of Her Autograph Materials in American Institutions," *Bulletin of Research in the Humanities* 81 (1978): 56–73.

——"Pitfalls and Rewards of the Solo Editor: Sophia Peabody Hawthorne," *Resources for American Literary Study* 11.1 (Spring 1981): 91–100.

Barthes, Roland. *Camera Lucida: Reflections on Photography*, trans. Richard Howard. New York: Hill and Wang, 1981.

Baym, Nina. *The Scarlet Letter: A Reading*. Boston: Twayne Publishers, 1986.

Bennet, Betty T. and Stuart Curran, eds. *Mary Shelley in Her Times*. Baltimore: Johns Hopkins University Press, 2000.

Brown, Gillian. *Domestic Individualism: Imagining Self in Nineteenth-Century America*. Berkeley: University of California Press, 1990.

Coale, Samuel. "The Romance of Mesmerism: Hawthorne's Medium of Romance," in *Studies in the American Renaissance*, ed. Joel Myerson. Charlottesville: University Press of Virginia, 1994. 271–88.

Conger, Syndy M., et al. *Iconoclastic Departures: Mary Shelley after Frankenstein: Essays in Honor of the Bicentenary of Mary Shelley's Birth*. Madison, NJ: Farleigh Dickinson Press, 1997.

De Man, Paul. "Autobiography as De-Facement" in *The Rhetoric of Romanticism*. New York: Columbia University Press, 1984. 75–77.

De Salvo, Louise. *Nathaniel Hawthorne*. Brighton, Sussex: Harvester Press, 1987.

Eagleton, Terry. *Ideology of the Aesthetic*. Oxford: Blackwell, 1990.

Emerson, Ralph Waldo. "Nature" (1844), in *Selected Writings of Emerson*, ed. Donald McQuade. New York: Modern Library, 1981.

Hawthorne, Nathaniel. *Passages from the American Note-Books of Nathaniel Hawthorne*, ed. Sophia Hawthorne. Boston: Ticknor and Fields, 1868.

—— *Passages from the English Note-Books of Nathaniel Hawthorne*, ed. Sophia Hawthorne. Boston: James R. Osgood & Company, 1871.

Herbert, T. Walter. *Dearest Beloved: The Hawthornes and the Making of the Middle Class Family*. Berkeley: University of California Press, 1993.

Hurst, N. Luanne Jenkins, ed. "Sophia Hawthorne as Literary Critic and Educator: A Letter," *The Nathaniel Hawthorne Review* 18.2 (Fall 1992): 5–8.

Idol, John L., Jr. and Buford Jones, eds. *Nathaniel Hawthorne: The Contemporary Reviews*. Cambridge: Cambridge University Press, 1994.

Idol, John L., Jr. and Melinda M. Pinder, eds. *Hawthorne and Women: Engendering and Expanding the Hawthorne Tradition*. Amherst: University of Massachusetts Press, 1999.

James, Henry. "Nathaniel

Hawthorne," in *Essays on Literature: American Writers, English Writers*, ed. Leon Edel. New York: The Library of America, 1984. 315–457.

Kauffman, Linda. *Discourses of Desire: Gender, Genre, and Epistolary Fictions*. Ithaca: Cornell University Press, 1986.

Keats, John. *Selected Letters of John Keats*, ed. Grant F. Scott. Cambridge, Mass.: Harvard University Press, 2002.

Kermode, Frank. *The Genesis of Secrecy: On the Interpretation of Narrative*. Cambridge: Harvard University Press, 1979.

Kesselring, Marion L. *Hawthorne's Reading, 1828–1850: A Transcription and Identification of Titles Recorded in the Charge-Books of the Salem Athenaeum*. Folcroft, PA: Folcroft Press, 1969.

Koestenbaum, Wayne. *Double Talk: The Erotics of Male Literary Collaboration*. New York: Routledge, 1989.

London, Bette. *Writing Double: Women's Literary Partnerships*. Ithaca: Cornell University Press, 1999.

MacKay, Carol Hanbery. "Hawthorne, Sophia, and Hilda as Copyists: Duplication and Transformation in The Marble Faun," in *Browning Institute Studies: An Annual of Victorian Literary & Cultural History* 12 (1984): 93–120.

McDonald, John, ed. "A Sophia Hawthorne Journal, 1843-1844," *The Nathaniel Hawthorne Journal* (Washington, D.C.: NCR Microcard Editions, 1974): 1–30.

Mellow, James R. *Nathaniel Hawthorne in His Times*. Baltimore: Johns Hopkins University Press, 1998.

Miller, Edwin Haviland. "A Calendar of the Letters of Sophia Peabody Hawthorne," in *Studies in the American Renaissance*, ed. Joel Myerson. Charlottesville: The University Press of Virginia, 1986. 199–281.

Miller, J. Hillis. *Hawthorne and History: Defacing It*. Cambridge: Blackwell, 1991.

McGann, Jerome J. *The Textual Condition*. Princeton: Princeton University Press, 1991.

Melville, Herman. "Benito Cereno," in *Piazza Tales*, ed. Egbert S. Oliver. New York: Hendricks House, 1948.

Melville, Herman. *Pierre*, ed. Henry A. Murray. New York: Hendricks House, 1949.

Norko, Julie M. "Hawthorne's Love Letters: The Threshold World of Sophia Peabody," *American Transcendental Quarterly* 7.2 (June 1993): 127–139.

Person , Leland S., Jr. *Aesthetic Headaches: Women and a Masculine Poetics in Poe, Melville, and Hawthorne*. Athens: University of Georgia Press, 1988.

——. "Hawthorne's Love Letters: Writing and Relationship," *American Literature* 59.2 (May 1987): 211–227.

Peters, John Durham. *Speaking into the Air: A History of the Idea of Communication*. Chicago: University of Chicago Press, 1999.

Reiman, Donald H. *The Study of Modern Manuscripts: Public, Confidential, and Private*. Baltimore: The Johns Hopkins University Press, 1993.

Ricoeur, Paul. *Hermeneutics and the Human Sciences: Essays on Language, Action, and Interpretation*, trans. John B. Thompson. Cambridge: Cambridge University Press, 1981.

Royle, Nicholas. *Telepathy and Literature: Essays on the Reading Mind*. London: Basil Blackwell, 1990.

Simons, Judy. *Diaries and Journals of Literary Women from Fanny Burney to Virginia Woolf*. London: Macmillan, 1990.

Smith, Martha Nell. *Rowing in Eden: Rereading Emily Dickinson*. Austin: University of Texas Press, 1992.

Stewart, Randall. "Editing Hawthorne's Notebooks: Selections from Mrs. Hawthorne's Letters to Mr. and Mrs. Fields," *More Books* XX (Sept. 1945): 299–315.

——, ed. *The English Notebooks*. New York: Modern Language Association, 1941.

Stillinger, Jack. *Multiple Authorship and the Myth of Solitary Genius*. New York: Oxford University Press, 1991.

Tanselle, G. Thomas. *A Rationale of Textual Criticism*. Philadelphia: University of Pennsylvania Press, 1989.

Valenti, Patricia Dunlavy. "Sophia Peabody Hawthorne's *American Notebooks*," in *Studies in the American Renaissance*, ed. Joel Myerson. Charlottesville: University Press of Virginia, 1996. 115–185.

Werner, Marta. "Entre censure et contre-écriture: Emily Dickinson, Traversée et traces de rapture" in *Genèse, censure, autocensure*, ed. Catherine Viollet and Claire Bustarret. Paris: C.N.R.S. Editions, 2005: 131–148.

Index

The Common Journal of Nathaniel and Sophia Hawthorne

www.ingramcontent.com/pod-product-compliance
Lightning Source LLC
Chambersburg PA
CBHW081139300726
48982CB00006B/1004

* 9 7 8 0 8 7 1 6 9 2 5 6 6 *